COLORADO

OFF THE BEATEN PATH®

OFF THE BEATEN PATH® SERIES

THIRTEENTH EDITION

COLORADO

OFF THE BEATEN PATH®

DISCOVER YOUR FUN

CHRISTINE LOOMIS

Globe
Pequot

Essex, Connecticut

All information in this guidebook is subject to change. We recommend that you call ahead to obtain current information before traveling.

Globe
Pequot

An imprint of Globe Pequot, the trade division of
The Rowman & Littlefield Publishing Group, Inc.
4501 Forbes Blvd., Ste. 200
Lanham, MD 20706
www.rowman.com

Distributed by NATIONAL BOOK NETWORK

British Library Cataloguing in Publication Information available

Library of Congress Cataloging-in-Publication Data: This title is a serial and is covered under LCCN: 2002208433

ISBN 9781493070220 (paperback) | 9781493070237 (ebook)

∞™ The paper used in this publication meets the minimum requirements of American National Standard for Information Sciences—Permanence of Paper for Printed Library Materials, ANSI/NISO Z39.48-1992.

Contents

Acknowledgments

This book was written with the assistance of many people. The author thanks Gaylene Ore, Ore Communications; Maureen Poschman, Promo Communications; Aspen Chamber Resort Assoc.; Kim Farin, Visit Boulder; Lauren Swanson, GoBreck; Heidi Barfels, Visit Estes Park; PK Knickerbocker, Pikes Peak Region Attractions; Visit Colorado Springs; Elizabeth Fogarty, Visit Grand Junction; Nancy S. Hale, Historic Georgetown; Britny Kalule, Acclimate PR; Joy Meadows, Meadows PR; Visit Golden; Silverthorne, Colorado; Laura Soard, Steamboat Chamber; and Kira Rose Riley, Boulder hiker/researcher extraordinaire.

About the Author

Christine Loomis is a travel writer, editor, and photographer and was the first travel editor at *Parents* magazine. She also covered travel for *Family Life* magazine and was editor in chief of *Scientific American's Explorations*. She has written and edited for many websites, including *USA Today 10Best* (where she serves as a Denver expert). Christine has also provided family, adventure, and romance travel content and photo essays for websites like Away and Orbitz, and her freelance articles have appeared in many publications, including *Endless Vacation, AAA* magazines, *Roads to Adventure, Corporate & Incentive Travel*, and more. She is the author of three travel books and sixteen children's books. Her essay "Vincent's Room" was included in the anthology *A Mother's World* (Travelers' Tales), and her essay "Oscar's Dreamland" was included in *The Best Women's Travel Writing*, volume 11. In addition to destination coverage, Christine writes about fishing, health & wellness, and food. She is a long-time member of the Society of American Travel Writers and resides in Denver.

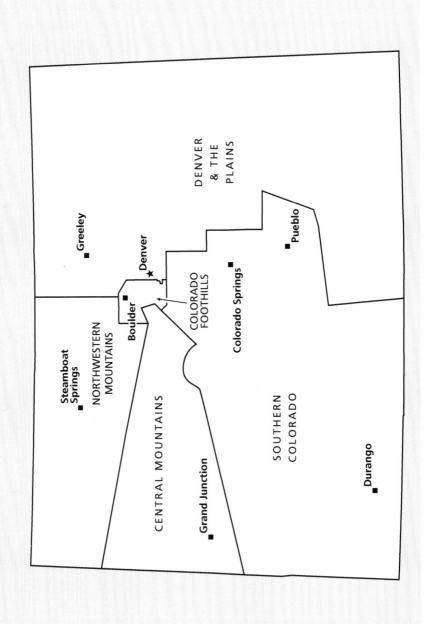

COLORADO

Introduction

Colorado is a four-season destination offering unparalleled adventure and recreational pursuits, a thriving arts scene, a rich cultural heritage, restaurants helmed by acclaimed chefs, and renowned ski areas and resorts. The state's inspiring landscape boasts natural hot springs, the headwaters of 7 major rivers, many peaceful lakes and reservoirs, 12 national parks and monuments, and 54 mountain peaks that top 14,000 feet.

It's no wonder that Colorado's cities and small towns frequently appear on those "Best Places to Live in America" lists. The state has so much to offer that many people come to visit and never leave. Even longtime residents constantly find new things to love about the state.

The mountains are perhaps the biggest draw. Each spring wildflowers fill the meadows, streams and rivers flow, and life returns to the high country. Summer means long, warm days, afternoon thundershowers, and exploring the forests and alpine reaches. In the fall, aspen shimmer golden against electric blue skies, and bull elk gather in the meadows to bugle and herd their cows. Winter is the time for thrilling downhill runs through fresh powder, quiet snow-shoeing or cross-country ski tours deep into the woods, or sitting by a crackling fire in a cabin as snow swirls outside.

But there's more to the state than mountains. Colorado is the true West, and just outside any town or city another world begins, where ranches, farms, and scattered rural communities represent the Western rural lifestyle. Much of the state's early pioneering history is rooted in agriculture on the plains and across valleys.

Colorado's Great Sand Dunes are the tallest in North America. The Pawnee National Grasslands buttes protect a Great Plains geography largely gone from the American landscape. Dinosaur bones can be inspected at Dinosaur National Monument. Rivers run through canyons, awaiting exploration by raft. Historic ghost towns and ancient Native American ruins remain to remind visitors of the first people to call this place home.

Along with the open spaces and natural beauty, Colorado is also a renowned cultural destination. Front Range cities are blessed with world-class performing arts, cuisine to satisfy any palate, a thriving music scene, a high concentration of microbreweries, extensive bike paths and parks, multiple major league sports teams, and top-notch universities. And perhaps best of all, within easy access of each of these cities await the Rocky Mountains.

Colorado Off the Beaten Path travels to the far corners of the state and covers most points in between. It offers a mix of singular, less-known destinations and well-known locales. Both visitors and residents will find new places to explore to keep them busy for years to come.

A word about Amendment 64 and the growing niche market of "pot tourism." As of January 2014, it's legal in Colorado for those over the age of 21 to use marijuana *privately* and to possess it in very limited quantities—up to 1 ounce for Colorado residents and a quarter ounce for visitors. The big challenge for the Colorado Tourism Office is educating visitors about the laws.

In spite of what you may have heard, Colorado is not a free-for-all of pot smoking. The law specifically bans public consumption of marijuana. Using it in public areas is illegal, and that is being enforced. Public areas include business and residential areas, city sidewalks, ski areas, city parks, state parks, national parks, and all public lands. What this means for visitors is that they can purchase marijuana legally in a legal dispensary selling recreational pot, or in a medical dispensary if they have a medical marijuana card, but unless they're staying in marijuana-friendly or private lodging, there's no place they can legally use it.

It is absolutely illegal to take marijuana across state borders or on airplanes—even on flights to other Colorado cities—and security personnel at Colorado's airports actively look for it and confiscate it when found. Before arriving in Colorado with plans to purchase and use marijuana, educate yourself. One good resource is denvergov.org/Government/Agencies-Departments-Offices/Agencies-Departments-Offices-Directory/Marijuana-Information/Marijuana-Information-for-Residents-Visitors-and-Business-Owners. If your vacation plans include legal use of marijuana, do your research to comply with laws and to find authorized dispensaries and marijuana-friendly lodging. Doing so will keep you and others safe and your vacation positive.

This book is divided into five regions, with each chapter covering a region of the state.

Chapter 1 deals with the Front Range foothills area west of the Denver/Boulder corridor, where much of the state's population lives. Chapter 2 explores the state's northwestern mountains, including Rocky Mountain National Park, Trail Ridge Road, and Steamboat Springs. In chapter 3 you follow one of Colorado's main arteries—I-70—through historic Georgetown and Glenwood Springs to the Western Slope city of Grand Junction, with side trips along the way. Chapter 4 goes into the state's vast southern region, including the spectacular San Juan Mountains, the ruins of Mesa Verde, and the unique towns of Telluride, Cortez, and Durango. Finally, chapter 5 covers cosmopolitan Denver and the sprawling Plains. Throughout the book you will discover unique, hidden places overlooked by the casual traveler.

Happy trails!

Author's Note

After attending the University of Oregon in the 1970s, I headed to New York to be a magazine editor. Fate intervened. I stopped to visit friends in Colorado—and stayed for nearly five years. Eventually I reached New York and served as editor on several national publications, though Colorado remained in my heart and mind. After sixteen years working in Manhattan, I moved to Boulder with my family, where I stayed for another sixteen years before moving to Northern California. Yet once again I was drawn back to Colorado.

Blame it on Chief Niwot's Curse, famously interpreted by locals as, "Once you see the beauty of the Boulder Valley, you will always come back." No matter how many historians point out that the eloquent leader of the Southern Arapahoe didn't say exactly that, the curse—or blessing—lives on. Like many others, I've succumbed over and over to the extraordinary beauty, vibrancy, quirkiness, and evocative mix of urban sophistication and backcountry accessibility that is Colorado. Chief Niwot can rest where I'm concerned. This time, I'm back for good, and proud to share my Colorado with you.

Fast Facts about Colorado

COLORADO'S MAJOR NEWSPAPERS

The Denver Post (daily), denverpost.com
Westword Newspaper (weekly), westword.com

TRANSPORTATION: REGIONAL TRANSPORTATION DISTRICT (RTD)

RTD has an extensive bus system in addition to light-rail.

1600 Blake St.
Denver, CO 80202
(303) 299-6000
rtd-denver.com

Weather Overview

Residents claim that old cliché about the weather—if you don't like it, wait an hour—started in Colorado. The state is known for its ability to go from clear skies to thunderstorms, tornadoes, flash floods, and back before you've had time to complain about any of it. Temperatures can drop 30 degrees in a matter of hours, and just when you thought it was Indian summer in October, a blizzard can dump 3 feet of snow in two days' time. It never hurts to keep an eye on the sky, especially when traveling in the mountains.

The following best sums up the climate in Colorado:

- Semiarid

- Short springs

- Dry, often hot summers with brief periods of rain with thunder and lightning

- Warm, clear fall days with cool nights

- Mild winters, except in mountains

Average highs and lows in Denver (degrees Fahrenheit)

Jan 43/16	Apr 61/34	July 88/58	Oct 66/36
Feb 46/20	May 70/43	Aug 85/56	Nov 52/25
Mar 52/25	June 81/52	Sept 76/47	Dec 44/17

For more information about Colorado, contact the tourism office at:

Colorado Tourism Office
1600 Broadway, Ste. 2500
Denver, CO 80202
(800) 265-6723 or (303) 892-3840
colorado.com

Where to Stay & Where to Eat Price Codes

Listed at the end of each chapter are area accommodations and restaurants you'll want to check out.

The rating scale for hotels is based on double occupancy and is as follows:
Inexpensive: Less than $100 per night
Moderate: $100 to $200 per night
Expensive: More than $200 per night

The rating scale for restaurants is as follows:
Inexpensive: Most entrees less than $10
Moderate: Most entrees $10 to $20
Expensive: Most entrees more than $20

Colorado Foothills

Front Range

When you first come upon the 70-million-year-old amphitheater at **Red Rocks Park,** west of Denver, the primeval scene takes your breath away. Huge reddish sandstone formations jut upward and outward. Each is higher than Niagara Falls. The view conjures up dinosaurs, sea serpents, and flying reptiles; indeed, tracks of those long-extinct creatures remain embedded in nearby rock, along with valuable fossil fragments. The saturated colors rival those of the Grand Canyon, and the tortured geology is evidence of earth-shattering, monolith-building cataclysms, retreating ancestral oceans, violent upwelling, and centuries of water erosion. Geographers once considered this site one of the Seven Wonders of the World.

Long before the first settlers arrived, the Ute tribe favored the area for camping. The US Geographical Survey began the first surveys in 1868. By 1906 financier *John Brisben Walker* had acquired the land, claiming the acoustics of these rocks would be perfect for an amphitheater. Walker eventually donated the land to the community, and in 1927 it was incorporated into the **Denver Mountain Parks System.**

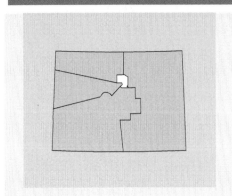

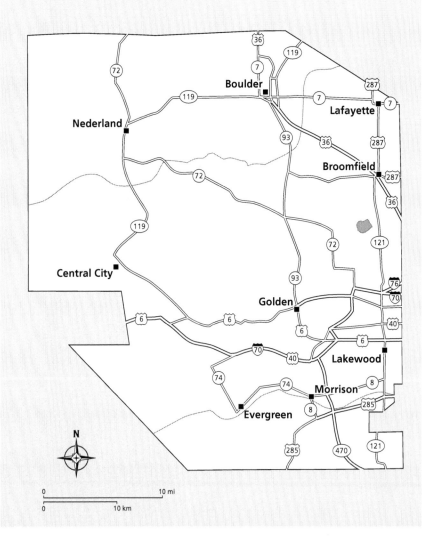

Construction started a few years later, followed in 1941 with the dedication of the tiered outdoor area. The local symphony came, producing perfect sound and aesthetic inspiration against a magnificent backdrop of Denver and the plains far below. Triumphant ballet performances and celebrated orchestras wowed audiences. Over the years improvements were made to the stage and seating.

However, the cost of bringing in large groups of classical musicians and opera companies proved to be financially draining. What's more, performers sometimes fought with winds that would tear away the orchestra's notes or with summer downpours that would drench the singers.

Since 1961 classical music has rarely been heard at the amphitheater. In 1964 the Beatles showed up, and along with an admission price of $6.60, rock and roll arrived at Red Rocks. From the 1970s forward to today, the summer season is packed with an assortment of rock, pop, blues, folk, jazz, and country-western stars—often with sellouts of the 9,525 seats. The stage is now covered, and tickets can be expensive, but the magical setting brings fans regardless of price.

Red Rocks is truly one of the world's great open-air stages. Many famous groups return year after year, claiming this venue among their favorite places to perform. For music lovers, sitting down to a summer show at Red Rocks as the sun sets and stars sparkle overhead is one of life's perfect moments.

At all other times, admission is free to Red Rocks. Many locals come here during the day for a vigorous workout of running or walking up and down the amphitheater stairs. An ***Easter Sunrise Service*** has been a strong Denver tradition for several decades. A 30,000-square-foot underground ***Red Rocks Visitor Center,*** entered from the top of the amphitheater, features an excellent exhibit on the venue, with its geological history and a chronological list of every performance over the last 50 years. Featuring sweeping views from terraces, elevator access for people with disabilities, and new restrooms, the visitor center is open to the public free of charge year-round. Also included are event spaces (email eventsatredrocks@aramark.com for details) and a restaurant.

Hiking trails in the park surrounding the amphitheater offer hours of exercise or just quiet contemplation among the birdlife, browsing deer, and ancient geology. Mere minutes from the Denver suburbs, the splendor of Red Rocks can feel like another world.

Red Rocks, located at 16352 CR 93 in Morrison, is easy to reach via numerous routes. From Denver you can take West Alameda Avenue west, drive US 285 west to CR 470 to Morrison Road, or follow I-70 west and watch for the marked exit. The total distance varies between 14 and 17 miles, depending on

trivia

Long ago, a vast inland sea, which contained sediments that gradually built up on its floor, covered the Colorado area. After the sea receded, the sediments hardened and the forces of geology and erosion went to work over the next few million years to sculpt the formations you see at Red Rocks today.

your route. Hours on non-event days are one hour before sunrise to one hour after sunset. On event days the park closes in the afternoon, with the specific time dependent on show time. Hours for the trading post and **Colorado Music Hall of Fame** are 10 a.m. to 6 p.m. daily. **Ship Rock Grille** is open daily 10:30 a.m. to 2:30 p.m. For more information go to redrocksonline.com.

You can see the amphitheater from the hiking trails of **Mount Falcon Park,** a protected sanctuary in the foothills just above Red Rocks. In the early 1900s, John Brisben Walker, financier, entrepreneur, and visionary, built a mansion on a promontory high above the surrounding hills. His next project was to be a Summer White House for US presidents, but Walker's fortunes ultimately waned. The Summer White House was never built, and the financier's own castle-like home was struck by lightning and burned down in 1918. The stone walls, fireplaces, and chimneys remain—an interesting destination for hikers.

The Mount Falcon area is surrounded by mountains, and in the distance you can spot Mount Evans (elevation 14,264 feet) and the Continental Divide. Other vistas of the 2,130-acre park include the Colorado plains and, with a little imagination and a clear day, Kansas.

The park is surprisingly serene; it is so vast that walkers, mountain bikers, and the occasional horseback rider easily spread out. No motorcycles are permitted, and cars are restricted to two parking lots. The well-marked foot trails are often shaded by conifer forests. In the winter, cross-country skiers, snowshoe enthusiasts, and anyone looking for a quick escape from the city come here to enjoy the views and explore the quiet trails.

Picnic tables entice families to the park, and the meadows are popular with kite-fliers and butterfly fans. Hikers find solitude among the daisies, scrub oak, and spruce. Here, at 7,750 feet above sea level, summers are cooler here than down below in Denver. Far from traffic, you hear only the light Colorado wind in the pines.

Mount Falcon Park is accessible via Highway 8 to Morrison (turn west on Forest Avenue and north on Vine Avenue) or via US 285 and the Indian Hills exit (stay on Parmalee Gulch Road for 5 miles to Picutis Road, and then follow signs to the parking area). Be prepared for a brief dusty road to the park entrance. For more information contact Jefferson County Open Space at (303) 271-5925; jeffco.us/1332/Mount-Falcon-Park.

Beaver Brook Trail
(303) 271-5925
jeffco.us/open-space/parks/
windy-saddle-park

Central City Opera House
(303) 292-6700
centralcityopera.org

Colorado Shakespeare Festival
(303) 492-0554
coloradoshakes.org

Chautauqua Park
(303) 442-3282
bouldercolorado.gov/parks-rec/
chautauqua-park

Eldorado Canyon
(303) 494-3943
cpw.state.co.us/placestogo/parks/
EldoradoCanyon

Golden History Tours
info@goldenhistorytours.com
Goldenhistorytours.com

Lookout Mountain Nature Center & Preserve
(720) 497-7600
jeffco.us/open-space/parks/
lookout-mountain-nature-center

Matthews/Winters Park
(303) 271-5925
jeffco.us/open-space/parks/
matthews-winters-park

Mount Falcon Park
(303) 271-5925
jeffco.us/open-space/parks/
mount-falcon-park.

NoBo Art District & First Fridays
info@noboartdistrict.org
noboartdistrict.org

Pearl Street Mall in Boulder
(303) 449-3774
boulderdowntown.com

Red Rocks Park and Amphitheatre
(303) 697-4939 (Visitor Center)
redrocksonline.com

Trident Booksellers & Café
(303) 443-3133
tridentcafe.com

Waterton Canyon
(303) 893-2444
denverwater.org/recreation/
watertoncanyon

Mount Falcon Park and Red Rocks feel far from the city, but they are only 20 minutes west of Denver. Just south of Red Rocks, **Morrison Road** winds through the foothills toward higher country. It's a popular route into the mountains, but along the way there are little gems to be discovered.

One such place is the town of **Morrison.** On any given weekday, neighbors meet on the street corners to catch up on local news. Bicyclists ride the paths along Bear Creek and stop at a cafe for lunch. Visitors browse eclectic boutiques and people-watch the steady stream of locals, tourists, and on weekends, bikers. Indeed, at times, Morrison is very Norman Rockwellesque.

But along with a pleasant atmosphere, this community offers a treasure trove of antiques that will please collectors and browsers alike. Old Western memorabilia, crafts, and unusual one-of-a-kind items pack tiny stores. Drop by any of several antiques shops along Bear Creek Avenue or on side streets. Whatever your pleasure—buying, selling, or window-shopping—Morrison is a pleasant place to spend an hour or two and enjoy lunch or an ice-cream cone. For more information call the town of Morrison at (303) 697-8749 or visit town .morrison.co.us.

A 5-minute uphill drive from Morrison will take you to the much-photographed locale of **The Fort,** a replica of Bent's Fort, an 1834 early Colorado fur-trading post. The thick, picturesque adobe building contains a small shop that sells authentic Native American jewelry and other items. But The Fort is best known as an award-winning restaurant, popular among locals for impressing out-of-town guests. The walls are covered with Western oil paintings and original etchings celebrating the West. The cuisine features foods of the American West, both old and contemporary, with appetizers such as roast bison marrow bones, braised bison tongue, buffalo empanadas, and Rocky Mountain "oysters" (bull testicles). Entree selections include elk, buffalo, lamb, beef, salmon, and quail prepared a variety of ways and accompanied by sides, an extensive wine list, and original desserts. The Fort is located at US 285 and Highway 8. The restaurant is open for dinner Mon through Wed starting at 5:30 p.m., last reservation at 8 p.m; Thur to Sun starting at 4:30 p.m., last reservation at 8:30 p.m.. For reservations call (303) 697-4771 or visit thefort.com.

Close to Denver, **Matthews/Winters Park** and the adjacent **Hogback** are popular for wildlife viewing, hiking, and **mountain biking.** The trails range from easy to moderately difficult. The park is a mixture of undulating grasslands, trails, and fields of silver-green sage, purple thistles, wild roses, and wild plums. Trails run through rabbitbrush and tall dill, and a short walk away from the parking lot the highway noise fades, replaced by birdsong and serenity.

Tracks in Time

A visit to the Morrison area would not be complete without a stop at the outdoor museum known as **Dinosaur Ridge.** View more than 300 dinosaur footprints, all preserved in the sandstone of the Dakota Formation on the east side of the hogback. This National Natural Landmark is open for free viewing year-round, with interpretive signs providing information about the tracks and other fossils found in the area. Visitors can also arrange for a guided tour with the visitor center ($3 per person) or call ahead or check the website to find out about the next Dinosaur Discovery Day, held monthly on Saturdays from Apr through Oct. During these days guests enjoy free guided tours and activities at the center. For more information, call (303) 697-3466 or visit dinoridge.org.

The Hogback, with its twisted geography running north–south, dramatically separates the mountains and the plains. Red Rocks Park is nearby. Serious bikers can cross the road from the park and find a variety of paths. On the eastern face at 16831 W. Alameda Pkwy. is the Dinosaur Ridge main visitor center. The Dinosaur Ridge Trail is a 1.5-mile path leading past hundreds of dinosaur tracks, a quarry of dinosaur bones, and unusual geologic formations. Call (303) 697-3466 or visit dinoridge.org for more information.

The park lies astride the entrance to **Mount Vernon Canyon,** which is one of the early routes to the goldfields of Central City and South Park. The big year here was 1859. Stagecoaches and wagons rolled through, and the nearby town of **Mount Vernon** had a 150-horse corral. For a while Mount Vernon became a stage stop. An inn, a saloon, and a schoolhouse were built, used, and abandoned. Once boasting 44 registered voters, the town of Mount Vernon lost its place in history after the railroads arrived.

Sunflowers, chokecherries, and willows now lean over the gravestones and crosses of long-gone pioneers: One marker reads I.I. DEAN, DIED AUGUST 12, 1860, AGED 31 YEARS, I AM AT REST. Not far from the few square gravestones that remain, picnic tables sit under leafy trees near Mount Vernon Creek.

Weekends and summer evenings at the park are the busiest times, and the small parking lot fills quickly. The parking area is located off Highway 26, just south of I-70, and lies within the Mount Vernon townsite. All Jefferson County Open Space parks are closed from 1 hour after sunset until 1 hour before sunrise unless otherwise noted by signage at individual parks. For more information contact Jefferson County Open Space at (303) 271-5925; jeffco.us/open-space.

Southwest of Denver, close to Chatfield Reservoir, is **Waterton Canyon** (denverwater.org/recreation/waterton-canyon-strontia-springs-resevoir). The canyon is popular with hikers and bikers, who walk or ride the gravel road that follows the South Platte River. It can get crowded on summer weekends, but Waterton Canyon is a delightful place anytime for a peaceful hour or two along the river.

trivia

Colorado's Front Range has an average of 300 days of sunshine per year—second only to San Diego, California, and Tampa, Florida.

To the west of Morrison, approximately 30 miles west of Denver on US 285, is the sign for **Meyer Ranch Park.** Here are 623 quiet acres with miles of well-maintained hiking trails winding through aspen groves and pine forests. Through the spring and summer, the meadows are home to Colorado's state flower, the columbine, shooting stars, lady's slippers, and the purple Indian paintbrush. The trail names fit the surrounding scenery: Owl's Perch, Lodge Pole, and Sunny Aspen.

In the winter the hill near the park parking lot becomes a popular sledding and tubing destination. Motorized vehicles are not permitted here at any time, and dogs belong on a leash. The Meyer Ranch Park area has a history of homesteading, haying, and grazing. According to local legend, during the late 1880s the animals of the P. T. Barnum circus wintered here. The handsome Victorian-style Meyer home—still occupied by the Meyers—stands proudly across the highway. For more information about the park, contact Jefferson County Open Space at (303) 271-5925; jeffco.us/openspace.

The same US 285 will take you to a truly offbeat family destination that even many Denverites don't know about. Around 25 minutes from the city is **Tiny Town,** a Lilliputian village and miniature railway.

Tiny Town appeals to children and anyone interested in miniature re-creations. Imagine about a hundred toy-size, handcrafted buildings to peek into, and sometimes even crawl into, and you get the picture. This town has old miniature log cabins, a fire station, a post office, a water tower, a flour mill, a bank, stables, a schoolhouse, a rooming house, farms, ranches, barns, windmills, mines, and miners' shacks. There's even a miniature train ride around the entire Tiny Town village loop.

The attraction is run on a not-for-profit basis by the Tiny Town Foundation, which donates a portion of its annual proceeds to local charities. The distance from Denver is about 12 miles via US 285, turning south at South Turkey Creek Road. Bring a picnic and be prepared to pay $5 for adults and $4 for children ages 2 to 12. Children younger than 2 are free. There is a $4 train fare per person. Open every day from Memorial Day weekend through Labor Day 10 a.m. to 5 p.m. Open weekends in May and Sept 10 a.m. to 5 p.m. For more information contact Tiny Town at (303) 697-6829; tinytownrailroad.com.

Just west of Denver, the plains of eastern Colorado end and the foothills of the Rockies begin. Nestled in a long valley with the jagged foothills rising on both sides, **Golden** is a historic town and home to the Colorado School of Mines.

Golden greets its visitors with a sign arched across Main Street that reads: HOWDY FOLKS! WELCOME TO GOLDEN, WHERE THE WEST LIVES. The concept of the West is among the most basic cornerstones of American folklore and legend. Its connotations extend well into the realms of history, geography, morality, and philosophy. To the traveler visiting the western states, it's an almost mythical sense of place blending with the past. Golden, with its 10 museums—a record for a town of its size—does not disappoint in either category.

The Golden story began back in 1859, when Tom Golden set up a hunting camp with a few men. Soon representatives of the Boston Company passed by on a wagon train, looking for a suitable place to establish a trading and supply base for the prospectors who were flooding the mining areas to the west. They liked the site and stayed.

Golden grew rapidly. Within a year it had a population of 700. By 1862 it became the territorial capital but lost this honor five years later to Denver. There was sporadic gold excitement in the immediate area but no big finds. Even today people still occasionally pan **Clear Creek** just west of town, and with the high price of gold, some of them even manage to pull a profit out of the fast-moving stream. Golden's early economy was built on trading. It was the major supply center for mining operations at Black Hawk, Central City, Idaho Springs, and other communities.

With the decline of mining, new economic bases emerged. Golden's present economy is based in part on two institutions, both of which have brought it international recognition: the Colorado School of Mines, for a century the leading school in the world devoted to mining and minerals, and Coors Brewery, the world's largest single-site brewery.

To the west of Golden you'll find range after range of mountains, each higher than the last. These mountains serve the practical purpose of limiting the size to which Golden can grow—it currently has about 19,000 inhabitants. Unlike with other Front Range cities, the Rockies have protected Golden from becoming part of an increasing urban sprawl.

Consider booking a Wild West Walking History Tour or ghost tour with Golden History Tours for an immersive, interactive look at the city's past, rife with shootouts, gold rushers, lawless frontiersmen, ghosts, and a host of characters. Learn more at goldenhistorytours.com.

To learn all there is to do in town, stop by the **Golden Visitors Center,** adjacent to the historic downtown at 1010 Washington Ave. Grab a cup of coffee there and browse through the informational touch-screen kiosk. The center, run by the Golden Chamber of Commerce, is open Mon through Fri from 9 a.m. to 5 p.m.; Sat from 10 a.m. to 4 p.m.; closed Sun. For more information call (303) 279-2282 or go to visitgolden.com.

trivia

Golden's Armory Building, built in 1913, is the largest cobblestone building in the country. Workers hauled 3,300 wagonloads of stream-worn boulders from nearby Clear Creek and quartz from Golden Gate Canyon to construct the building, which is located at 13th and Arapahoe.

The **Colorado School of Mines** has an interesting, kid-friendly museum that fits the theme of the college. **The Mines Museum of Earth Science,** on the corner of 16th and Maple on campus, is almost an art gallery. Murals by Irwin Hoffman depict many periods in the development and history of mining. See minerals from around the world, a rock from the Moon, Colorado's mining history, fossils, Colorado gem trails, and more. Regular hours are 9 a.m. to 4 p.m. Mon through Sat and 1 to 4 p.m. Sun; closed all CSM holidays and Sun during summer. Admission is free. Contact Colorado School of Mines, Department of Geology and Geological Engineering; (303) 273-3815; mines. edu/museumofearthscience.

Train buffs and anyone interested in old transportation and machinery will want to drop by the *Colorado Railroad Museum,* which displays many ancient, standard- and narrow-gauge locomotives and cars and even a small depot. The narrow-gauge railroads of Colorado made it possible for miners and other fortune seekers to access the mineral riches of the Rocky Mountains. These tracks also allowed the wealth to be carried out and sent across the country. The history of railroads in Colorado is preserved in the 15-acre Colorado Railroad Museum. Here you will see the original rolling stock, including locomotives. A rail spur allows the facility to "steam up" different engines throughout the year.

The building itself, a masonry replica of an 1880 depot, houses some 50,000 photographs and artifacts. The basement contains one of the state's largest HO-scale model railroad exhibits, open to the public on the first Thursday of each month. Famous relics of the museum include the Rio Grande Southern 1931 Galloping Goose No. 2 and the steel observation car used on the Santa Fe Super Chief, the Navajo. A bookstore sells more than 1,000 railroad-themed gifts, books and magazines, tapes, and mementos, while the *Robert W. Richardson Library* holds more than 10,000 railroad-specific publications.

Open every day except Thanksgiving, Christmas, and New Year's Day. Hours are 9 a.m. to 5 p.m. Admission is $10 for adults, $8 for seniors, and $5 for children ages 2 to 17 (children under 2 free). Contact the Colorado Railroad Museum at 17155 W. 44th Ave., Golden 80403; (800) 365-6263 or (303) 279-4591; coloradorailroadmuseum.org.

trivia

Golden once rivaled Denver; it was the capital of the Colorado Territory from 1862 to 1867.

Golden in its early days was the true West, home to pioneers who left the civilized East in search of a new life. They were risk-taking, self-reliant doers on the path toward something better. These days Golden folks embody this spirit of the West with their love of the outdoors, and the town has an abundance of campers, backpackers, cyclists, and off-road enthusiasts. For many here, life is more about "doing" than sitting back and watching.

Given the town's outdoorsy reputation, it should come as no surprise that Golden is home to the 47,000-square-foot *American Mountaineering Center,* located at 710 10th St. This center is the headquarters for the century-old American Alpine Club, the Colorado Mountain Club, the Outward Bound Wilderness, the Colorado Fourteeners Initiative, and the nonprofit organization

Climbing for Life, which uses rock climbing to have a positive impact on at-risk youth in the Denver metro area. Stop by the center for a visit to the **Henry S. Hall Jr. American Alpine Club Library.** The library, with more than 50,000 volumes specific to rock climbing and mountaineering, is open to the public for research (only club members can check out books). Hours are Wed, 10 a.m. to 6 p.m.; Thurs, 10 a.m. to 4 p.m.; Fri, 10 a.m. to 3 p.m.; Sat, noon to 4 p.m. For more information call (303) 384-0112 or visit americanalpineclub.org.

The center's museum, the **Bradford Washburn American Mountaineering Museum,** is the only one in the country devoted to the culture and spirit of mountaineering, and it houses numerous climbing exhibits and artifacts from the US and around the world. Admission is $5 for adults, $1 for children under 12. It's open Mon–Fri, 10 a.m. to 4 p.m. For more information, email museum@mountaineeringmuseum.org or visit mountaineeringmuseum.org.

Nearby **Golden Gate Canyon State Park** will give you an idea of how the foothills looked to the first miners who walked up here well over a century ago. Just 30 miles west of Denver, and with 132 campsites, 5 cabins, 2 yurts, 20 backcountry tent sites, 4 backcountry shelters, and 35 miles of trails, the park is a serene mountain escape for hiking, bicycling, relaxing, and enjoying more than 12,000 acres of hills, canyons, meadows, and woods. From Golden take Golden Gate Canyon Road for 13 miles to the park. For more information call (303) 582-3707 or visit cpw.state.co.us/placestogo/parks/GoldenGateCanyon.

After a day of touring the museums and riding the alpine slide, or biking and hiking the nearby trails, how about a cold one? The famous **Coors Brewery,** the world's largest single-site brewery, offers free, self-guided tours on a first-come, first-served basis. No reservations are taken. Plan to spend around 30 minutes on the tour, which includes a close-up look at the malting, brewing, and packaging process. Afterward, visitors gather for a short tasting session in the hospitality room to sip limited servings of Coors products. You must be 21 or over to sample beer; minors can enjoy nonalcoholic drinks.

The brewery is located at 12th Street and Ford Street in Golden. Summer tour hours are Mon through Sat, 10 a.m. to 4 p.m.; Sun, noon to 4 p.m. Winter hours are Thurs through Mon, 10 a.m. to 4 p.m.; Sun, noon to 4 p.m. Closed holidays. For more information contact (800) 642-6116 or (303) 277-2337; coorsbrewerytour.com.

trivia

Golden is where Jolly Rancher candy was first produced, back in 1949.

Before you leave Golden, ask yourself what could possibly epitomize the West more than the place where **Buffalo Bill** is buried? Buffalo Bill was a unique character of the frontier. And the museum that bears his name, 12 miles west of Denver on Golden's Lookout Mountain, has a uniquely

Western quality. Here are the mementos that bring a fascinating man to life: the paintings and posters that show him in full regalia on his white horse, with flowing white hair and beard, and a cowboy hat jaunty on his head. You can see his clothes, saddles, old weapons, a mounted buffalo, and numerous other artifacts at the *Buffalo Bill Grave and Museum.* More than half a million visitors come annually to see the exhibits and photographs that retrace his careers as a buffalo hunter, Indian fighter, army scout, and entertainer.

Born *William F. Cody,* Buffalo Bill led an extraordinary life. As a longtime Pony Express rider, he was pursued by Indians, escaping (as he wrote), "by laying flat on the back of my fast steed. I made a 24-mile straight run on one horse." On another occasion he rode 320 miles in some 21 hours to deliver the mail. (En route he exhausted 20 horses for the journey.) He had few rivals as a hunter and was said to have shot 4,280 bison in a period of one and a half years. His slogan: "Never missed and never will / always aims and shoots to kill."

The buffalo shooting had a purpose, though; the meat was needed to feed some 1,200 men who were laying track for the railroad. And though William Cody had his battles with the Indians, he later learned the Sioux language and befriended the Cheyenne, among other tribes.

William Cody may have had his best years as a circus rider, actor, and showman, gaining fame all over the world. The first "Buffalo Bill's Wild West" show opened in 1883. The extravaganza toured for nearly three decades, spreading myths and legends of the American West around the globe. Almost a hundred mounted *Sioux Indians* chased wagon trains and a stagecoach; Annie Oakley and *Johnny Baker* amazed audiences with their marksmanship; 83 cowboys rode bucking broncos, thereby formalizing a cowboy sport into rodeo; and the entire Battle of Little Big Horn was re-created. Spectators could see live elk and deer from Colorado. There were horse races and even a bison hunt, complete with a charging herd.

At its height, Buffalo Bill's show employed more than 600 performers. In one year he traveled 10,000 miles, performing in 132 cities in 190 days. Cody's flamboyant style and rifle-holding figure symbolized the Wild West in many European capitals. Buffalo Bill gave a command performance for Queen Victoria at Windsor Castle and amused Kaiser Wilhelm II in Berlin.

No fewer than 557 dime novels were written about Cody during his lifetime. His face beamed out from hundreds of thousands of posters. At his peak he was one of the most famous men in the world. Even today, the distinctive goatee and silver hair continue to make him as recognizable as the kings, generals, and presidents who may have honored him.

Cody made one of the first movie Westerns ever produced. Although near the end of his career, he also lived to see the start of the tourist industry as he opened the first hotel near Yellowstone National Park. Toward the end of his life, he turned into an entrepreneur and author. He gave most of his life's savings away to various good causes. His money ran out; his fame did not.

When Buffalo Bill died, President Woodrow Wilson wired his condolences. Former president **Teddy Roosevelt** called Cody "an American of Americans." The Colorado legislature passed a special resolution ordering that his body lie in state under the gold-plated rotunda of the State Capitol in Denver. Nearly 25,000 people turned out to pay their last respects and walk in his funeral procession on Memorial Day, June 3, 1917.

Buffalo Bill's grave is a few steps from the museum atop Lookout Mountain, with a good view of Denver and the plains. Anyone can come and see the burial place. It is marked by white pebbles. The simple legend reads: WILLIAM F. CODY 1846–1917.

The museum stands in a quiet conifer forest. First opened in 1919, it has been restored and improved over the years. The Pahaska Tepee Gift Shop sells original Western artwork and Western-themed toys, and serves food—including buffalo—in its large coffee shop.

Museum hours are 9 a.m. to 5 p.m. daily; closed Thanksgiving, Christmas, and New Year's Day. Call (720) 865-2160; write to 987½ Lookout Mountain Rd., Golden 80401; or visit buffalobill.org for more information. Admission is $5 for adults, $4 for seniors, and $1 for children ages 6 to 15 (children under 6 free). For the most scenic drive, take US 6 west of Denver to Golden, turn left on 19th Street, and proceed uphill via **Lookout Mountain Road,** also called Lariat Trail due to its winding loops, all the way up Lookout Mountain.

Whether or not the museum is your final destination, no visit to Golden would be complete without a trip up Lookout Mountain. The Lariat Trail drive twists and turns up hairpin curves and narrow roads, rewarding travelers with spectacular views of Golden and Denver. At night the city below sparkles bright beneath the radiance of hundreds of stars.

As you continue south on Lookout Mountain Road after leaving Buffalo Bill's grave, a sign on Colorow Road will direct you to turn right toward the **Lookout Mountain Nature Preserve and Center.** Situated on 77 acres

Home on the Range

The city of Denver has continuously maintained a herd of bison since 1914 at **Genesee Park,** just down the hill from the Buffalo Bill Grave and Museum. The buffalo roam free in their natural habitat and are best seen in fall, winter, and early spring, when park officials feed them daily. Take I-70 west to exit 254 (Genesee Park). The bulls and cows can be seen on either side of the highway—a tunnel under the road allows the animals safe passage.

of a fenced nature preserve, the center has a Discovery Corner, Observation Room, plant and animal displays, and a self-guiding nature trail (all wheelchair accessible). Admission is free. Nature center hours are 10 a.m. to 4 p.m. Tues through Sun year-round, and Sat and Sun 10 a.m. until 5 p.m. from Memorial Day weekend through Labor Day weekend; the facility is closed on Mon and holidays. The preserve is open 8 a.m. to sunset daily. Also offered is a wide variety of hikes, activities, and nature programs. Most sessions require preregistration. The nature center is located at 910 Colorow Rd., just off Lookout Mountain Road, Golden. Call (720) 497-7600 or go to https://www.jeffco.us/1281/Lookout-Mountain-Preserve-and-Nature-Cen.

Of the many trails that explore the foothills outside Denver, one has been traveled for centuries. ***Beaver Brook Trail,*** curving around Lookout Mountain, was first used by the ***Cheyenne*** and ***Arapaho Indians*** as a lookout. It is among the state's more interesting paths, yielding views of the gorges below as it dips and climbs through a varied landscape of deciduous trees and dramatic Douglas fir. Hillsides of yucca, aster, and wild rose bloom in summer. Although you're close to Denver, the trail quickly leads you away from civilization.

The Beaver Brook Trail includes scrambling across several small boulder fields, making it a challenging hike. The trail, a little more than 14 miles out and back, remains blissfully quiet during the week. Weekends are busy, but those starting early will find solitude. If you hike up here in June and July, you'll be surrounded by lots of blossoming color. On the trail you may also spot the state flower, the blue Rocky Mountain columbine, as well as deer and abundant birdlife.

Wildflowers bloom later at the higher elevations, so by the time plants have already wilted around Golden (elevation 5,675 feet), flowers on the Beaver Brook Trail are just beginning to unfold. The higher you climb, the later the growth, the smaller the flower, and the cooler the air.

Flying over Golden & Lookout Mountain

On warm weekday afternoons and during the weekends, the sky just southwest of Golden is the playground for daredevil hang gliders. The steep slopes of Lookout Mountain combine with steady updrafts to create the perfect location for launching hang gliders and riding the thermals for minutes, and sometimes an hour or more. Whenever cars fill the small roadside parking lot just before the Lookout Mountain Road, there's a good chance hang gliders will be soaring overhead.

Small Colorado plants appear and disappear with the seasons, go underground, or take many years to mature. Certain wildflowers can sleep peacefully under the thickest snow cover, biding their time until spring. In summer the mountain flowers on the Beaver Brook Trail are as profuse as any in the region. They are all fragile, so take care not to trample or disturb them so those coming after you can also enjoy them.

The Beaver Brook Trail is an easy drive from Denver. Follow US 6 into Golden, turn left at the first traffic light (19th Street), then drive up Lookout Road for 3 miles. Before you get to Buffalo Bill's grave, look for a sign on your right. Admission is free, and the trail is open 1 hour before sunrise until 1 hour after sunset year-round. For more information contact Jefferson County Open Space at (303) 271-5925; jeffco.us/facilities/facility/details/Beaver-Brook-Trail-92.

Around 30 miles west of Denver up I-70 is a remnant of the ice age. *St. Mary's Glacier* is actually an ice field, covering a steep year-round snow bowl about 10 acres. In summer, when Denver swelters in a 95°F heat wave, it's about 45°F on the glacier, and people come to ski and snowboard here in July and August. Other visitors to the famous snowfield bring platters or tire tubes or even race downhill on shovels. Hikers, campers, and backpackers can be spotted at the 11,000-foot level as they scramble uphill past the last scrub pines. Less-energetic visitors come to sit on rocks and soak up the Colorado sun.

The ever-present snow and ice make St. Mary's Glacier a refreshing warm-weather trip, luring city dwellers as soon as the hiking trail opens each spring. After exiting I-70, the road follows a creek flanked by stands of conifers and aspen. After about 8 miles the road steepens and leads into a series of challenging curves and serpentines. Then the valley widens and the forest thickens. During snowmelt you see several rushing waterfalls, and at around 10,400 feet the parking lot appears. Hike up the rocky jeep trail or follow the uphill footpaths through kinnikinnik (evergreen groundcover), past the many fallen trees that are returning nutrients to the soil as they decompose. On weekends you'll share the trail with plenty of hikers.

After half an hour of hiking you reach a cold lake, topped by the glacier. Don't be fooled by the harmless appearance. Mountain dwellers know the glacier's record; almost every year someone who skis too fast or careens downhill on a shovel gets bruised, bloodied, or even killed. On rare occasions cross-country skiers are buried by an avalanche. In winter, the ill-prepared and underclothed can get frostbitten at higher elevations. Prudent visitors know that the mountains are unforgiving and come prepared.

From I-70 just past Idaho Springs, take exit 238, known as Fall River Road. A 12-mile drive brings you to the parking lot and the trailhead to St. Mary's Glacier.

Richest Square Mile on Earth

At one point in history, **Central City** vied with Leadville for Colorado's mining bonanzas. They called Central City the Richest Square Mile on Earth. In all, some $75 million in gold was found there. Although the rich veins are long gone, tourists can still do a bit of gold panning in nearby creeks. Surrounding the town are the bleached mountainsides, old abandoned mounds of earth, and mines from another era. Both Central City and neighboring Black Hawk are now reaping profits of a different sort since legalized gambling started up. Black Hawk has three times as many casinos as Central City, and as a result, Central City has retained more of its original historical appearance, at least for now.

With an abundance of buildings well over a century old, Central City and the adjacent Black Hawk together form the Central City/Black Hawk National Historic District. In Central City, sloping, winding **Eureka Street** has been beautifully restored. The redbrick buildings look as well preserved as those of Denver's Larimer Square. Central City's pharmacy and several other stores display relics in the windows.

For an overview of the area's history, visit the **Gilpin History Museum,** located at 228 E. First High St. Housed in a brick building built in 1870 and used as a school until the 1960s, this two-story museum includes a replica of a classic Main Street of the past. The Gilpin History Museum is open 11 a.m. to 4 p.m. daily, Memorial Day through Labor Day. For another window back into days gone by, visit the **Thomas House Museum** at 209 Eureka St. This Greek Revival frame house was built in 1874 around the entrance to a mine. The Thomas House Museum is open 10 a.m. to 4 p.m. daily. Entrance to each museum costs $7. For more information contact (303) 582-5283; gilpinhistory.org.

The Gilpin History Museum, the Thomas House Museum, and the well-appointed Central City Opera House contrast dramatically with the miners' dwellings. The latter are small, modest cubes scattered across the pale gold, ocher, and russet slopes.

The first frame houses sprang up during the 1860s, along with the mine dumps. Gold was being discovered not just in the river but in the

Mother Cabrini Shrine

On a 900-acre hilltop on Lookout Mountain sits the Mother Cabrini Shrine. There is no charge to enter the famous little chapel, which was built in 1954 and devoted to Saint Frances Xavier Cabrini. The setting includes lovely fields, surrounding forests, and enough steps to make hikers happy. For more information call (303) 526-0758 or visit mothercabrinishrine.org.

mountain too. In 1859 a man named **John Gregory** had walked from Denver to 8,500-foot-high Central City, a trip of some 35 miles with an elevation gain of more than 3,000 feet. Gregory soon dug up a fortune. The word raced as fast as the spring waters of Clear Creek. Horace Greeley, a New York editor, heard about **Gregory Gulch** and traveled west to take a personal look. Greeley reported: "As yet the entire population of the valley, which cannot number less than four thousand, sleep in tents or under pine boughs, cooking and eating in the open air."

A mass of prospectors swarmed into the hillsides. Most never struck it rich and many left poorer than when they arrived, but some had a grand time. A theater was built. Sarah Bernhardt and Edwin Booth came to perform. The **Teller House Hotel** rose in 1872, built with care by fine craftsmen and artisans.

Large, carved bedsteads, marble-topped commodes, and tall rosewood and walnut highboys were ferried across the prairies and up the rough roads by teams of oxen and mules and on wood-burning trains. The fine hotel hosted famous people; President Ulysses S. Grant, Walt Whitman, Oscar Wilde, Baron de Rothschild, and assorted European noblemen and their wives all slept in Central City.

In 1874 most of the community burned down, but gold rebuilt it. Fewer than four years later there was a new opera house, which still stands. Built in 1878 by Welsh and Cornish miners, the **Central City Opera House,** located on Eureka Street, is home to the fifth-oldest opera company in the nation. This restored Victorian opera house holds an annual summer festival that draws patrons from nearly every state. Performances range from its popular one-act opera *The Face on the Barroom Floor,* which recounts the local lore behind the painting on the Teller House Bar floor, to classic operas such as Giuseppe Verdi's *La Traviata* and Puccini's *La Bohème,* as well as popular musicals such as *Oklahoma!* Central City Opera House invites opera buffs to sit back and relax in one of its 550 comfortable seats while taking in performances by known stars and future divas.

For show dates (performances are in summer), prices, and times, contact Central City Opera at (303) 292-6700; centralcityopera.org. Opening night remains a prominent Colorado social event. Cars and busloads of operagoers from nearby cities climb the road along **Clear Creek Canyon,** the same route taken by John Gregory more than 100 years ago.

These days gamblers also swarm to the area, since gaming was approved in the early 1990s for Central City and Black Hawk. New casinos have replaced many historic buildings and shops, and most visitors these days are more interested in games of chance than in the history of these former mining towns. Where parking was once hard to find, it is now almost impossible, but shuttle services run from Golden and areas in Denver on a regular basis.

If you want to try your luck, stop at some of these Central City establishments: Century Casino & Hotel, Famous Bonanza, Grand Z Casino Hotel, Dostal Alley, and Easy Street Casino. Down the road in Black Hawk, try Bally's Casino, Monarch Casino Resort Spa, Bull Durham, Gilpin Hotel, The Lodge Casino, and Isle of Capri.

Central City and Black Hawk are less than an hour's drive from Denver via US 6 and Highway 119. For more information, stop by the Central City Visitors Center, 103 Eureka St.; (303) 582-3345, or visit visitcentralcity.com.

If you're heading north from Central City to Estes Park, your route will take you along one of Colorado's oldest and most picturesque drives. The **Peak to Peak Highway** was established in 1918. Following Highways 72 and 7, it runs parallel to the Continental Divide, passing close to Golden Gate Canyon State Park, Arapaho and Roosevelt National Forests, and Indian Peaks Wilderness Area before reaching Estes Park and the entrance to Rocky Mountain National Park. Small towns along the way such as Nederland, Ward, and Allenspark have cafes, art galleries, and small shops. The Peak to Peak Highway is easily accessible from both Denver and Boulder.

Rock Canyons & Boulders

As you drive toward **Boulder,** the towering **Flatirons,** huge slabs of metamorphic sandstone thrust up by the same geologic forces that gave birth to the Rocky Mountains, dominate your view to the west. Now the city's trademark, the Flatirons—some of which reach heights of more than 1,000 feet—offer ample opportunities for rock climbers of all abilities. These monoliths also appeal to hikers and trail runners due to the abundance of trails through the meadows and hills surrounding the Flatirons. Forming the abrupt border between the plains and the Rocky Mountains, this stunning rock formation is a perfect destination for walking, wildflower watching, or sitting with friends and enjoying a warm Colorado afternoon. Located 22 miles northwest of Denver, Boulder is easily reached in about half an hour via the Boulder Turnpike, US 36.

Arguably in possession of the highest population of rock climbers per capita of any city or town in the US, Boulder enjoys its status as one of the centers of US **rock climbing.** This reputation becomes even clearer when you drive up nearby Boulder Canyon or Eldorado Canyon to watch the climbers clinging to the steep rock faces. Dozens of world-class climbing areas within several hours' drive, combined with two of the best indoor climbing facilities in the country right in Boulder, only add to the city's appeal. Rock climbing's popularity has grown tremendously since the early 1990s. Boulder's reputation as a climbing mecca spread quickly, attracting both experienced climbers and those eager to try their first ascent.

All Aboard!

The first train from Denver to Black Hawk rolled through on December 15, 1872. It took another six years for the line to extend to Central City. Regardless of the railroad's success, writer-explorer Isabella Bird once complained that she had never seen such "churlishness and incivility as in the officials of that railroad." She wrote of her disapproval in her excellent 1875 book about her adventures, *A Lady's Life in the Rocky Mountains*. Back then, the train traveled a 200-foot-per-mile grade through Clear Creek Canyon. Black rock walls rose more than a thousand feet on either side. You can still see those ominous walls if you travel US 6 through the area; it follows the same route as the railroad did.

Eldorado Canyon is one of the birthplaces of rock climbing in the US. Gorgeous sandstone cliffs soar above the canyon floor in shades of red speckled with greenish and golden-hued lichen that appears to take on its own luminescence when viewed in the right light. Formed of the same type of hardened sandstone that makes up the Flatirons—known as the Fountain Formation—the world-class walls of Eldorado Canyon enjoy international prestige within the rock-climbing community.

Hundreds of established routes await rock climbers of all abilities on the canyon walls, but none should be taken lightly. "Eldo," as climbers affectionately refer to the place, is known for its stiff grades, polished rock (especially on popular climbs), and sometimes scant protection. All of these factors mean that climbers should exercise caution when they first start out climbing in the canyon, perhaps choosing an easier route to allow themselves time to grow accustomed to the area.

Once a bastion for some of the state's hardest routes, Eldorado Canyon's heyday as far as pure difficulty for climbing moves has passed, but that doesn't relegate its challenges to second-tier status by any means. Exposure—that sensation you get when you can truly feel just how high above the canyon floor you are—is the name of the game on classic routes like the Naked Edge, the Yellow Spur, and even Bastille Crack. Easily identified as the crack that divides the Bastille formation (the crag that sits on the left of the road as soon as you start to drive up the canyon), it is an ever-popular classic; more likely than not you will see someone climbing it any given day, at any given time.

If scaling the walls isn't your idea of fun, Eldorado Canyon has plenty of other options. Tourists flock to the canyon in at least as many numbers as rock climbers, often clogging the narrow road up the canyon as they stop to gawk at tiny figures dangling from the walls high above. At the end of the canyon's road lies a lovely streamside picnic area with tables and barbecue grills, perfect for a family outing. Numerous hiking trails allow non-climbers to keep their feet on the ground while exploring the canyon's deeper realms. Kayakers and anglers delight in South Boulder Creek, which burbles its way down the canyon for most of the year, freezing over during winter months.

Mountain bikers (and hikers) get a solid workout as they slog their way up the unrelenting **Rattlesnake Gulch Trail,** a strenuous loop trail that challenges the rider with 1,200 feet of elevation gain during the 3.2-mile ride along some tight, technical singletrack. See the remains of the historic Crags Hotel and view the Continental Divide. To find the trail, turn left on the Fowler Trail after passing through the first parking area in Eldorado Canyon State Park. Visit trails.colorado.gov/routes/45.

trivia

Sherrill Milnes and Beverly Sills both got their operatic starts in Central City.

As with most Colorado destinations, weekdays here are almost always less crowded than weekends. To reach Eldorado Canyon State Park, 25 miles northwest of Denver, take the Boulder Turnpike to the Superior exit; turn south at the light and then turn right onto Highway 170, which will take you to Eldorado Springs. From Boulder, head south on Highway 93 and then take a right (west) on Highway 170 (Eldorado Springs Drive). The visitor center is located 1 mile up the canyon. Help with overcrowded summer weekends by riding the free Eldo Shuttle to Eldorado Canyon State Park instead of driving. It also accesses the Marshall Mesa, Doudy Draw, and South Mesa trailheads, which are popular hiking, sightseeing, climbing, and biking destinations south of Boulder. The shuttle makes multiple stops in Boulder along Broadway and at the McCaslin Blvd. and US 36 park-n-ride. The shuttle runs from late May to early Sept on Sat, Sun, and holidays from 8 a.m. to 7 p.m. For more info visit bouldercounty.gov/transportation/multimodal/eldoshuttle.

Eldorado Canyon State Park is open dawn to dusk year-round. A $10-per-vehicle charge is required for entry, and currently timed reservations are also required, plus a state park pass. Be aware that certain trails may be closed temporarily certain months to protect nesting golden eagles. For more information call (303) 494-3943 or go to cpw.state.co.us/placestogo/parks/EldoradoCanyon.

Another popular canyon destination is **Eldorado Springs** at the entrance to the canyon. This tiny, eclectic town not only serves as a gateway to the park but also is home to the **Eldorado Springs Pool** at the historic Eldorado Springs Resort, which makes for a great place to cool off during hot summer months.

Once a major tourist destination known as the "Coney Island of the West," Eldorado Springs Resort attracted more than 60,000 guests every summer during the early 1900s. The pool, built in 1906 and then advertised as the largest pool in the country, is filled to the brim with artesian water from the springs. The pool is under renovation through 2022, but management says it hopes to keep the historic resort open for another 114 years post renovation. Call (303) 499-1316 for more information, or go to eldoradosprings.com.

To find out more about the history of rock climbing, as well as mountaineering and skiing, stop by **Neptune Mountaineering** on your way into Boulder. There you can explore Gary Neptune's impressive collection of climbing and skiing artifacts while you stock up on hydration packs, hiking boots, climbing equipment, and energy bars. Make sure you grab an event schedule—Neptune Mountaineering hosts frequent evening audiovisual presentations on adventure sports, mountaineering, and travel. The slide shows are generally low in cost and high in fun. Leave time to relax in Neptune's bar-cafe and soak in the spirit of outdoor adventure that permeates the whole place.

The store (633 S. Broadway, Ste. A) is located on the upper level of the Table Mesa Shopping Center at the corner of Broadway and Table Mesa in Boulder. From Eldorado Springs, take Highway 93 north (it turns into Broadway). Open Mon through Wed, 10 a.m. to 7 p.m.; Thur and Fri, 10 a.m. to 8 p.m.; and Sat and Sun, 10 a.m. to 6 p.m. For more information call (303) 499-8866 or check the website at neptunemountaineering.com.

After stopping at Neptune's, continue along Broadway to Baseline Road, turning west to head up **Flagstaff Mountain,** the perfect place to mingle with rock climbers while taking in some beautiful scenery. Bouldering—a type of rock climbing that involves short, intense movements up the sides of the boulders, with the climber normally staying low to the ground—is a popular pastime on Flagstaff, and for good reason. Plenty of high-quality boulders dapple the flanks of Flagstaff, serving up myriad challenges that both delight and frustrate the numerous rock climbers who flock to the sharp, rough sandstone. Pull out at any of a number of locations along the road and follow the paths back to the boulders, where you'll likely find some climbers who have come to test their skills for an afternoon. It's said that necessity is the mother of invention. Case in point: crash pads. You'll see bouldering enthusiasts carrying crash pads on their backs or stacking them at the foot of their next route.

Boulder Hiking

The **Mesa Trail,** one of Colorado's most scenic introductions to year-round hiking and trail running, is easily accessible. From Denver, drive the Boulder Turnpike (US 36) to the Louisville/McCaslin Blvd. exit; head southwest to Highway 170. Go 1.7 miles until you see the South Mesa Trailhead sign on the right. This takes you on a northbound 6.7-mile trek along Boulder's foothills and through a landscape of sumac bushes, ferns, and sedges. The uphills are gentle enough, leading into impressive pine forests with views of the Flatirons. The Mesa Trail winds up in Boulder's Chautauqua Park. In winter the trail is popular with cross-country skiers.

TOP ANNUAL EVENTS IN BOULDER COUNTY

MAY
Bolder Boulder 10K Race
Memorial Day
(303) 444-7223
bolderboulder.com

Boulder Creek Festival
Memorial Day weekend
(303) 449-3137
bceproductions.com

Chautauqua Summer Concerts and Events
May to Sept
(303) 442-3282
chautauqua.com

JUNE
Colorado Music Festival
Boulder Chautauqua Park
June through early Aug
(303) 449-1397
comusic.org

Bands on the Bricks
1300 block of Pearl Street
Wednesday evenings, mid-June to early Aug
boulderdowntown.com/events/bands-on-the-bricks

JULY
Shakespeare Festival
University of Colorado Boulder campus
July through Aug
(303) 492-0554
coloradoshakes.org

AUGUST
Lafayette Peach Festival
Old Town Lafayette on Public Rd.
lafayettecolorado.com

OCTOBER
Open Studios Tour
Artist studios across Boulder
(303) 444-1862
First three weekends in Oct
openstudios.org

The ingenious concept was created by, of course, a couple of freewheeling, bruised boulderers in need of a softer landing. A few pieces of carpet and foam launched an industry. Continue strolling along one of the mountain's marked trails, or just grab a seat on one of the surrounding smaller boulders and relax in the shade of ponderosa pines while you watch the fun. The jagged ridge of the First Flatiron pokes out above the trees to the south, and obstructed views of the city of Boulder can be seen to the east.

trivia

President Dwight Eisenhower and his wife, Mamie, spent their honeymoon in Eldorado Canyon.

For more information on hiking or biking Flagstaff Mountain, contact the City of Boulder Open Space and Mountain Parks Department, 66 S. Cherryvale Rd., Boulder 80303; (303) 441-3440; bouldercolorado.gov/osmp. Daily parking permits can be purchased for $5 from any of the six well-marked self-service stations located along Flagstaff Road.

For a treat, make dinner reservations at the **Flagstaff House,** one of Boulder's revered dining establishments. Nestled on the side of Flagstaff Mountain, this lovely restaurant is sure to delight even the most discriminating food lover. It's one of the pricier area eateries (entrees start at $38), but in return you get gourmet New American cuisine complete with impeccable service, occasional complimentary appetizers from the chef, and a terrific wine list, not to mention sweeping views of Boulder. The Flagstaff House (1138 Flagstaff Rd.; 303-442-4640) is on the right as you drive up the mountain. Visit them at flagstaffhouse.com.

After dinner, walk off your meal with your date by taking a romantic moonlit stroll at **Panorama Point** (1 mile up Flagstaff Road from the base of the mountain) or at one of the many other overlooks that line Flagstaff Road. If you're still feeling guilty about your marvelous dinner the next morning, you can always come back and bike up Flagstaff Road; it's one of the most popular workouts for local mountain and road bikers.

trivia

Tightrope walker and all-around daredevil Ivy Baldwin made 86 journeys across Eldorado Canyon on a tightrope suspended 582 feet above the ground. He made his last walk (and survived!) in 1948, at the ripe young age of 82.

The tree-lined campus of the **University of Colorado–Boulder** (known to locals as simply "CU") warrants a visit, particularly in the summer when the university stages its annual **Colorado Shakespeare Festival.** During the season, you'll notice banners proclaiming the performances—and telling you to keep quiet—along Broadway as you head toward downtown Boulder. The festival performs several Shakespeare plays in July and August. National auditions attract actors from all over. Contact the festival organizers at (303) 492-8008 or coloradoshakes.org.

Valmont Bike Park

Boulder is home to the largest free urban bike park in America. Opened in 2011, Valmont Bike Park is a 42-acre off-road bike park with competition-grade racing trails, big dirt jumps, a network of singletrack trails, dual-slalom tracks, and more. Equivalent to the size of 30 football fields, the park offers off-road riding for all levels of riders. A trike track, kid's play area, learning loop, and restrooms make this a family-friendly park. Located at the corner of Valmont and Airport Roads. For more information go to bouldercolorado.gov/locations/valmont-bike-park.

Macky Auditorium Concert Hall, also on the CU campus, hosts performances by the Boulder Philharmonic, the College of Music, visiting musicians participating in the Artists Series, and concerts by nationally known groups. For information call (303) 492-8423 or visit colorado.edu/macky.

Boulder also hosts the *Colorado Music Festival* from June through August. Visiting performers and composers lend their talents and energy to the festival. Performances are set in historic Chautauqua Auditorium, built in 1898 as part of the expansion of culture and adult learning offered at Chautauquas across the country and beyond in the late 19th and early 20th centuries. Reservations are required. Call (303) 665-0599 or visit comusic.org.

trivia

The pure, 76°F water of Eldorado Springs flows at a constant rate of 200 gallons per minute. Bottled at the source, Eldorado Springs drinking water is available for purchase at grocery stores around the state.

Hopefully you haven't tired of rock formations yet—Boulder still has more to offer in this department. Turn west from town for a drive up *Boulder Canyon.* Tall granite outcroppings line Highway 119 as it wends its way up toward the rustic town of Nederland and the *Peak to Peak Highway.* Find the canyon via Broadway (Highway 93) in Boulder. Head west on Canyon Boulevard (Highway 119)—you can't miss it. Stop at the pullout 11 miles up the canyon on your left to park, and then cross the street for a short walk back to the falls. Free; open from dawn to dusk May 1 through October 31. For more information contact City of Boulder, Open Space and Mountain Parks Department, 1777 Broadway, Boulder 80302; (303) 441-3440; bouldercolorado.gov/osmp.

You'll probably catch glimpses of rock climbers on the formations as you drive up the canyon, weather permitting. In winter you're more likely to see

trivia

Boulder is the only US community that uses its own city-owned glacier, Arapahoe Glacier, for its water supply.

people with crampons (metal-toothed attachments) on their boots and ice axes in their hands hacking their way up frozen waterfalls and sheets of ice—Boulder Canyon attracts ice climbers, too. But with its classic rock climbs, both traditional and sport, the canyon most likely sees far more climbing traffic from those who like to feel the rock instead of ice beneath their fingers and under their feet in warmer weather. After all, some claim that the canyon's famous Country Club Crack (5.11c) was the hardest rock climb in the country for a period of time!

Seeing all this rock climbing around Boulder might spark your interest in trying out rock climbing yourself—but don't head out there uninformed. Though rock climbing is a relatively safe sport, you should receive proper instruction and learn the safety basics before trying it out on your own. Rock climbing also requires specialized equipment that can take a big bite out of your wallet. To get a thorough understanding of ropes and gear, novices take lessons or get an experienced climber to show them the ropes, so to speak. Boulder has a number of local schools and workshops that teach safe climbing.

A reputable, established place to learn rock climbing in Boulder is the *Colorado Mountain School.* Affiliated with *Boulder Rock Club,* the AMGA-accredited school offers a wide range of classes for all ages and ability levels. Pretty much anybody can take a beginning climbing class—rippling abs and bulging biceps are not prerequisites. Especially at the more moderate levels of the sport, technique, balance, and flexibility count just as much as, if not more than, sheer strength.

Beginner classes often start in the indoor climbing gym. The school provides all necessary climbing equipment, allowing the student to sample rock climbing without making any monetary investment beyond the price of the class.

trivia

Boulder has no shortage of trails to explore: The city's Open Space and Mountain Parks Department maintains 145 miles of trails in its open space program, used by walkers, hikers, bicyclists, horseback riders, dog walkers, birders, and photographers.

Contact the Boulder Rock Club/Colorado Mountain School for details at (800) 836-4008 or visit coloradomountainschool .com. The facility is located at 2829 Mapleton Ave. Take US 36 into Boulder, and then head east on Mapleton. The club is on the north side of the street. Call for class schedules and to reserve a space.

For a tamer introduction to Boulder's famous monoliths, head up to pretty *Chautauqua Park.* This popular park has large, grassy meadows perfect for selfies and views of town. Hiking trails meander into the woods and up to the Flatirons. It's the location for the Colorado Music Festival, weddings, and summer film and music events. Follow Baseline Rd. west from Broadway to 900 W. Baseline Rd.

One of the best places to feel the eclectic mood of Boulder is on a stroll along the pedestrian *Pearl Street Mall.* Take Broadway north from the Canyon Boulevard intersection; the mall crosses Broadway a few blocks up. Locals and visitors mingle among boutiques, bookstores, and restaurants, many of which feature outdoor patios. Sculptures, fountains, cozy seating, and children's play areas along this 4-block thoroughfare help to make it one of the nation's

Sip, Read, Relax

Trident Booksellers & Café has been a beloved Boulder staple for more than 40 years. If you're passionate about independent bookstores, fast disappearing in this country, be sure to visit Trident at 940 Pearl Street. Now owned by a group of long-time employees, Trident is still thriving and still the labor of love it has always been. Peruse new and used books, sit out back and savor coffee or tea, and chat with Trident's many ardent local fans. Call (303) 443-3133 or visit tridentcafe.com.

most successful open-air pedestrian malls. Find a bench and enjoy some of the most colorful people-watching in the state. Talented musicians, jugglers, magicians, and other street performers entertain, especially on weekends and during the summer. The mall has been closed to auto traffic since the 1970s.

On the first Friday of the month, head up to NoBo (North Boulder) to get a firsthand look at the depth and breadth of artistic endeavors in Boulder on a free, self-guided tour of artists' studios and creative businesses. NoBo Art District is a collection of more than 200 creative industries and professional working artists in private studios on and around North Broadway between Pearl Street and Lee Hill. Open studios on First Fridays can number well over 20, plus food trucks, musical performances, and more. The art district not only introduces the public to neighborhood artists, photographers, sculptors, designers, and artisans; the community-focused organization provides a network of support for the artists themselves. Learn more at noboartdistrict.org.

If you have a sudden, uncontrollable craving for ice cream, head straight to locally based *Glacier Homemade Ice Cream & Gelato.* There are two locations: 3133 28th St., 1 block north of Valmont, (303) 440-6542, and 4760 Baseline Rd., Ste. C, (303) 499-4760; glaciericecream.com. Glacier makes more than 1,000 flavors in total, each one made fresh in the stores using premium ingredients. Popular flavors include coffee caramel crunch, death by chocolate, pralines 'n' cream, and coconut chocolate melt; many flavors are gluten-free. Want your own sundae bar for a celebration? Glacier offers catering, too.

trivia

CU-Boulder's mascot is a live buffalo named "Ralphie." Six Ralphies—all females—have trotted around the football field since the original Ralphie made her debut in 1966.

Between the university and the city, you'll find plenty to keep you busy in any season. Find out what's happening in town by picking up a copy of the *Boulder Weekly* newspaper, available for free at many businesses around town, or peruse it online at boulderweekly.com.

Traditional vs. Sport Climbing

Most of the rock climbing done in Eldorado Canyon falls under the definition of "traditional climbing," meaning that climbers place and remove virtually all the pieces of protection that they utilize on any given climb. These days, "sport climbing" has taken off in a variety of locations, including Boulder Canyon. In sport climbing, climbers hook devices called quickdraws into preplaced expansion bolts that are relatively permanent fixtures to the rock face, meaning that the bolts remain in the rock for the use of future parties.

Boulder is no longer the only star in Boulder County. Many residents have moved east for a less crowded, less expensive lifestyle but with easy access to all Boulder offers as well as easy access to Denver. As a result, the county's eastern towns have grown, becoming attractive to entrepreneurs who open breweries, restaurants, and art galleries for far less money than they could in Boulder, and that has bolstered and renewed some of the towns' older businesses, too.

Tiny **Lafayette** is one such town, just 11 miles east of Boulder via Arapahoe or Baseline Rd. Public Road, Lafayette's main street, has experienced a renaissance of sorts since folks have moved in and built new houses or renovated old ones, but the history and heart of Lafayette, and many of its longtime residents, remain part of the small-town, steadfast culture here. It's well worth an afternoon or evening escape from Boulder for a slice of original Colorado.

Lafayette was at first a ranching and farming community, then a major coal-mining town from the 1880s to the 1930s, helping supply heat and power to the Front Range. The Simpson and Cannon Mines were just two of the mines once worked in what is now Old Town Lafayette. Though little evidence of the area's mining history remains, which is mostly a good thing, it's said that there is still a network of tunnels beneath Lafayette and neighboring Louisville. Get insight into this largely hidden part of Boulder County's heritage at the **Miner's Museum,** open Wed to Fri, 10 a.m. to 2 p.m., and Sat from 8 a.m. to noon. The museum is housed in a historic mine company cottage. For tours contact the museum at 108 E. Simpson St.; (303) 665-7030; lafayettehistoricalsociety.org/visit.

A little gem among Denver Metro Area's breweries is **Odd 13 Brewing** (301 E. Simpson St.; 303-997-4164; odd13brewing.com). The excellent tap list changes regularly, so there's always a new brew to taste. Food is supplied by a revolving selection of food trucks out back.

The Post Chicken & Beer-Lafayette (105 W. Emma St.; 303-593-2066; postchickenandbeer.com/lafayette) is a full-on restaurant and brewery housed

South Boulder Creek Trail

Rain or shine, summer and winter, one of the most popular walkways in Boulder is the South Boulder Creek Trail. Located east of the main part of town, the trail doesn't tackle any of Boulder's hilly terrain but rather offers a nice, flat, 3.5-mile dirt path alongside South Boulder Creek. This route winds through trees and grasslands, offering interpretive signs along the way as well as the opportunity to see wildlife, from coyotes to entire prairie dog towns. Each season brings a different mood to the trail. In fall the trees burst into glorious shades of orange and yellow, while winter finds them stark and bare and the trail covered with snow. With spring come budding greenery, songbirds, and the fragrant scent of new growth. In summer the walk bursts with life. From Broadway in Boulder, head east on Baseline. The Bobolink trailhead is on the right about 1 mile past Foothills Parkway, with plenty of parking. Located on City of Boulder Open Space, you can also catch the trail on Highway 93, about ½ mile south of Greenbriar Boulevard. It's a 3.4-mile (each way) there-and-back trail, with access to the Highway 36 bike path as well. Visit bouldercolorado.gov/trail/south-boulder-creek.

in the town's former VFW Post 1771 building. In addition to cold beer, The Post is all about good fried chicken, though meats and fish are also on the limited menu.

In spite of what Boulder residents may think, *Efrain's* in Lafayette (101 E. Cleveland St.; 303-666-7544; facebook.com/efrainsmexrest) is the original of the family-owned restaurants. Set in an older house, it has served up Northern Mexican cuisine in Lafayette for more than two decades, and it remains as popular as ever.

Two excellent coffee shops, both in the historic downtown area, provide a sense of local community and camaraderie. *East Simpson Coffee Company* (201 E. Simpson St.; 720-502-7010; eastsimpsoncoffee.com) opened in 2013 and is part of the revival of Simpson St., once Lafayette's main thoroughfare, which had fallen on hard times. Some residents on the street have lived there for decades; others are new to the charms of Lafayette. In addition to excellent modern coffee drinks, patrons here enjoy homemade soups, locally made pastries and more. *Cannon Mine Coffee* (210 S. Public Rd.; 303-665-0625; cannonmine .com) honors Lafayette's mining history with its name. Coffee, breakfast burritos, and pastries are enjoyed against a backdrop of artwork and photography by locals. Wednesday, Friday, and Saturday Cannon Mine stays open into the evening and presents live music along with beer, wine, coffee cocktails, and a full bar. Learn more about Lafayette by contacting the Lafayette Chamber of Commerce, 304 W. Baseline Rd.; (303) 666-9555; lafayettecolorado.com.

Places to Stay in the Colorado Foothills

BOULDER

Boulder Adventure Lodge
91 Fourmile Canyon Dr.
(303) 444-0882
a-lodge.com
Inexpensive to Moderate
Geared toward outdoor adventurers, this community-focused lodging connects guests with local adventures and gives them a comfortable, convivial base to return to. Mix of nicely appointed rooms and very affordable shared hostel accommodations. Hot tubs by creek, seasonal swimming pool.

Boulder Twin Lakes Inn
6485 Twin Lakes Rd.
(303) 530-2939
twinlakesinnboulder.com
Moderate
Less than 7 miles from downtown, Twin Lakes Inn is peaceful, budget-friendly respite in a parklike setting with complimentary breakfast, hot tub, and free Wi-Fi.

The Bradley Boulder Inn
2040 16th St.
(303) 545-5200 or
(800) 858-5811
thebradleyboulder.com
Moderate to Expensive
Located steps away from the Pearl Street Mall, this is a 12-room luxury inn with full gourmet breakfast, evening wine and cheese, snacks throughout the day, and free wireless internet. Some rooms include fireplaces, Jacuzzis, balconies with mountain views. No children under 14.

Courtyard Boulder
4710 Pearl East Circle
(303) 440-4700
marriott.com
Moderate to Expensive
Pool, free wireless internet, 2 miles from Pearl Street Mall.

Colorado Chautauqua Cottages & Lodges
900 Baseline Rd.
(303) 952-1611
chautauqua.com/cottages-and-lodges
Moderate to Expensive
Colorado Chautauqua, a National Historic Landmark, offers studio- to three-bedroom cottages built between 1899 and 1954. Rooms can also be booked in historic Columbine Lodge. Guests have access to 40+ miles of trails (start out early before the crowds arrive), complimentary Wi-Fi throughout the park, cultural programming, the Dining Hall, and a small general store. Few settings in Boulder match Chautauqua's allure.

Hotel Boulderado
2115 13th St.
(303) 442-4344 or
(800) 433-4344
boulderado.com
Expensive
Historic luxury hotel with Victorian decor in the heart of downtown and 1 block from Pearl Street. Free wireless internet.

Hyatt Place Boulder/Pearl Street
2280 Junction Place
(303) 442-0160
hyatt.com/en-US/hotel/colorado/hyatt-place-boulder-pearl-street/denzb
Expensive
Contemporary and typical of the brand; clean, easy to access with a pool, complimentary breakfast and free Wi-Fi. Zeal, a restaurant at Hyatt Place is an excellent option for vegan and vegetarian dishes but also meat and tasty ethnic dishes.

St. Julien Hotel & Spa
900 Walnut St.
(720) 406-9696 or
(877) 303-0900
stjulien.com
Expensive
Independently owned luxury hotel 1 block from Pearl Street offering an infinity pool, whirlpool and spa, and free Wi-Fi.

GOLDEN

Origin Hotel Red Rocks
18485 West Colfax Ave.
(303) 215-0100 or
(833) 674-4461
originhotel.com
Expensive
Part of a tiny chain seeking to foster meaningful connections in each community for its staff and guests, Minutes from downtown Golden, it's

also the official hotel of Red Rocks Amphitheatre. Contemporary and upscale, it offers a nice counterpoint to the rugged adventures guests can access just outside the doors.

Table Mountain Inn
1310 Washington Ave.
(303) 277-9898 or
(800) 762-9898
tablemountaininn.com
Moderate
Southwestern decor and 74 guest rooms make this a Golden favorite. The award-winning Table Mountain Grill & Cantina is part of the inn. Free wireless internet and complimentary access to nearby community center.

The Eddy Taproom & Hotel
1640 8th St.
(720) 442-8150 or
(877) 226-3898
theeddygolden.com
Expensive
Casual retreat with 49 guest rooms for outdoor enthusiasts and others who want a base camp at the foot of the Rocky Mountains from which to discover Clear Creek Valley and the history, attractions and friendly, small-town vibe of Golden.

The Golden Hotel
800 11th St.
(303) 279-0100 or
(800) 233-7214
thegoldenhotel.com
Moderate
Overlooking Clear Creek, close to Coors Brewery and downtown, live music Thursday evenings,

complimentary local shuttle, free wireless internet, pet-friendly. Bridgewater Grill in hotel offers a daily full menu.

Places to Eat in the Colorado Foothills

BLACK HAWK/ CENTRAL CITY

Millie's Restaurant
120 Main St., Central City
(303) 582-5914
famousbonanza.com
Inexpensive
Appetizers, soups, salads, burgers, sandwiches, entrees.

BOULDER

Boulder Dushanbe Teahouse
1770 13th St.
(303) 442-4993
boulderteahouse.com
Moderate
Popular restaurant housed in an authentic, craftsmen-built Tajikistan teahouse. The menu includes a wide variety of international entrees for breakfast, lunch, and dinner, plus an extensive tea selection. If you want to book afternoon tea—and you should—do so well in advance.

Flagstaff House
1138 Flagstaff Rd.
(303) 442-4640
flagstaffhouse.com
Expensive
Fine French-American

dining with breathtaking views of Boulder, extensive wine cellar.

The Kitchen
1039 Pearl St.
(303) 544-5973
thekitchencommunity.com
Expensive
Popular community eatery serving innovative American cuisine inspired by European bistro fare.

Oak at Fourteenth
1400 Pearl Street
(303) 444-3642
Expensive
Menu of seasonal and local items built around the restaurant's oak-fired oven and grill. Chic and comfortable with an excellent menu.

Rio Grande
1101 Walnut St.
(303) 444-3690
riograndemexican.com/ boulder
Inexpensive to Moderate
Loud, fun Mexican restaurant with wicked-good margaritas and freshly prepared entrees. Indoor dining and rooftop patio.

Southern Sun Pub & Brewery
627 S. Broadway, Ste. E
(303) 543-0886
mountainsunpub.com
Moderate
Pub fare in South Boulder, plus a brewery that brews about 75 different beers in a year. Southern Sun is part of a small restaurant/ brewery group with several locations.

The Sink
1165 13th St.
(303) 444-7465
thesink.com
Moderate
On the hill, near the university, The Sink is old Boulder and new Boulder, a place that has changed yet stayed the same. Many will tell you the Sinkburger is the best burger in Boulder. Decide for yourself. Take time to scrawl your name on the crowded wall and search for President Obama's signature while you're at it. No surprise, The Sink has also been celebrated by Guy Fieri and Anthony Bourdain.

GOLDEN

Ali Baba Grill
109 Rubey Dr.
(303) 279-2228
alibabagrill.com
Moderate
Tasty Lebanese and Persian cuisine cooked fresh daily in a friendly setting.

Bridgewater Grill
800 11th St.
(303) 279-2010
bridgewatergrill.com
Moderate to Expensive
Salads, steaks, seafood, burgers, and American classic dishes at the Golden Hotel. Live music in the lounge on Thursday evenings.

Buffalo Rose
1119 Washington Ave.
(720) 638-5597
Moderate
Buffalo Rose is housed in a collection of historic buildings in the heart of Golden, offering food, drink, entertainment, and a palpable sense of Western history and culture. Regional American cuisine with Latin and Western flair.

Golden Mill
1012 Ford St.
(720) 405-6455
Inexpensive to Moderate
A food emporium where multiple vendors sell their own dishes from separate stalls. Mexican, sushi, fried chicken, and ice cream are among the choices. Self-pour tap walls offer a huge variety of beverages; check in first at the host stand to get your Golden Mill RFID then start tasting.

Sherpa House Restaurant
1518 Washington Ave.
(303) 278-7939
sherpa.house
Moderate
Authentic Tibetan, Nepalese, and Indian cuisine with decor based on a traditional sherpa home in Nepal.

Table Mountain Inn Grill & Cantina
1310 Washington Ave.
(303) 277-9898
tablemountaininn.com
Moderate
Fresh Southwestern and American cuisine.

LAFAYETTE

Efrain's
101 E. Cleveland St.
(303) 666-7544
facebook.com/ efrainsmexrest
This is the original of Boulder County's Efrain's restaurants, serving Northern Mexican cuisine in a casual setting for more than 20 years.

95a Bistro & Co.
1381 Forest Park Circle
(303) 665-3080
Moderate to Expensive
95abistroandsushi.com
American, Latin, Asian, and Mediterranean influences; tapas and small plates.

Odd 13 Brewing
301 E. Simpson St.
(303) 997-4164
Odd13brewing.com
The tap list changes regularly, so check the website. A revolving selection of food trucks out back offer food to take inside, and there's live music most Saturdays.

The Post Chicken & Beer
105 W. Emma St.
(303) 593-2066
postbrewing.com
Cold beer and fried chicken with a few other dishes added in.

MORRISON

The Fort
19192 Hwy. 8
(303) 697-4771
thefort.com
Expensive
Historic, award-winning restaurant combines flavors of the early West with contemporary cuisine. Wide range of game, meats, Southwestern flavors, and an extensive wine list.

FOR MORE INFORMATION

BOULDER
Visit Boulder
2440 Pearl St., 80302
(303) 442-2911
bouldercoloradousa.com

CENTRAL CITY/BLACK HAWK
Central City–Black Hawk Visitor
Center
103 Eureka St.
Central City 80427
(303) 582-3345
colorado.gov/pacific/centralcity/
visitor-information-1

GOLDEN
Visit Golden
1010 Washington Ave., 80401
(303) 279-2282
visitgolden.com

LAFAYETTE
Lafayette Chamber of Commerce
309 S. Public Rd., 80026
(303) 666-9555
lafayettecolorado.com

OTHER ATTRACTIONS WORTH SEEING IN THE COLORADO FOOTHILLS

BOULDER
University of Colorado at Boulder
(303) 492-1411
colorado.edu

CENTRAL CITY
Coeur d'Alene Mine Shaft House
(303) 582-5283
gilpinhistory.org/coeur-d-alene-mine

GOLDEN
Coors Brewery
(303) 277-2337 or (800) 642-6116
coorsbrewerytour.com

Golden Gate Canyon State Park
(303) 582-3707
cpw.state.co.us/placestogo/parks/
GoldenGateCanyon

LAFAYETTE
The Miner's Museum
108 E. Simpson St.
(303) 665-7030
cityoflafayette.com

Northwestern Mountains

Rocky Mountain National Park Territory

If you come to **Estes Park** during the high summer season—and want to be above the melee—you might consider the short uphill drive to the **Stanley Hotel.** It stands above the busy town like a white castle. The 140-room Stanley reminds you of those old Swiss Grand Hotels—aristocratic, flawlessly kept up, frequently restored, and a monument to good taste and good manners.

The hotel is all stately white columns, Victorian furniture, fireplaces crackling in the lobby, rooms with impeccable white linen, polished cherrywood furniture, and antique dressers. The handwrought leaded-glass windows, spotless tablecloths in the elegant dining room, and highly regarded whiskey bar—said to have Colorado's largest collection of whiskey, with more than 1,000 labels—add to a feeling of being on vacation. Miles of walks can be accessed from the hostelry, which is at an elevation of 7,500 feet.

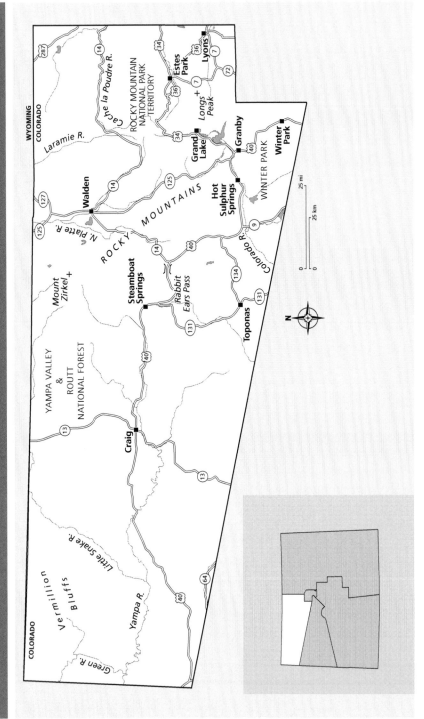

The historic hotel was built by one of the inventors of the Stanley Steamer automobile. Back in 1905, doctors gave **F. O. Stanley,** who had tuberculosis, only a few months to live. Stanley gathered his wife, her maid, and his controversial Steamer and left Massachusetts, heading for the Colorado Rockies. Stanley lived another 37 years, to the age of 91. His palatial hotel opened in 1909, and the "all-electric" hotel charged $8 a day, gourmet meals included. Celebrities such as Theodore Roosevelt, John Philip Sousa, and Molly Brown came, adding to the grandeur. More recently, novelist Stephen King found inspiration for his novel *The Shining* while staying at the hotel.

The hotel still hosts guests with deluxe accommodations. Nonguests can enjoy the Cascade Restaurant, admire the architecture and the views, and sign up for daily tours that focus on the hotel's history and reputed paranormal activity. Contact Stanley Hotel at 333 Wonderview Ave., Estes Park 80517; or call (970) 577-4000 or visit stanleyhotel.com.

The town of **Estes Park** (elev. 7,522 feet) is the eastern and most popular gateway to Rocky Mountain National Park. For those not camping in the park, the town offers a variety of lodging options, including hotels, motels, vacation homes, and cabins. The main thoroughfare through town is lined with an eclectic collection of shops and boutiques, as well as craft breweries, and the scenic river walk is an inviting place to stroll. During July and August downtown traffic can slow to a crawl. Those in a hurry to get to the park should look for the sign just inside the town limits for the bypass road that circumvents the business area.

Although tourist traffic downtown can be heavy, Estes Park has much to offer the many thousands of visitors who arrive each summer. Shoppers have fun browsing for Native American crafts and jewelry, trendy fashions, and quality outdoor gear. Kids ride go-karts, take on the challenge of a high-ropes course, or speed down a giant slide. Fishing and golf are close by. And there's a full calendar of music, cultural, and entertainment events throughout the year. Just keep in mind that you will be sharing the town with plenty of others—including many elk in the fall, which wander everywhere. To avoid the crowds, plan your visit for late spring or weekdays in the fall, or in summer arrive by midmorning.

Estes Park is 65 miles northwest of Denver and easy to reach via the Boulder Turnpike (US 36) through **Lyons.** For more information contact Visit Estes Park, 500 Big Thompson Ave., Estes Park 80517; (970) 577-9900 or (800) 443-7837; visitestespark.com.

Many people who come to Estes Park do so with another destination in mind. The east entrance to **Rocky Mountain National Park** is just a few miles beyond the town. Go beyond the bustle of town to step into the natural grandeur of the park with its high peaks, meadows, and rivers, and you will see the reason you came here. With almost no commercial activity inside the park, the landscape looks much as it did when Mr. Stanley first arrived more than 100 years ago.

With 415 square miles of park, there's no shortage of acreage to explore. The park has 98 peaks over 11,000 feet. The highest is **Longs Peak** at 14,259 feet. Surrounding those mountains is a vast wonderland of lakes, waterfalls, streams and rivers, meadows, forests, and tundra.

The best way to explore the park is to leave your car and walk some of the 350-plus miles of hiking trails. Trails ranging in difficulty from easy to extreme lead to remote valleys, sprawling meadows, and granite peaks. Several popular ones are short, level paths to beautiful lakes and waterfalls. Some trails to consider: Nymph, Dream, and Emerald Lakes; Ouzel Falls; Adams Falls; Bear Lake; Lulu City; Deer Mountain.

Frequent nature presentations and guided walks sponsored by the park are a great way to get kids interested in their surroundings. Backpackers obtain permits and disappear into the mountains for days at a time. The streams and lakes offer trout fishing. For many, sitting next to a meadow or river and watching the afternoon go by is reward enough.

In the summer, wildlife watchers may spot deer, elk, bighorn sheep, beavers, coyotes, pikas, and many bird species. Afternoon lightning and thunderstorms are not uncommon, cooling the air with rain before they blow to the east. In the winter, bundle up and choose from dozens of cross-country skiing and snowshoeing destinations.

For many, autumn is the best time of all, with its seemingly endless string of clear, warm days. The evenings turn crisp and the nights are chilly, so bring an overcoat.

Visitors in the fall get two bonuses: Aspen turn golden, and elk gather in the meadows to defend harems and bugle their high-pitched calls. Both events begin in September and last into mid-October. For many Coloradans, coming to the park to hear the elk and watch the fall colors is an annual tradition. The park visitor center can provide forecasts in early fall on foliage and elk activity.

One of the park highlights is the drive along spectacular **Trail Ridge Road** (US 34), the highest continuously paved highway in the US. Climbing more than 4,000 feet from Estes Park, the road winds along for 48 miles before dropping down to Grand Lake. Eleven miles of the road are above tree line in an arctic tundra environment, with the high point at 12,183 feet. Up here the air is thin and the ultraviolet rays are strong. It's a fragile world of tiny plants and flowers, alive in summer with birds, small mammals, and often snow.

Like most important Colorado highways, Trail Ridge has a long history. The first human travelers along this route were Utes and other Native American tribes following the already marked trails of wild animals. Miners used it in

Estes Park: The Best Views

The **Estes Park Aerial Tramway**, west on US 34 to Moraine Park Road, carries summertime visitors to the 8,896-foot summit of Prospect Mountain for an unmatched look at the community and surrounding mountains. Ride in one of two suspended cabins and view the Continental Divide, and then picnic at the summit. For more information call (970) 475-4094 or visit estestram.com.

the 1880s. In 1929 Congress approved the highway, and in 1932 the road was finally completed.

Multiple parking areas along the way are the starting points for exploring the area. To truly experience this unique ecosystem, leave the car and set out on one of the designated trails. Keep an eye on the weather to avoid lightning storms; the first half of the day is generally less prone to storms. Stay on trails to avoid damaging the fragile flora underfoot.

The season is short for a drive on the road, though. Deep snows and snowdrifts cover Trail Ridge all winter and spring. The road is open from around Memorial Day until the first heavy snowfall, usually in mid-October.

Rocky Mountain National Park is one of the busiest national parks, third in the country in 2019, with over 4.6 million visitors. Visitor crowding and congestion at RMNP have led to increased negative impacts to visitor and staff safety, resource protection, visitor experience, and operational capacity. For those reasons, RMNP has implemented a timed-entry reservation system. Plan ahead, especially if you want to camp within the park. The best way to avoid crowds is to visit before Memorial Day or after late September, when children are in school.

The park entrance fee is $30 for a one-day private vehicle. The Rocky Mountain Annual Pass at $70 is good for a year. Travelers age 62 and older can purchase the Annual or Lifetime Senior Pass for $20 or $80, respectively.

You have four options for getting to the park from Denver. One of two quickest routes is driving through Boulder and Lyons (use US 36); from Boulder it's about 34 miles to Estes Park and the east gate to the national park. The other is to travel some 70 miles north from Denver on I-25 north to Highway 66, then west on 66 until it joins US 36 to Estes Park.

trivia

The Stanley Hotel earned some of its more recent notoriety as the setting that inspired Stephen King's novel *The Shining*. King wrote roughly half of the manuscript for the novel while staying in Room 217 at the hotel. He returned to the Stanley Hotel in 1997 to make the ABC miniseries version of *The Shining* (the motion picture was filmed elsewhere).

You can also come on the spectacular ***Peak to Peak Scenic Byway*** (Highways 119, 72, and 7) from Black Hawk. The drive is especially enjoyable in late fall when aspen trees burst into gold. Plan on 2 to 3 hours, depending on sightseeing stops, to reach the national park via this route. For a more leisurely course, head west from Denver on I-70, cross Berthoud Pass via US 40, and then get to Rocky Mountain National Park via Grand Lake. You can do a loop by returning to Denver using one of the previous two routes. For more information contact Rocky Mountain National Park, 1000 Hwy. 36, Estes Park 80517; (970) 586-1206; nps.gov/romo.

After spending the day on Trail Ridge Road (have warm clothes handy even in summer), you can continue west and drop into a wide river valley with meadows and thick stands of pine, spruce, and aspen. After exiting through the park's west entrance, you will come to the town of ***Grand Lake,*** which skirts the shores of Grand Lake itself. This unusually blue lake—the largest natural lake in the state—will be dotted with sailboats in August, its marinas filled with yachts. At an elevation of almost 8,400 feet above sea level, Grand Lake boasts the "World's Highest Yacht Club." The high surrounding peaks stand over a stunning, Swiss-like scene.

The first people to visit here many centuries ago were Paleo-Indians, crossing the high mountain passes in search of game. In the 1800s, Arapaho, Sioux, and Cheyenne began venturing here, resulting in fierce conflicts with the Utes who lived throughout the area. Trappers, traders, and explorers trickled in, and in 1875 gold, silver, copper, and lead discoveries touched off a mining boom. Ten years later the boom went bust, and the population dropped from 600 to 80 year-round residents.

But the beauty of the area was not forgotten. Tourists, ranchers, and sportsmen began coming to the lake, and when Rocky Mountain National Park was designated in 1915, the future of Grand Lake as a tourist destination was firmly sealed.

Break the Ice: Ice Climbing near Estes Park

The *Colorado Mountain School (CMS),* one of six concessionaires permitted to guide rock and ice climbs in Rocky Mountain National Park, offers classes out of their Estes Park location. Wintertime is the perfect season to test yourself on the park's frozen waterfalls under the watchful eyes of one of CMS's expert guides. They also offer instruction in mountaineering, backcountry skiing, and other outdoor activities. From introductory one-day courses to an intensive, multiday advanced course, CMS has classes appropriate for all skill levels. Contact CMS at 341 Moraine Ave., Estes Park 80517; (720) 387-8944 or (800) 836-4008; coloradomountainschool.com.

Today Grand Lake can serve as an overnight getaway or the base for a week of exploring the area. The lake is a major landlocked sailing destination with frequent regattas. It's also a haven for dozens of classic wooden Chris-Craft boats, and during the warm months they're often out on the water. During the summer marinas rent kayaks, canoes, rowboats, paddleboats, and motorboats. Lakes and nearby streams give anglers numerous places to wet a line, while mountain trails provide a scenic route for horseback rides.

With mountains on all sides, there's no shortage of hiking trails. The East Inlet Trail leads to a spectacular set of cascading falls, continuing into a mountain valley with a river and large meadows. Just inside the west park entrance are a variety of hikes to choose from, including the trail to Lulu City, an abandoned mining town with only a few foundations remaining from a once-thriving settlement.

If you arrive in Grand Lake and realize you've forgotten an essential piece of outdoor equipment, there's a good chance that ***Never Summer Mountain Products*** on Grand Avenue will have what you need. They're open year-round, and the store is also a good resource for advice on local hiking, camping, and fishing.

But Grand Lake is about more than outdoor pursuits. The town is an idyllic setting to spend a lazy summer day just wandering. The last 6 blocks of Grand Avenue, the town's main street, are filled with boutiques, restaurants, and shops. The beach area has plenty of benches and grassy areas to sprawl with a good book. Stop by the ***Kauffman House Museum*** for a fascinating peek into the past. Exhibits, photos, books, and descriptions of the area over the last century help bring to life the history of a region that was anything but dull. Volunteer docents answer questions and share information about the collection of antiques and memorabilia. The museum is open from 11 a.m. to 5 p.m. daily from Memorial Day to Labor Day. It's located in a log house on the hill overlooking the lake, just above the beach. Admission is $5; children under 13 free. For more information go to grandlakehistory.org/museums/kauffman-house-museum.

After a day spent outdoors, you'll also be happy to return to Grand Lake to choose from a handful of restaurants. At Sagebrush Barbecue and Grill, a basket of peanuts arrives as soon as you're seated. Follow the crowd and toss your discarded shells on the floor. Several ice-cream parlors offer cool, creamy desserts, but locals claim the best is the homemade ice cream

trivia

RMNP is home to more than 60 species of mammals, including elk, bighorn sheep and moose, and more than 280 bird species have been recorded in the park. You can also find 6 amphibians, 11 species of fish, and countless insects. But just one reptile calls the park home: the harmless garter snake.

at little Myauchi's Snack Bar across the street from the beach. Blue Water Bakery has homemade baked goods and tasty coffee. For a hearty brunch or lunch, visit Huntington House Tavern at Grand Lake Lodge, where the views are as delicious as the food.

In winter most of the handsome, wooden summer homes along the lake are abandoned. The souvenir shops along the boardwalk close down; only a few saloons and a tiny grocery stay open. Trail Ridge Road is closed. At the same time, the cross-country skiing and ice-fishing possibilities are plentiful. The Rocky Mountain National Park entrance is only a mile away, and you see Nordic skiers even on the golf course. Noisy snowmobile enthusiasts show up with their machines. Winter tourists stay in one of several year-round motels or cabin resorts or in nearby **Granby,** such as Granby Ranch or River Run Resort; those not on a budget head to the C Lazy U Ranch.

trivia

The 1,000-foot east face of Longs Peak, a vertical granite cliff known as the Diamond, attracts rock climbers from all over the world.

Grand Lake in winter is popular for riding snowmobiles. But the roaring engines and blue exhaust fumes quickly shatter the deep stillness that winter brings to the Rockies. One place to escape the snowmobiles is the ***Grand Lake Nordic Center*** (1415 CR 48, Grand Lake 80447; 970-627-8008; grandlakerecreation.com/nordiccenter). From the intersection of Highway 40 and Highway 34 go east on 34 for 16 miles to Country Road 48 and turn left at the sign marked "Golf Course Road." Yes, under all that snow is a golf course! The Nordic Center is set in beautiful terrain, and the 35 kilometers of trails are immaculately kept up. Some of the runs are surprisingly steep—especially for a golf course!—but other trails are gentle enough for beginners. The center is open daily through the winter from 9 a.m. to 4 p.m. For more information contact Grand Lake Area Chamber of Commerce, PO Box 429, Grand Lake 80447; (970) 627-3402 or (800) 531-1019; grandlakechamber.com.

trivia

Legend says the Utes shunned Grand Lake, believing its mists were the spirits of the women and children who drowned in the lake during an attack by the Cheyenne and Arapaho.

For a memorable retreat from the outside world, try the ***C Lazy U Ranch*** in the Willow Creek Valley. This is no ordinary dude ranch. Private, secluded, and open year-round, the 8,000-acre ranch offers endless outdoor activities and gourmet Western cuisine. In summer and fall, choose from horseback riding (with a personal horse during your stay), fishing, hiking, mountain biking, yoga, tennis, swimming, and trap shooting. Winter means downhill skiing over at Winter Park, cross-country skiing, ice skating, sledding, horseback riding, and warming up in the heated outdoor pool or hot tub. Even though you can get cell phone reception here, this luxurious ranch is a perfect place to unwind, relax, and be pampered.

Rates are high and commensurate with the ranch's amenities and all-inclusive package. C Lazy U is open year-round. Take I-70 to exit 232, then along US 40 to Highway 125. You'll see the sign. For more information and to make reservations, contact C Lazy U Ranch, 3640 CO 125, Box 379, Granby 80446; (970) 364-0411; clazyu.com.

A 10-mile drive west from Granby along US 40 toward **Kremmling** will take you to **Hot Sulphur Springs Resort.** Once used by the **Ute Indians** as a place for bathing and healing, the resort has been in operation for 140 years. Facilities include 21 pools and private baths and a summer swimming pool. Anyone staying at the resort gets free use of the outdoor pools. Massages, body treatments, and facials are available. For those not staying at the resort, guests 12 and older can soak in the outdoor pools for $26 a day; the price is $12 for kids age 4 to 14 (four pools) and free for children 3 and younger (four pools). Private, adults-only pools are $16 per hour per person. Open every day from 8 a.m. to 10 p.m. Reservations are recommended for all services; call for details. Hot Sulphur Springs Resort, 5609 CR 20, Hot Sulphur Springs 80451; (970) 725-3306 or (800) 510-6235; hotsulphursprings.com.

Another guest ranch offering a true Colorado experience is **Devil's Thumb Ranch.** Located about a 10-minute drive north of Winter Park, this upscale resort has a new lodge, cabins in the woods, and two restaurants. Guests enjoy horseback riding, mountain biking, trout fishing, and exploring 5,000 acres of meadows, forests, and streams. In winter the ranch opens its Nordic center with 100+ kilometers of groomed trails for some of the best cross-country skiing in the country. From Winter Park, take US 40 past Fraser. About 2 miles after Fraser, turn right on Highway 83. The road forks a short

Grand County Fishing

Grand County has some of the largest bodies of water in the state: natural Grand Lake and man-made reservoirs Lake Granby and Shadow Mountain Lake. They are home to rainbow, brook, brown, and cutthroat trout and mackinaw (char). The area is also popular for winter ice fishing. Local streams are also well-known for **fly fishing.** Try Willow Creek, the Fraser River, and the Colorado River in the area west of Granby for brook, rainbow, cutthroat, and brown trout.

distance after this; turn onto the right-hand fork and follow it for 3 miles. For more information, contact Devil's Thumb Ranch Resort & Spa, 3530 CR 83, PO Box 750, Tabernash 80478; (970) 726-7000; devilsthumbranch.com.

Winter Park

Winter Park is one of Colorado's most beloved ski resorts, and for good reason: great runs for all skill levels, consistent snowfall, and close proximity to Denver. But just like elsewhere in the state, Winter Park is a year-round destination. In summer and fall the ski slopes and surrounding mountains transform into a playground for mountain bikers, with over 600 miles of marked and mapped trails, from singletracks to backcountry roads. Hikers, fishing enthusiasts, and lovers of the outdoors find plenty to do in the surrounding national forests. Festivals and special events fill the calendar during the warm months. Colorado's longest alpine slide is here. In town, a variety of unique restaurants keep locals and visitors well-fed. Kids are welcome everywhere, and there's easily enough to keep vacationers busy for several days.

Three of the Winter Park Resort lifts that move skiers up the mountain all winter haul a different load in summer: mountain bikers and their bikes. Miles of trails include jumps, obstacles, and fast downhill runs, along with more leisurely rides. For information and directions to other bike routes in the area, drop by one of several area bike shops or the Winter Park Visitor Center and get a free Winter Park/Fraser mountain biking trail guide.

Yes, biking is big here. The area is a mecca for riders who want to tackle more than 600 miles of gravity-fed trails throughout Winter Park and Fraser. The resort is also home to Trestle Bike Park, where riders of all levels, kids to adults, can ramp up their skills. The Winter Park and the Fraser Valley Chamber of Commerce website at playwinterpark.com lists dates for this and other local events, such as the Winter Park Jazz Festival and Alpine Art Affair. Both these events have been held here for more than 30 years.

The main drag through the towns of Winter Park and Fraser is a series of strip malls and shopping complexes that's not especially conducive to strolling. But it's worth browsing to find places like **Winter Park Trading Company,** a sporting goods consignment store, **B Jammin' in Cooper Creek Square,** for fun family souvenirs, **Epic Mountain Sports** (78737 US 40) for outdoor gear, and several thrift stores with excellent merchandise in Fraser.

A hearty, healthy breakfast is a wise prelude to an active day in the mountains. **Carvers Bakery Cafe** on US 40 in town, **Rise and Shine Cafe** downtown next to the Conoco station, and **Wake N' Bacon** in the Park Place Shopping Center are all local favorites. For friendly local coffeehouses, try **Winter Perk** along the main drag or **Bake Haus 232** in Cooper Creek Square.

Lunch and dinner in the area offer a range of choices, including Mexican, Nepalese, Indian, sushi, barbecue, Italian, and contemporary American.

Winter Park Resort, with 142 runs, has the fourth-largest terrain area of any ski resort in Colorado. Neighboring **Mary Jane** ski area is famous for its ski moguls, and if you want to learn how to master moguls, there's no better place. There's no celebrity parade here, and not much in the way of wild nightlife. But the amount of snow and the varied terrain make this a Colorado favorite year after year.

trivia

Grand Lake is also known as the "Snowmobile Capital of Colorado" due to its more than 300 miles of trails.

With advance reservations, nonskiers can take a 2-hour ride to the summit in a heated vehicle called a snowcat, stopping at the top for a hot chocolate and photos before heading back down the mountain. Cross-country skiing and snowshoeing are available at **Devil's Thumb Ranch** (970-726-7000; devilsthumbranch.com), **Snow Mountain Ranch/YMCA of the Rockies** (ymcarockies.org), or along many of the area's easily accessible trails. Horse-drawn sleigh rides through a quiet winter landscape are offered by **Dashing Thru the Snow** (970-389-2977).

To avoid the hassle of renting a car, many visitors take advantage of **Home James Transportation Services,** with frequent shuttle vans that run from **Denver International Airport (DIA)** directly to lodging properties in Winter Park. The cost is $86 for adults, with discounts for groups of three or more. Children ages 2 to 11 are $43. They also go to the YMCA, Devil's Thumb, and Grand Lake. Contact them at PO Box 279, Winter Park 80482; (970) 726-5060 or (833) 274-3397; ridehj.com.

In decent weather the 67-mile drive from Denver to Winter Park will take less than 2 hours. Go west on I-70, then north on US 40 over Berthoud Pass. Winter Park Resort opens in Nov and closes in Apr. Resort hours are 9 a.m. to 4 p.m. Mon through Fri and 8:30 a.m. to 4 p.m. Sat, Sun, and holidays. For more information on summer and winter activities, contact Winter Park–Fraser Valley Chamber of Commerce; (970) 726-4221; playwinterpark.com; or Winter Park Resort; (970) 726-4781; skiwinterpark.com.

Colorado's Winter Park Ski Resort is home to the **National Sports Center for the Disabled (NSCD),** one of the world's largest therapeutic programs for skiers and riders with disabilities. More than 1,000 volunteers join the NSCD staff to provide over 3,000 lessons to participants each year. The NSCD provides services for people with almost any disability. For more information, contact the National Sports Center for the Disabled, PO Box 1290, Winter Park 80482; (970) 726-1518 or (303) 316-1518; nscd.org.

Yampa Valley & Routt National Forest

In 1875 *James Crawford,* the first white settler of *Steamboat Springs,* arrived here from Missouri with two wagons, his family, his horses, and a few head of cattle. He was attracted to the area by a newspaper article. The author of the piece described his view from the top of the Park Mountain Range as "a wilderness of mountain peaks and beautiful valleys, dark forests and silvery streams—a deserted land except for immense herds of elk and deer and buffalo which had not yet learned by experience to shun the presence of man."

The Yampa Valley's idyllic setting and mild climate made the eventual "presence of man" inevitable. Even before Crawford built his log cabin along the west bank of *Soda Creek,* the Yampa Valley had sheltered Ute Indians and, later, French and English fur trappers.

Cattle ranchers found Steamboat's emerald-green slopes ideal for fattening their herds en route to market. Hot and cold running water in the forms of three creeks, numerous hot springs, and the flow of the **Yampa River** lured more and more settlers to the valley.

Recreational skiing first came here in the early 1900s, when Norwegian Carl Howelsen introduced the sports of ski jumping and ski racing to the community.

Today Colorado's northernmost ski town is a delightful blend of Western ranch culture and outdoor adventure, where tourists come for a taste of mountain life. Along with fleece and skiwear, you will see plenty of jeans, Stetsons, cowboy boots, and saddles. Skiing is a strong tradition in Steamboat. The town has produced numerous world-class skiers, and many Olympians first cut their ski teeth here.

In summer, the fields outside town are ripe with hay. Horses graze in sprawling meadows. The Yampa River flows through the valley, and mountains rise on all sides. Tourists come to browse the shops along Lincoln Avenue, float down the Yampa on inner tubes, ride the gondola for some high-altitude hiking, and fish area streams and lakes. Dude ranches offer guests horseback riding and the experience of a working ranch. Especially in summer, the town is a tranquil blend of rural Colorado and relaxing tourist destination.

Like other Colorado ski towns, Steamboat has no dearth of kitschy tourist stores. But tucked between the fast-food joints and T-shirt shops, or hidden down quiet backstreets, are little gems waiting to be discovered. Get into the Western spirit by visiting historic **F.M. Light & Sons**, which has been at 830 Lincoln Ave. for more than 100 years, outfitting customers in authentic Western wear.

But you didn't come to Steamboat just for shopping. Perhaps the most unique way to explore the valley is to rent an inner tube from one of several shops in town and float down the Yampa River. The trip takes 45–60 minutes, depending on stops, allowing floaters to meander lazily downstream. Local guidelines require "tubers" to start below Fletcher Park, which has a parking lot and easy access to the river. Takeout is around the 13th Street bridge. Several commercial outfits offer tubes and shuttle service back to your car. Although the water is tame, this is a natural river with an unpredictable flow. Life jackets or helmets are suggested, especially for weak swimmers and children. Local

Fishing Steamboat

The area around Steamboat Springs offers numerous fishing opportunities. Three local shops—Straightline, Steamboat Flyfishers (owned by Nordic combined Olympic silver medalist Johnny Spillane), and Bucking Rainbow—offer guided trips, float trips, gear, and advice on where to wet your line.

tubing rules include no littering, glass, or dogs, and respecting the marked quiet zones along three residential areas. Go early in the day to avoid the crowds and afternoon thunderstorms.

One of the area's more popular hikes begins close to town. **Fish Creek Falls** is a cascading 283-foot waterfall that crashes over a cliff and drops into the canyon creek below. A quarter-mile trail leads to the falls. From there, a 6-mile hike goes past the Upper Falls, up switchbacks, and around a meadow area to Long Lake. Along the way hikers will get stunning views of the Yampa River and town. The waterfall runs heaviest during the spring runoff. As the snowpack disappears from the high peaks in early to midsummer, the flow decreases. Reach the trailhead by heading east on Lincoln Avenue, then turning left on 3rd Street. At the next stop sign turn right onto Fish Creek Falls Road. Continue for 3 miles to the parking lot. The Forest Service charges $5 per vehicle per day.

Howelsen Hill ski jump is famous worldwide among the ski jumping community. Its long, steep jump has launched many world records. But you don't have to wait for winter to watch jumpers racing down the steep run. When the snow melts, a porcelain surface on the jump gives young skiers a place to practice during the warm months. They lift off at the end of the jump and soar impossible distances before alighting in the grass below. They practice throughout the week and on weekends. The jump is located across the Yampa River next to the rodeo arena. Ask for directions around town.

During the warm months the **Howler Alpine Slide** at Howelsen Hill is open for business. A chairlift takes you up the hill and high above town. At the top, climb onto a plastic sled for an exhilarating ride curving and bending down a 2,400-foot track. Proceeds from the alpine slide benefit the young athletes of the Steamboat Springs Winter Sports Club.

For a combination sightseeing ride and hike, take the gondola ride up **Mount Werner** at the ski resort. Within minutes the town and valley to the

Ride the Divide

For an exhilarating winter adventure, take a snowmobile tour with **Grand Adventures** (grandadventures.com) from Winter Park to the Continental Divide. Topping out at almost 12,000 feet, the tour is perfect for beginner and intermediate riders, offering a thrilling ride and sweeping views of the Winter Park ski area and Fraser Valley.

Grand Adventure Balloon Tours

Passing through Winter Park in the summer and looking for a fun adventure? Try a hot air balloon flight. Launching in Fraser, the tour takes you and your companions soaring above the treetops with aerial views of the surrounding mountainous terrain. For reservations and information, contact Grand Adventure Balloon Tours, 220 CR 522, Fraser 80442; (970) 887-1340; grandadventureballoon.com.

west shrink to a tiny panorama far below. Eliminate the cawing ravens, drop some cows on the hillsides, and squint just a bit, and this could be the Swiss Alps. At the top, hiking trails fan out in every direction, and you can explore the surrounding alpine landscape before returning on the gondola or heading down the mountain on foot. A network of mountain bike trails also crisscross the mountain, but you have to make it to the top under old-fashioned human power as the resort's gondolas currently don't take bikes. But the reward for all that hard pedaling to the top is a sweeping panorama and the thrill of conquering the challenging trails down to the bottom. Bring your own bike, or rent one at any of several places around town or the ski resort.

Yes, Steamboat does have springs. A walking tour downtown will take you past 10 hot springs, easily identified by their pungent smell. In town you can visit *Old Town Hot Springs* (oldtownhotsprings.org) with eight hot spring-fed pools, two waterslides, massages, and a fitness center. For a more rustic hot springs experience, check out *Strawberry Park Natural Hot Springs* (970-879-0342; strawberryhotsprings.com), located about 7 miles outside of

Playground for Cross-Country Skiers

After a 10-minute drive north from Winter Park, near Tabernash you come to the turnoff for the year-round *Snow Mountain Ranch/YMCA of the Rockies.* Thanks to more than 100 kilometers (62 miles) of cross-country skiing, the ranch has become one of Colorado's most popular Nordic ski centers. The setting is quiet and remote: no shops, restaurants, or movie theaters in the vicinity; no television in the rooms; and for dinner you line up with other guests for simple, wholesome meals. Apart from cross-country skiing, you can try snowshoeing, tubing, ice skating, swimming in an indoor pool, and in summer, a wide variety of outdoor activities and family programs. For more information contact YMCA of the Rockies, 1101 CR 53, Granby 80446; (970) 887-2152; ymcarockies.org/Locations/Snow-Mountain-Ranch.

Located north of Kremmling, *Latigo Ranch* has 60 kilometers (37 miles) of groomed trails ranging from flat track to challenging advanced. Surrounding the ranch is over 200 square miles of national forest awaiting backcountry skiers. For more information call (970) 724-9008 or go to latigoranch.com.

downtown Steamboat Springs. With three main pools varying in temperature and gorgeous stonework, this special place warrants a visit. The unpaved upper part of the road can be challenging if wet or snowy; four-wheel drive with snow tires or chains required Nov 1 to May 1. Ask in town for directions. Reservations are a must. Hours are 10 a.m. to 10 p.m. (admission until 9:30 p.m.). Admission to the pools is $20 per person, all ages, and only cash is accepted. After dark, only adults are admitted, and clothing is optional. Dogs are not permitted anywhere on the property, including in the parking lot or your car.

When it comes to quirky mountain town festivals and events, Steamboat Springs doesn't disappoint. Several times each winter, spectacular torch-lit parades stream down the ski slopes at the Torchlight Parades & Fireworks. The *Cowboy Downhill* each January is the result of placing 70 professional rodeo cowboys and cowgirls, many with questionable skiing skills, on skis and snowboards instead of horses and bulls. Locals and visitors cheer on their favorites, who are dressed in chaps and cowboy hats during slalom races, roping and saddling in the snow, and a wacky cowboy stampede race at the end. In February, the Steamboat Winter Carnival, more than 100 years old, celebrates the season with ski jumping, slaloms, a tubing party, the Diamond Hitch parade, madcap street events for kids on snow-covered Lincoln Avenue, and a brilliant fireworks display at Howelsen Hill, with the famous Lighted Man.

One of the year's most anticipated celebrations is *Springalicious.* Each April as the winter ski season winds down, the mountain heats up with free concerts featuring national acts, a super-affordable four-day ski pass, the splashdown pond skimming competition, and more. The highlight of the festival, which marked 40 years in 2022, is the *Cardboard Classic,* Steamboat's traditional rite of spring. Piloting homemade crafts constructed only from cardboard, glue, string, masking tape, and duct tape, contestants race down Stampede Run at the base of the Steamboat Ski area to a hysterical and chaotic finish. Information for these and other events can be found at steamboat.com.

For a truly authentic event celebrating Steamboat's Western and ranching history and culture, the *Steamboat Springs Pro Rodeo Series* (steamboatprorodeo.com) runs on Friday and Saturday evenings most weekends during the summer from June through Labor Day. Some of the best cowboys from Colorado and Wyoming compete in bull riding, team roping, steer roping, barrel racing, and bareback riding. Come early for the barbecue and live entertainment.

trivia

One of North America's largest elk herd ranges is near Steamboat Springs.

If you find yourself hankering for yet more cowboy culture, consider the *Annual Cowboy's Roundup Days,* going strong since 1903. Held over several days leading up to and including the Fourth of July, this is small-town Independence Day

Yampa Street

Running parallel to the Yampa River, Yampa Street in downtown Steamboat is a compact, pleasant stretch of trendy restaurants, bars, shops, and stores. It's popular with bicyclists, walkers, and anyone who enjoys relaxing next to a mountain river. Take a stroll, bring lunch to a riverside overlook, and enjoy some of the town's best free entertainment.

celebrated in true Western style. From all-you-can-eat pancake breakfasts, parades, and free concerts to evening rodeos and ranch rodeo competitions, this is a mountain party unlike any other in Colorado.

The Saturday Farmers' Market on 7th Street between Lincoln and Yampa brings locals in search of buffalo meat, organic peaches, gourmet bakery breads, sheep cheese, barbecue pork sandwiches, and other edible specialties and local handicrafts. The market is open from 8 a.m. to 2 p.m., beginning in June and running through Aug.

Steamboat Springs is also home to one of the country's best automobile driving schools. But don't expect to learn how to parallel park here. The ***Bridge-stone Winter Driving School*** is patterned after similar facilities at European ski resorts. In operation since 1983, the school is open from mid-Dec through early March. The track is a snow- and ice-covered course with enough turns, loops, and straights to satisfy anyone who envisions being a race-car driver.

But this is not play. You often share your class with law enforcement officers and ambulance personnel. Although these people are professional drivers, they recognize the need for practice, and many return every year. But every skill level is welcome.

The school's three tracks are designed for safety and forgiving of mistakes. In case of a spinout—and there will be spinouts!—the snow walls catch the car and hold it safely with no injury to driver or machine.

After the one-day class, you will feel confident in your ability to avoid collisions due to ice- and snow-covered roads. Six levels of instruction are available in half-day and full-day sessions to match your winter driving skills. Costs start at $339 for a half day of instruction. For more information contact the Bridgestone Winter Driving School at (970) 879-6104 or (800) 949-7543; winterdrive.com.

Steamboat Springs is closer to Denver (around 156 miles) than Aspen (approximately 200 miles). From Denver, the 3-hour

trivia

More Olympians—100 at last count—have emerged from Steamboat Springs than from any other town in the US. The reason? World-class skiing and an almost endless supply of the area's famous Champagne Powder® snow.

drive follows I-70 west to the Silverthorne exit (exit 205). Head north on Highway 9 to Kremmling, and then west on US 40, which takes you over Rabbit Ears Pass and into Steamboat. Arrival by air is also possible; daily direct flights land at **Yampa Valley Regional Airport,** near Hayden, which is 22 miles from the ski area. For information on year-round Steamboat Springs, contact Steamboat Springs Chamber Resort Association, 125 Anglers Drive, PO Box 774408, Steamboat Springs 80477; (970) 879-0880; steamboatchamber.com. For ski resort information, contact Steamboat Ski & Resort Corporation, 2305 Mt. Werner Circle, Steamboat 80487; (800) 922-2722 or (877) 237-2628 (reservations); steamboat.com.

The **Vista Verde Guest & Ski Ranch** sits at the end of a rugged road, 30 miles north of Steamboat Springs. Another standout among Colorado dude ranches, it's among the best choices in the state for a family or couples vacation. More than 500 acres of ranch to explore, and thousands more in the surrounding Routt National Forest, mean riders, cyclists, and hikers have an almost unlimited choice of trails. Apart from horseback riding, this dude ranch offers supervised hiking, cycling, fly fishing, whitewater rafting, and even rock-climbing instruction. In winter, you can cross-country ski, backcountry ski, sled, snowshoe, and

trivia

Ten national ski-jumping records have been set on Howelsen Hill.

Winter in Steamboat Springs

With 165 trails over almost 3,000 acres of terrain, giant **Steamboat Ski Area** has something for everyone. Its northern location is blessed with some of the highest annual snowfall in the state. Plenty of lifts, short lines, a prestigious ski school, and a top-notch ski patrol all add to the resorts' quality. Free mountain tours are offered daily at 10:30 a.m. starting outside the upper gondola terminal at the top of Vagabond. Choose from runs like Tomahawk, Buddy's Run, Stampede, Giggle Gulch, Last Chance, High Noon, Calf Roper, and Chutes.

Five Nordic centers—Steamboat Touring Center, Haymaker, Howelsen Hill, Steamboat Lake, and Lake Catamount—cater to cross-country skiers. In addition, many public lands are open and free for use, such as the popular Rabbit Ears Pass area.

With national forests on all sides, Steamboat abounds with free snowshoeing opportunities for the whole family. Both the Steamboat Ski Touring Center (970-879-8180) and Haymaker Nordic Center (970-879-9444) offer snowshoe rentals, passes, lessons and more. The Haymaker Center is located a short drive from the ski area.

Downhill All the Way

No, it's not about skiing, but about the annual *Steamboat Springs Marathon,* which takes place in early June. Starting out at an elevation of 8,128 feet and finishing at 6,728 feet, the marathon really is mostly downhill, but don't let that fool you. Though *Runner's World* magazine cited this course as one of the "10 Most Scenic Marathons of the Year" and one of the "Top 10 Destination Marathons in North America," it's still quite a challenge. Spectators stand along Lincoln Avenue or at the finish line at the courthouse lawn. The marathon is limited to 500 runners, and it fills early. For those who don't want to run a full marathon, or any marathon for that matter, the event also includes a half marathon and 10K race. For more information call (970) 879-0880 or visit steamboatchamber.com/signature-events/steamboat-marathon.

ride horses. Enthusiastic staff make sure there's never an idle moment, unless of course you prefer to read a book, soak in your private hot tub, or just find a quiet meadow and enjoy the secluded surroundings. For more information contact Vista Verde Guest & Ski Ranch, Inc., PO Box 770465, Steamboat Springs 80477; (800) 526-7433 or (970) 879-3858; vistaverde.com.

Continuing west on US 40 past Craig and Maybell, you will eventually reach the out-of-the-way ***Dinosaur National Monument,*** which straddles the Utah border. You get to it via the small town of Blue Mountain or via Dinosaur, another small town.

A visitor center has exhibits and displays describing the Jurassic environment and its inhabitants, and the auditorium shows films about the monument. Built over the world-famous ***Carnegie Dinosaur Quarry,*** the nearby ***Quarry Exhibit Hall*** provides public access to the 1,500 fossilized dinosaur bones that were deposited here around 149 million years ago. But it's the surrounding area, once a real-life Jurassic Park (without the Hollywood actors, of course), that is true dinosaur fossil bone country. Even without the visitor center, it's hard to ignore this magnificent landscape of giant sandstone cliffs, gray-green sage, juniper, and piñon pine. And the spectacular Yampa River is never far away. A variety of hikes and two self-guided driving tours take visitors deeper into this unusual park.

trivia

Steamboat Springs received its name in the early 1800s from French trappers, who mistakenly thought that they heard the chugging steam engine of a steamboat. In fact, they were hearing a natural mineral spring.

To access the Quarry Exhibit Hall, visitors must first stop at the Quarry Visitor Center located approximately a quarter of a mile from the exhibit hall. For more information contact Dinosaur National Monument, 4545 E. Hwy. 40, Dinosaur 81610; (435) 781-7700; nps.gov/dino. Entry to the monument is $25 per vehicle, $20 per motorcycle, $15 for cyclists and walk-ins.

trivia

Steamboat boasts more than 100 natural hot springs.

Anglers will love **Steamboat Lake State Park,** which allows fly, lure, and bait fishing for its cutthroat and rainbow trout year-round. Camping, waterskiing, swimming, and boating are available. Take US 40 west through Steamboat Springs for 2 miles, and then turn north on CR 129 and go another 26 miles. Cost is $9 for a vehicle day pass; $18–$36 per night for camping. For information contact (970) 879-3922; cpw.state.co.us/placestogo/parks/SteamboatLake. To the south of town, **Stagecoach State Park** offers fishing, boating, waterskiing, camping, biking, and, in the winter, cross-country skiing and ice fishing. Go 4 miles east of Steamboat on US 40, then south on Highway 131 for 5 miles to Routt CR 14. Drive 7 miles south on CR 14 to the park entrance. A daily pass is $9; camping is $18–$36 per night. For information contact (970) 736-2436; cpw.state.co.us/placestogo/parks/Stagecoach.

Fishing licenses may be purchased from most sporting goods and convenience stores in Colorado. A one-day license costs $17.64 and a five-day license costs $33.53 for nonresidents. An annual fishing license costs $36.71 for residents and $102.40 for nonresidents.

Places to Stay in the Northwestern Mountains

ESTES PARK

Mountain Village at Lake Estes
1700 Colorado Peaks Dr.
(970) 473-5735
mountainvillageestespark.com
Expensive
A collection of two-bedroom, two-bath cabins overlooking the lake. The look is rustic, but these upscale accommodations have everything you need for a fantastic mountain getaway, including lots of room, a private hot tub, and an indoor-outdoor fireplace. If you're looking for a winter holiday retreat for the family, the cabins and setting evoke everything magical about the season. Each cabin sleeps 8.

Ponderosa Lodge
1820 Fall River Rd.
(970) 586-4233

ponderosa-lodge.com
Inexpensive to Moderate
On the banks of the Fall
River, quiet, individually
decorated rooms, riverside
picnic area with patio and
grills.

River Rock Cottages
311 Virginia Dr.
(970) 586-2760
theriverrockcottages.com
Moderate
Eight nicely appointed
modern housekeeping
cottages include
complimentary Wi-Fi,
kitchens, grill areas, and
easy access to nearby
trailheads.

The Stanley Hotel
333 E. Wonderview Ave.
(970) 577-4000
stanleyhotel.com
Expensive
Elegant, historic, built and
preserved in the tradition
of the grand hotels from a
past era. Restaurant and
cafe on-site, free Wi-Fi, and
a spectacular view across
the valley.

GRANBY

Bar Lazy J Guest Ranch
447 CR 3, Parshall
(970) 725-3437 or
(800) 396-6279
barlazyj.com
Expensive
All-inclusive dude ranch on
the banks of the Colorado
River offers meals,
horseback riding, "Gold
Medal" fly fishing, hayrides,
mountain biking, campfires,
kid's programs, and more.

C Lazy U Ranch
3640 CO 125
(970) 364-0411
clazyu.com
Expensive
All-inclusive dude ranch
with gourmet meals,
luxury lodging, horseback
riding, fly fishing, hiking,
whitewater river rafting and
canoeing, in-house spa,
and more.

Devil's Thumb Ranch
PO Box 750
3530 CR 83
Tabernash 80478
(970) 726-5632
devilsthumbranch.com
Expensive
Two good restaurants, a
spa, some of America's
best cross-country skiing in
winter, and an abundance
of mountain scenery make
this an easy yet luxurious
place to unwind.

Drowsy Water Ranch
PO Box 147
Granby 80446-0147
(970) 725-3456 or
(800) 845-2292
drowsywater.com
Expensive
All-inclusive dude ranch on
600 acres with horseback
riding, swimming, Western
dancing, campfires,
children's programs, and
more.

Snow Mountain Ranch at YMCA of the Rockies
1101 CR 53
(970) 887-2152
snowmountainranch.org
Inexpensive to Moderate
Affordable lodging, many
activities for families,

excellent cross-country
skiing in winter, hiking in
summer. Pay-as-you-go
buffet dining options.

Sun Outdoors Rocky Mountains
1051 Summit Trail
(970) 557-0200
sunoutdoors.com/
colorado/sun-outdoors-
rocky-mountains
Inexpensive to Expensive
Stay your way. Lodging
options include RV sites,
vacation home rentals,
luxury covered wagons,
Airstreams, tent sites, and
cabins. Resort amenities
range from pools and
hot tubs to a yoga lawn,
planned activities, bowling,
and more.

Trail Riders Motel
215 E. Agate Ave.
(970) 887-3738
Moderate
Affordable lodging, clean
and quiet, run by friendly
management.

GRAND LAKE

Gateway Inn
200 W. Portal Rd.
(970) 627-2400
gatewayinn.com
Moderate
Spacious rooms, internet
access.

Grand Lake Lodge
15500 US 34
(970) 627-3967
grandlakelodge.com
Expensive
Choose from full- or
half-cabin accommodations
or solar-powered Jupes,

outfitted with a Nectar mattress and wood floors. Huntington House Tavern serves as the resort restaurant.

The Rapids Lodge & Restaurant
210 Rapids Ln.
(970) 627-3707
rapidslodge.com
Moderate to Expensive
Lodge rooms, suites, and condominiums located just off Main Street. The Rapids Restaurant offers riverside dining.

Western Riviera Lakeside Lodging and Events
419 Garfield St.
(970) 627-3580
westernriv.com
Moderate
Lakeside accommodations, free internet.

Winding River Resort
Road 491 outside Grand Lake
(970) 627-3215
windingriverresort.com
Moderate
Cozy, quiet lodge and cabins on the North Fork of the Colorado River. Camping and RV facilities also available.

KREMMLING

Latigo Ranch
201 CR 1911
(970) 724-9008
latigoranch.com
Expensive
All-inclusive dude ranch includes 3 meals, horseback riding and instruction, overnight pack

trip, rafting, children's program, gratuity, and more.

Muddy Creek Cabins
315 River Lane
(970) 724-9559
muddycreekcabins.com
Moderate
Ten cabins at the base of the Kremmling Cliffs along Muddy Creek. Kitchenettes with minifridge, free wireless internet; most cabins have gas fireplace.

Bear Claw Condominiums
2420 Ski Trail Ln.
(970) 871-9100
steamboatelevated.com/
steamboat-springs-condos/
bear-claw
Moderate to Expensive
Located at the ski slope, with heated swimming pool, sauna, whirlpool, and courtesy shuttle during ski season.

The Ptarmigan Inn
2304 Apres Ski Way
(970) 879-1730 or
(888) 236-2163
theptarmigan.com
Inexpensive to Moderate in summer, Moderate to Expensive in ski season
Slopeside location offers ski-in/ski-out convenience; hot tub and heated pool.

Rabbit Ears Motel
201 Lincoln Ave.
(970) 879-1150 or
(800) 828-7702
rabbitearsmotel.com
Moderate
Family owned since 1971, affordable and pet-friendly with free wireless internet.

Sheraton Steamboat Resort
2200 Village Inn Ct.
(970) 879-2220
marriott.com
Expensive
Steamboat's full-service resort with ski-in/ski-out convenience, one of the area's top restaurants and golf.

Trailhead Lodge
1175 Bangtail Way
(970) 879-9000
vacasa.com
Expensive
Highly rated condominium property with its own gondola; amenities include fitness center, pool, hot tubs, guest shuttle, in-unit washer and dryer, complimentary wireless internet, and fully equipped kitchens.

Vista Verde Guest Ranch
5800 Cowboy Way, Clark
PO Box 770465, 80477
(970) 879-3858
vistaverde.com
Expensive
Luxury all-inclusive dude ranch in a secluded setting with gourmet meals, beer and wine, horseback riding, rock climbing, rafting, and more all included.

WINTER PARK

Beaver Village Condominiums
(800) 979-7907
winterparkresort.com/plan-your-trip/lodging/beaver-village-condominiums
Moderate to Expensive
Condos, cabins, and

townhomes in town and next to the ski resort.

The Viking Lodge & Ski Shop
78966 US 40
(970) 726-8885
skiwp.com
Moderate
Cozy, eclectic, somewhat dated but affordable ski resort accommodations in downtown Winter Park.

The Vintage Hotel
100 Winter Park Dr.
(800) 472-7017
winterparkresort.com/plan-your-trip/lodging/vintage-hotel
Moderate to Expensive
Located at the entrance to Winter Park Resort, pet-friendly, with free wireless internet, an outdoor pool, sauna, and hot tub.

Winter Park Central
Reservations
(800) 979-7907
winterparkresort.com
Moderate to Expensive
Variety of condos, townhomes, and hotel rooms at Winter Park Resort.

Zephyr Mountain Lodge
201 Zephyr Way
winterparkresort.com/plan-your-trip/lodging/zephyr-mountain-lodge
(970) 726-8400 or
(800) 979-7907
Moderate to Expensive
Luxury ski-in/ski-out condos at the base of Winter Park ski slopes with outdoor hot tubs, heated underground parking, free wireless internet.

Places to Eat in the Northwestern Mountains

ESTES PARK

Brunch & Co
Stanley Hotel
(970) 577-4104
stanleyhotel.com/brunchco
Book a table for a decadent brunch, along with a creative cocktail pairing. Whether your go-to brunch is eggs Benedict, waffles, loaded biscuits, steak, or fried chicken, it's here in a light, airy space in the Lodge at Stanley, next door to the main hotel.

Mama Rose's
338 E. Elkhorn Ave.
(970) 586-3330
mamarosesrestaurant.com
Moderate to Expensive
Casually elegant Italian cuisine with homemade pastas and sauces, extensive wine and regional beer list.

The Rock Inn Mountain Tavern
1675 Hwy. 66
(970) 586-4116 or
(970) 308-8786
rockinnests.com
Moderate to Expensive
Set in a 1937 dance hall, Rock Inn offers up steaks, salmon, burgers, veggies, greens, hand-rolled pizza, and bluegrass music. Fine Colorado spirits, craft beer, and a nice wine list round out the options.

Smokin' Dave's BBQ & Brew
820 Moraine Avenue
(970) 577-7427
smokindavesq.com
Moderate
St. Louis–style pork ribs, aged rib eye, smoked brisket, Grandma's Tater Salad, southern catfish, smoke-shack Caesar salad, and more along with the town's largest selection of microbrews.

Twin Owls Steakhouse at Taharaa Mountain Lodge
3110 S. St. Vrain Ave. Ste B
(970) 586-9344
taharaa.com/twin-owls-steakhouse
Expensive
Casual fine dining in a charming 1920s log cabin serving organic, grass-fed beef, game, seafood, poultry, pork.

FRASER

Elevation Pizza
551 Zerex Ave., Ste. C-106, in the Fraser Valley Center
(970) 726-0066
elevationpizzaco.com
Inexpensive
Freshly made dough, homemade tomato sauce, and a variety of familiar and signature toppings.

Sharky's Eatery
221 Doc Susie Ave.
(970) 726-8646
Inexpensive to Moderate
Breakfast, sandwiches, salads, burgers, and sides.

GRANBY

Brickhouse 40
320 E. Agate Ave.
(970) 887-3505
brickhouse40.com
Moderate to Expensive
Greek focus but also
steak, burgers, salads,
and creative small plates
served up in a historic brick
building.

Fat Cat Cafe
185 E. Agate Ave.
(970) 887-8987
Inexpensive to Moderate
Friendly breakfast and
lunch cafe run by an expat
Brit. The weekend buffet
brunch here is legendary,
among the best in
Colorado.

Granby Ranch Grill
1000 Village Rd.
(970) 887-5200
granbyranch.com
Moderate
Seasonal menu of
Italian-inspired fare
with specialty salads,
daily specials, and
entertainment.

Java Lava
200 W. Agate Ave.
(970) 887-9810
Inexpensive
Good breakfast
sandwiches and burritos,
full coffee and tea selection.

Simply Coffee Company
100 E. Agate Ave.
(970) 660-8450
Inexpensive

Friendly walk-in or
drive-through coffee
and espresso place with
affordable prices.

Maverick's Grille
15 E. Agate Ave.
(970) 887-9000
mavericksgrille.com
Moderate
Family dining with steaks,
chicken, burgers, and
game along with Colorado
microbrews and wine.

GRAND LAKE

Blue Water Bakery
928 Grand Ave.
(970) 627-5416
Inexpensive
Breakfast and lunch with
good sandwiches, pastries,
and coffee.

The Rapids Lodge & Restaurant
210 Rapids Ln.
(970) 627-3707
rapidslodge.com
Moderate to Expensive
Sandwiches, small plate
entrees, elk, prime rib,
steak, trout, salmon;
streamside dining for lunch
and dinner.

One Love Rum Kitchen
928 Grand Ave.
(970) 798-8067
onelovecateringwp.com
Caribbean-inspired
sandwiches, fish tacos,
wraps and salads, plus
beer wine and the kind of
cocktails that demand an

umbrella. Taking a cue from
Bob Marley, One Love's
website tells us, "everything
is gonna be alright."

Sagebrush Barbecue and Grill
1101 Grand Ave.
(970) 627-1404
sagebrushbbq.com
Moderate
Barbecue, salads and
soups, steak, fish, and
game. Occasional evening
musical entertainment.

The World's End Brewpub
813 Grand Ave.
(970) 509-9970
worldsendbrewpub.com
Casual brewery on the
boardwalk with indoor and
outdoor seating.

STEAMBOAT SPRINGS

Back Door Grill
825 Oak St.
(970) 871-7888
thebackdoorgrill.com
Moderate
Old-fashioned burgers and
brews with a contemporary
focus on fresh, natural
ingredients. Rumor has
it the onion rings are to
die for.

Cafe Diva
1855 Ski Time Square Dr.
(970) 871-0508
cafediva.com
Expensive
Eclectic, creative kitchen
with a seasonally changing

menu offers a variety of nouveau cuisine and traditional entrees.

Creekside Cafe & Grill
131 11th St.
(970) 879-4925
rexsfamily.com/creekside
Moderate
Hearty breakfast and lunch menu with popular entrees such as eggs Benedict and green chili.

Laundry
127 11th St.
(980) 870-0681
rexsfamily.com/the-laundry-restaurant
Expensive
This is the place for a splurge.

Mazzola's Italian Restaurant
917 Lincoln Ave.
(970) 879-2405
rexsfamily.com/mazzolas
Moderate to Expensive
Casual Italian dining and a varied menu in a diner atmosphere.

Ore House at Pine Grove
1465 Pine Grove Rd.
(970) 879-1190
orehouse.com
Expensive
Steak, seafood, and game.

Salt & Lime
628 Lincoln Ave.
(970) 871-6277
rexsfamily.com/salt-lime
Inexpensive to Expensive
Cheerful Mexican eatery

with classic dishes and some unexpected treats.

Sauvage
910 Yampa St., #104
(970) 761-3737
sauvage-restaurant.com
Expensive
Choose from a 3- or 6-course meal.

The Shack Cafe
740 Lincoln Ave.
(970) 879-9975
steamboat-dining.com
Inexpensive to Moderate
Popular with locals, breakfast and lunch at affordable prices.

WINTER PARK

Casa Mexico
Cooper Creek Sq.
(970) 726-9674
Inexpensive to Moderate
Mexican and Tex-Mex cuisine.

Carvers Bakery Cafe
78336 US 40
(970) 726-8202
carvers-wp.com
Inexpensive
Serving breakfast and lunch for over 30 years. Large menu and good food.

Deno's Mountain Bistro
78911 US 50
(970) 726-5332
denosmountainbistro.com
Moderate to Expensive
Fine dining with steaks, chops, seafood, chicken, pasta, pork, and an award-winning wine list.

Fontenots Fresh Seafood and Grill
78336 US 40
(970) 726-4021
fontenotswp.com
Moderate to Expensive
Seafood, steaks, and original dishes with a New Orleans Cajun accent.

Hernando's Pizza and Pasta Pub
78199 US 40
(970) 726-5409
hernandospizzapub.com
Inexpensive to Moderate
Variety of pastas, pizzas, and Italian sub sandwiches.

Rise and Shine Cafe
78437 US 40
(970) 726-5530
Inexpensive to Moderate
Deservedly popular cafe for homemade baked goods, breakfast, and sandwiches.

Tabernash Tavern
72287 US 40
(970) 726-4430
tabernashtavern.com
Expensive
Creative, well-rounded international menu of appetizers, entrees, soups, salads, and desserts.

TOP ANNUAL EVENTS IN THE NORTHWESTERN MOUNTAINS

FEBRUARY
Winter Carnival
Grand Lake
Jan or Feb
(970) 627-3402 or (800) 531-1019
grandlakechamber.com

ALL SUMMER
Rocky Mountain Repertory Theatre
Grand Lake
(970) 627-5087
rockymountainrep.com

Steamboat Springs Pro Rodeo Series
(970) 879-1818
steamboatprorodeo.com

JULY
Cowboy Roundup Days
Steamboat Springs
July 4 weekend
(970) 879-0880
steamboatchamber.com/
signature-events/july-4th-celebration

Rocky Grass Bluegrass Festival
Lyons
late July
(800) 624-2422
bluegrass.com/rockygrass

Rooftop Rodeo
Estes Park
mid-July
(970) 586-6104
rooftoprodeo.com

Winter Park Jazz Festival
(970) 726-4118 or (800) 903-7275
playwinterpark.com

SEPTEMBER
Longs Peak Scottish Irish Festival
weekend after Labor Day
(970) 586-6308 or (800) 903-7837
scotfest.com

FOR MORE INFORMATION

VISIT ESTES PARK/ESTES PARK VISITOR CENTER
500 Big Thompson Ave.
Estes Park 80517
(970) 577-9900
visitestespark.com

DINOSAUR NATIONAL MONUMENT
4545 US 40
Dinosaur 81610
(435) 781-7700
nps.gov/dino/index.htm

YMCA OF THE ROCKIES
Estes Park Center: (970) 586-3341
Snow Mountain Ranch: (970) 887-2152
ymcarockies.org

WINTER PARK RESORT
85 Parsenn Rd.
Winter Park 80482
(970) 726-5514
winterparkresort.com

Central Mountains

Beyond the Front Range

Most travelers in a hurry to cross Colorado take I-70, the wide, fairly straight thoroughfare that cuts east–west across the upper third of the state. Yes, it's the quick route between Grand Junction and Denver, and as far as highway scenery goes, it's probably one of the prettiest drives in the country. But those rushing through will miss out on the central mountains that contain some of the state's highlights.

Although the region deserves weeks of exploring to do it justice, many of the places of interest on the eastern side can be seen during a day trip from Denver. Each fall, when aspen begin changing and entire mountains turn shimmering gold, locals around the state hit the roads and trails to appreciate the fleeting magic of this brilliant display. Everyone has his or her favorite route, but one of the more popular ones is a loop trip: Denver, Idaho Springs, Silver Plume, Breckenridge, Fairplay, and back to Denver. The trip can be done in a day, or easily stretched into two or more days with stops along the way. But don't wait for September and October to take this drive; no

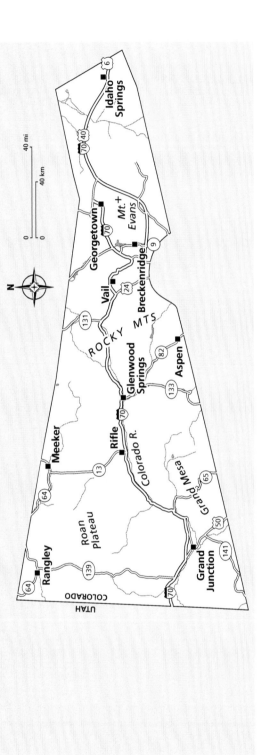

matter when you go, it's a diverse sampling of small mountain towns, western geography, and stunning scenery.

Beginning in Denver, head west on I-70 toward the mountain community of Idaho Springs (altitude 7,524 feet). Those wanting to explore the eastern side of the Mount Evans Wilderness can turn south here, climbing up into the high country above the tree line. Continue west past Georgetown, the historic mining town of beautifully preserved Victorian homes that's worth a visit on its own. This is also the access point to the western side of Mount Evans and dramatic Guanella Pass at over 10,000 feet.

As you continue along I-70, the mountains rise steeply and the valley turns narrow. Spruce, fir, and aspen blanket the mountains. Shortly before the Eisenhower-Johnson Memorial Tunnel—weather permitting, of course—turn off on US 6 at the sign for **Loveland Pass** and head up to the **Continental Divide** (11,990 feet). The views are unbeatable from up here, so stop and take in the alpine panoramas, including meadows of wildflowers in the summer. Afterward, cruise down the mountain past Keystone ski resort to Dillon Reservoir.

The reservoir area is popular with boaters, anglers, cyclists, and the ospreys that nest annually along the lake. Linger here and stretch your legs at the picnic and camping grounds on the south side of the lake beyond the marina and away from I-70, or follow the signs to Frisco, staying on the road around the lake. After Frisco, swing left onto Highway 9 and head down the valley to Breckenridge.

This former mining community is in the middle of another bonanza. In 1859 it was gold. Now it's skiing, vacation homes, and mountain life. Stay the night to enjoy the restaurants and shops, or continue driving through thick forests past beaver ponds to **Hoosier Pass.** You're surrounded by 14,000-foot peaks—Quandary Peak, Mount Lincoln, Mount Sherman—as you drop down into Placer Valley, leaving the subalpine terrain and returning to forests and streams.

At the town of Fairplay, turn north on US 285 through South Park (Fairplay, not South Park, is reportedly the visual influence for the TV show *South Park*). Keep an eye out for pronghorn in the surrounding grasslands and approach the steep incline toward Kenosha Pass. Dropping into the valley along the South Platte River, the road twists through a valley of pastures and grazing horses before coming to the tiny settlement of **Grant** and, 11 miles later, **Bailey.** It's there you'll find historic Glen Isle Resort, which underwent a multiyear closure and renovation. Lodging is in rustic cabins or tranquil tent sites on the 100-acre property, providing access to endless outdoor activities or time to simply enjoy nature. Just under 50 miles from Denver, it's a world away in every sense, the perfect Colorado respite from city life (573 Old Stagecoach Rd., Bailey 80421;

303-816-0790; glenisleresort.com). From Bailey, you climb up Crow Hill, then pass communities whose names signify Colorado: Pine Junction, Deer Creek, Conifer, Indian Hills, Aspen Park. Then it's a quick drop out of the foothills back to Denver, where you began your circle tour 175 miles ago.

Idaho Springs is a short drive west on I-70 from Denver, and the area makes an interesting half-day trip. Stroll along the short main street and browse the shops, some of which are in historic buildings from the mining days. Take a walking tour with the Historical Society of Idaho Springs (303-567-4382) to learn more about the history and mining past of the area. Two museums, the *Heritage Museum* and Visitor Center (open daily; 2060 Miner St.; 303-567-4382; historicidahosprings.com) and the *Underhill Museum* (1416 Miner St.; 303-567-4709) offer interesting tidbits, artifacts, and memorabilia about the area's colorful past.

If you decide to spend the night, keep in mind that the local motels, while not fancy, are among the lowest-priced in Colorado. A quick drive down Colorado Boulevard will give you a dozen or so to choose from. If you reach the area around lunch- or dinnertime, *Beau Jo's Pizza* is well-known in Colorado for its varieties and its "pizza by the pound." You can build your own pizza here as well (1517 Miner St.; 303-567-4376; beaujos.com). Open Sun through Thurs from 11 a.m. to 9 p.m. and Fri and Sat from 11 a.m. to 9:30 p.m.

Another excellent dining choice is *Two Brothers Deli.* For fast, quality sandwiches, breakfast wraps and specials, soup, salad, smoothies, hot drinks, and free wireless, this is a smart stop before or after hiking, skiing, or exploring the town. Located at 1424 Miner St. (303-567-2439; twobrothersdeli.com). Open weekdays 9 a.m. to 5 p.m., weekends 8 a.m. to 5 p.m.

The gold rush may be long over, but at the *Phoenix Gold Mine,* located at the west end of Idaho Springs, anyone can try a hand at what brought thousands of men to Colorado back in the 1800s . . . gold panning!

This is the only working gold mine in Colorado that is open to the public. Take a tour guided by actual miners. Better yet, dig your own samples—you even get to keep what you find. Gold panning costs $14 for adults, $12 for ages 4 to 12. Walking tours with panning cost $18 for children 4 to 12, $24 for adults. Open daily year-round; Mon to Thur 10 a.m. to 5 p.m., Fri to Sun until 6 p.m. *NOTE:* The temperature in the mine is only 42–54°F, so dress accordingly.

To get to the Phoenix Gold Mine, take I-70 eastbound to exit 239, and then take Stanley Road southwest to Trail Creek Road. For more information call (303) 567-0422 or email phoenixtourmine@gmail.com; phoenixgoldmine.com.

Most of Colorado's highest places can only be attained by a long, arduous hike. The rewards are worth the effort: sweeping views of the Rockies for miles in all directions, alpine wildflowers, and the shrill whistle of marmots and pikas.

But there are several places around the state where you can enjoy these grand views with little more effort than steady pressure on the gas pedal and both hands on the steering wheel.

The road to 14,264-foot-high **Mount Evans** is the highest paved auto road in the US. Starting in Idaho Springs, it winds steadily upward, rising through spruce and pine forests. As you go higher, the views only get better. You will pass through several ecological zones, an ancient bristlecone pine forest, and alpine lakes before reaching the summit. Keep an eye out for mountain goats and bighorn sheep that are often seen near the summit. And be prepared for cold weather at the top. It can be 90°F in Denver and 40°F on top of the mountain. The vista from the viewing platform is one of Colorado's premier scenic overlooks.

The road to the top of Mount Evans usually opens in May and stays open until the first significant snowfall of the year—meaning that if you want to tackle the peak in winter, you'll need to plan accordingly by packing snowshoes or cross-country skis and having the necessary wilderness skills to do so safely.

Once the road has been opened for the season, it is accessible 24 hours a day. Cost is $15 for a three-day vehicle pass, plus a $2 nonrefundable reservation fee. Timed tickets are required. Seventy-five percent of timed tickets go on sale 30 days in advance; the remaining 25 percent go on sale two days prior. Visit recreation.gov/timed-entry/10087438 for information on purchasing tickets.

Any sunny summer day will do to make your drive up to the summit, but weekdays are preferable if you want to avoid the crowds. In addition, visiting very early or very late in the day increases your chances of seeing the many animals that call Mount Evans home.

If you're starting your journey in Denver, you can choose to approach the mountain via Bergen Park and return via Idaho Springs, or vice versa. Expect to see stunning Colorado scenery along the way, including large, fertile meadows, dense lodgepole pine forests, aspen trees, ponderosa pine, Douglas fir, and thick bushes of wild raspberries in season, as well as the occasional chipmunk or squirrel.

Placid **Echo Lake** makes for a nice stopping point en route to the summit. Park and stretch your legs, and perhaps enjoy a picnic lunch, do some fishing, or join hikers on one of several trails heading into the woods. If you're visiting after Thanksgiving, expect to see a vast frozen expanse—the lake often freezes completely, and you can glide across it on cross-country skis, reaching numerous trails that yield great views. But even in summer it gets cool up here, so dress warmly and bring extra layers. Theoretically, for every 1,000 feet of elevation gain in the Rockies, you can compare your journey to traveling 200 miles north. Of course, this means you get to experience the cooler air in each zone on the way up, not to mention the shifting vegetation.

Above Echo Lake, a beautiful and complex world lies at your feet. Follow trails through alpine tundra, stooping to study the small grasses, sedges, herbs, and the almost microscopic plants with their tiny flowers. These plants grow close to the ground in order to withstand the harsh conditions at this altitude.

At one point on the way up you will see posted signs for the bristlecone forest hunkered on both sides of the road. If you take a close look at the twisted forms of these ancient trees, you can read the story of their struggle for survival in this unforgiving setting. Each dwarfed bristlecone and leaning Douglas fir in this area shows the signs of withstanding blizzards and summer storms as well as coping with blazing sunlight followed by rains. This wild weather destroys most exposed buds and conifer seeds, limiting the trees' reproduction. Some trees are bent and twisted from the relentless wind, while others are bleached from the sun or blackened and split by lightning strikes. At timberline, the already small array of trees becomes even sparser, with only single, isolated soldiers standing to face the elements.

Above timberline, in Colorado's alpine life zone, the fauna changes, too. Marmots often show themselves sunning on warm boulders. Well-camouflaged

AUTHOR'S FAVORITES IN THE CENTRAL MOUNTAINS

Colorado National Monument
(970) 858-2800
nps.gov/colm

Georgetown
(303) 569-2840
historicgeorgetown.org

Glenwood Canyon
(970) 945-6589
glenwoodchamber.com

Gore Range/Pass
(970) 945-2521
fs.fed.us

Grand Mesa National Forest
(970) 856-4153
visitgrandjunction.com/
exploring-grand-mesa-national-forest

Lake Dillon Marina
(970) 468-5100
townofdillon.com

Mount Evans Welcome Station
(303) 567-4382
recreation.gov

**Museums of Western Colorado–
Museum of the West**
(970) 242-0971
museumofwesternco.com

Rifle Falls State Park
(970) 625-1607
cpw.state.co.us/placestogo/parks/
RifleFalls

Safe Travel in Colorado

Colorado is renowned for its afternoon thunderstorms that proliferate during the summer months but are possible year-round. For this reason, outdoor activities—particularly those involving a long distance from safe shelter—should be done only with careful planning and attention to time. If you do find yourself caught up in a thunderstorm, take refuge in a car (with the windows up) or a substantial building—not a shallow cave or rock outcropping. If no safe shelter is available, seek a low-lying area or trench with shrubs or trees of similar stature. Avoid lone trees, open spaces, higher exposed ground, water, and contact with two different objects (such as rock and ground). Also maintain a 15-foot distance from others. Crouch low to the ground with both of your feet together and cover your ears. For more safety tips, visit the National Lightning Safety Institute's website at lightningsafety.com.

Flash flooding can pose a real danger in narrow canyons, even on days that begin with clear skies and sunny weather. Be sure to check weather reports for thunderstorm predictions, and always have a backup plan.

Drinking water from lakes, rivers, and streams is not exactly the wilderness treat it once was. Unless you want to find out just how nasty a bout of giardiasis can be—think diarrhea, stomach cramps, and a visit to the doctor—avoid drinking water from lakes, streams, or rivers unless you purify it first. Bring adequate drinking water (minimum of 2 liters per person per day) and, for backcountry trips, a water purification filter, which can be purchased from most sporting goods stores. You can also purify water by boiling it for at least 20 minutes to kill all disease-causing organisms.

ptarmigan can be spotted browsing among the grasses or leading their brood of chicks across the tundra. Tiny pikas scurry between rocks as they gather grasses for the long winter. Mountain goats are frequently seen up here, and once in a while you'll spot a bighorn sheep. Don't feed any animals; they stay much healthier with a natural diet.

Mount Evans's upper reaches are also dotted with lakes. At 11,700 feet, you'll spot Lincoln Lake; it's 800 feet below the highway. Then at 12,830 feet, Summit Lake awaits, complete with a short trail overlooking the picturesque Chicago Lakes, some 1,400 feet below. The Forest Service warns parents not to let their children run around in this area due to the sudden drop-offs—the highway has few guardrails.

Finally, complete the journey by pulling into the parking lot at 14,130 feet. Get out of your car and hike that last 134-foot gain in altitude to the summit via a quarter-mile hike along a trail. Catch your breath—the air is much thinner up here than it is on the plains, so visitors from the flatlands should walk slowly and take in the scenery. And if the thin air doesn't take away your breath, the views surely will.

Start your tour to Mount Evans on I-70. Take exit 240 in Idaho Springs onto the Mount Evans Highway (Highway 103). After Echo Lake, pay your fee and head onto Highway 5, which will take you to the summit. For a change of pace on the way back, continue west along Highway 103 to Bergen Park, and then take Highway 74 and I-70 to Denver. The distances are moderate—it's only 28 miles from Idaho Springs to the summit of Mount Evans, but the drive is thrilling (or terrifying, according to some). For more information call the Clear Creek Ranger District at (303) 567-4382 or visit fs.usda.gov.

Idaho Springs is home to the *Edgar Experimental Mine,* where students and faculty from the Golden-based Colorado School of Mines try their hands at traditional mining methods and put to use the most recent technological advances. Open to the public for tours throughout the year from Mon through Fri, 8 a.m. to 4 p.m. Admission is $20 for adults, $15 for children ages 12 and under. To reserve a tour, call ahead at (303) 567-2911 or visit mining.mines. edu/edgar-experimental-mine.

In autumn the wind whistles through the well-kept streets of *Georgetown,* rattling the windows of its many Victorian houses. The winter snows pile up high here, and spring is slow to come at an elevation of 8,500 feet. The mountains rise so steeply on all four sides of Georgetown that even the summers are cool; the sun shines on the town for only a few hours a day.

Yet this community 45 miles west of Denver has more ambience, more sightseeing, and more genuine concern for preserving its past than many other Colorado cities. The city officials have spent substantial sums to rebuild and preserve the pink-brick houses, the old-time saloons, and the museums that conjure up the 19th century of gold and silver riches. The antiques shops, silversmiths, and weavers are among the best in the state. The craft shops are unique and worth browsing, and often offer better deals than those of Vail, Aspen, and other ski resorts to the west.

Unlike Vail, which rose from a cow pasture, Georgetown is a historic community. And residents are proud of it. On a clear spring day in 1859, two prospecting brothers, George and David Griffith, struggled their way up Clear Creek searching for minerals.

Unsuccessful at the other mining camps in Colorado, the two prospectors reached out for new, untried land, and this time they had luck—they found gold.

After their discovery the Griffith brothers did a highly unusual thing for gold or silver seekers of the time—instead of just digging up the mountain and leaving with their wealth, they brought their entire family out from Kentucky to live permanently in their valley. The tiny settlement they founded became known as George's Town, and although no more significant strikes were made, it grew steadily for five years.

Little-Known Facts about Idaho Springs

- Some of Colorado's earliest gold strikes took place here in 1859.

- The Ute Indians were the first to discover and use its famous hot springs.

- When it was completed after 17 years in 1915, Argo Tunnel was the world's longest mining tunnel. The 5-mile-long tunnel once ran all the way to Central City, another gold rush town. Unfortunately, only a portion of the tunnel remains, and it is not open to the public.

- The highway that runs to the summit of Mount Evans from Idaho Springs is the highest paved driving road in North America.

Then in 1864 assays showed an extremely high silver content. The boom was on. Over the next 30 years, the mines in and around the town produced more than $200 million worth of silver. The town became known as the Silver Queen of the Mountains—and in 1868 it was renamed Georgetown.

By 1880 some 10,000 people made the city their home. Fortunes and reputations flourished. Elaborate mansions were built. Hotels served fine cuisine in gilt rooms with elegant furniture. An opera house brought Broadway productions and favorite classical operas to the wealthy.

All this came to an abrupt end when the silver panic of 1893 hit, with silver prices dropping to almost nothing. Almost overnight, mines, mills, and livelihoods vanished. The town became a ghost of its past glory.

Georgetown languished this way for more than six decades. As more people moved to the state, tourism followed, and interstate highways transported millions of travelers to the mountains. People discovered the beautiful old Victorian homes and set about restoring them to their former grace. Unlike other Colorado mining towns, Georgetown was never totally destroyed by fire, so today it has more than 200 carefully preserved historic buildings.

Luckily for Georgetown, forward-thinking residents and town officials passed a historic preservation ordinance many years ago. The local historical society actively watches over its Victorian treasures to ensure they will be around for many years. One of Georgetown's landmarks is the French-style ***Hotel de Paris Museum,*** full of Tiffany fixtures, lace curtains, and hand-carved furniture. Open from Memorial Day through Labor Day 10 a.m. to 4 p.m. and on Sat noon to 4 p.m. Adults are $10, seniors and children ages 7–17 are $5, and ages 6 and younger are free. Before visiting in person, take a virtual 3-D tour on the museum's website. Contact (303) 569-2311; hoteldeparismuseum.org.

Georgetown is a perfect town for parking and wandering. Walk in any direction and discover dozens of well-preserved homes well over a century old. The small business district has a mix of antiques shops, art galleries, a bookstore, and several restaurants. During the first two December weekends, a well-known Christmas market with small booths and outdoor stalls is a popular place for holiday shopping.

Georgetown is a good base for travelers who plan to explore the ***Continental Divide*** in summer or ski country in winter. It's also the best starting point for the spectacular drive to 11,669-foot ***Guanella Pass.*** Running through forests of aspen, fir, and spruce at lower elevations, the road climbs up a glaciated valley past meadows and cascading creeks. Camping, hiking, fishing, fall aspen foliage, and winter cross-country skiing and snowshoeing are some of the attractions. At the pass, tundra and willow thickets replace the forest, and in summer tiny wildflowers add color to the landscape. Look for ptarmigan in all seasons, white in winter and mottled brown in summer.

Mount Bierstadt, one of Colorado's "fourteeners," is the large mountain looming to the east. The trail to the summit starts from the parking lot. Other trails lead hikers across the tundra. Passenger cars can easily traverse the well-graded road, but it will be too narrow in places for RVs. Remember to bring warm clothes; the weather at the pass is often much colder than in Georgetown. For more information, visit colorado.com/articles/colorado-scenic-byway-guanella-pass-mount-bierstadt.

Georgetown is about an hour west of Denver via I-70. For information about Georgetown, contact ***Historic Georgetown,*** 305 Argentine St., PO Box 667, Georgetown 80444; (303) 569-2840 or (800) 472-8230; historicgeorgetown.org.

Want to experience a bit of the Colorado West? Then plan a vacation at one of Colorado's dude ranches. Imagine riding horseback with family and friends through an aspen grove to a sunny meadow full of wildflowers. Along the way you pass weathered settler's cabins with caved-in roofs and sagging door frames, the wood bleached and cracked by a century in the sun. The trail leads across brooks, through willow thickets, and then slowly down a steep, rocky slope. The riders move with care, savoring the moment as they hang on firmly. A light warm breeze blows through the pines. Alone with their thoughts, far away from crowds and freeways, they find rhythm in the creak of the leather saddles and the clicking of the hooves. Arriving at a sunny forest clearing, everyone finds a log to sit on. Coffee steams. The cowboys fry up eggs and sausage. It's morning in the Rockies.

Ask dude ranch visitors what's so special about staying in one of these places and they'll mention the informality, the quiet seclusion, the good food, and the friendliness of the place. With an average of 20 to 80 guests, it's easy to become acquainted with the staff and guests. The mood is calm and relaxed. But there's also plenty to do: horseback riding, fishing, hiking, mountain biking,

TOP ANNUAL EVENTS IN THE CENTRAL MOUNTAINS

APRIL

Fruita Fat Tire Festival
late Apr/early May
(970) 858-7220
fruitafattirefestival.com

JUNE

Aspen Music Festival and School
June through Aug
(970) 925-3254
aspenmusicfestival.com

Grand Junction Farmers' Market
Thurs June through Sept
(970) 245-9697
downtowngj.org/events/market-on-main/

Strawberry Days Festival
Glenwood Springs
mid-June
(970) 945-6589
glenwoodchamber.com/strawberry-days

JULY

Colorado Lavender Festival
June/July
Downtown Palisade
coloradolavender.org

AUGUST

Breckenridge International Festival of Arts (BIFA)
Mid-Aug
(970) 453-3187
BreckCreate.org/BIFA

Peach Festival
Palisade
Mid-Aug
(970) 464-7458
palisadepeachfest.com

SEPTEMBER

Breckenridge Film Festival
Mid-Sept
(970) 453-6200
breckfilmfest.com

Breckenridge October Fest
Mid-Sept
GoBreck.com

and just relaxing with a good book are a few of the many options. You can stay as busy as you like, or you can do nothing at all. Either way, you'll be well taken care of.

The names say a lot: C Lazy U Ranch, Tumbling River Ranch, Drowsy Water Ranch. They are just a few of the many endearing places set in romantic, isolated Colorado locations. Some of them still breed cattle or horses. A Colorado dude-ranch vacation is one of the most satisfying, genuine holidays available today. The air is clean, days are warm, evenings cool, and the mountain scenery is absolutely spectacular. Most dude ranches are family-oriented, with separate programs especially for kids.

Accommodations range from rustic to deluxe. Colorado has some 40 dude ranches, generally located in the scenic mountain regions. These are small, self-contained worlds that feel far from city life. There are lots of horse trails for novices, guided breakfast rides, ghost-town trips, and even extended rides into the wilderness. Some dude ranches arrange river-rafting trips, or you can rent a jeep. Archery, boating, rock climbing, fishing, and even golf are possibilities. And there are usually hot tubs and plenty of soft lounge chairs.

Dude-ranch vacations often cost less than you'd expect. A week at an average, all-inclusive guest ranch can run considerably less than other types of family vacations because meals, activities, and accommodations are included. Some ranches also offer programs by the day for those who can't take an entire week. **North Fork Ranch** in Shawnee, Colorado, sits along a half-mile stretch of the North Fork of the South Platte River where fly fishing and hiking is phenomenal. Lodge rooms are available at a nightly per-person rate that includes three meals, pool, hot tub, and more. Internet comes with the room, too, but this is a place to turn off the technology and embrace nature. A la carte activities include Orvis Fly Fishing Clinic, trap and skeet shooting, riding, bow and arrow, and guided hikes. You can hike on your own as well. For more information contact North Fork Ranch, P.O. Box B, 55395 US 285, Shawnee 80475; (303) 838-9873; northforkranch.com.

The **Tumbling River Ranch** in Grant seems hewn out of native rock and local wood. At night you can hear the tumbling river outside your window. The ranch stands at 9,200 feet, and most evenings the stars shine brighter than in any city sky. The ranch features not only trail riding but also a handsome outdoor heated pool. The food is excellent, and there are enough activities to keep you busy all summer.

Grant is a short trip southwest from Denver via US 285. For more information contact Tumbling River Ranch, 3715 CR 62; (303) 838-5981 or (800) 654-8770; tumblingriver.com. Open mid-June through the end of August.

To explore the many dude ranch choices across the state, contact the **Colorado Dude & Guest Ranch Association,** 56403 US 285, Shawnee 80425; (866) 942-3472; coloradoranch.com.

Driving east on Highway 70, after you've climbed out of steep Glenwood Canyon and dropped down from Vail Pass into **Summit County,** you'll see a large lake on your right. If you're coming west from Denver, you'll cross the Continental Divide at 11,158 feet and after a quick drop into Summit County, the road straightens out, and there it is—**Lake Dillon,** aka Dillon Reservoir.

No matter which direction you're coming from, this lake is hard to miss. With its 26-mile shoreline, the water on a summer day is often a deep blue, dotted by white sails, and alive with small motorboats, canoes, and kayaks skimming the surface. Anglers fish from shore for rainbow trout. Ospreys nest here each year. Bike paths run the length of the lake, continuing all the way to Breckenridge, 10 miles away.

Loveland in Wintertime—or All Year Long

Loveland Ski Area — which is nowhere near the city by the same name — has always been a favorite ski spot for Front Range residents. A big plus is Loveland's proximity — just 55 miles from Denver via I-70. There are no passes to cross and no Eisenhower Tunnel, either (which Loveland publicists call "a big bore").

Snowboarding is big here, and the ski area has excellent instructors. If you've been a skier your whole life, try snowboarding. It's definitely a different experience from skiing, and worth it to discover the distinction. Many Colorado skiers start snowboarding and never return to skiing.

The ski center shuts down in late spring when the snow melts, and since Loveland Ski Area does not have hotels or offer condominiums, that's it for winter sports. In summer the slopes fill up with mountain flowers and hikers out to enjoy the high country.

To arrange snowboarding lessons or for more information contact Loveland Ski Area, PO Box 899, Georgetown 80444; (303) 571-5580 or (800) 736-3754; skiloveland .com. Loveland Ski Area is open from Nov through Apr; lift tickets are priced lower than other more well-known ski areas in the region, plus kids 5 and younger ski free.

Mountains surrounding the lake are the domain of climbers, hikers, and horseback riders. Streams are everywhere: Blue River, Snake River, Ten Mile Creek. Almost all the water spills into the reservoir, flowing toward Denver, through the unseen Harold D. Roberts Tunnel, not far from ***Dillon.*** Highway traffic along I-70 moves fast along the north side of the lake, and if you're in a hurry, you may miss the sign for Dillon and continue toward Denver, 78 miles to the east.

Once you pull off the highway and drive into town, you leave the road noise behind. Dillon is a convenient base for exploring Lake Dillon and the surrounding mountains, and the ski destinations of Breckenridge, Copper, and Keystone are a short drive away. But unlike other Colorado mountain towns, there are no old buildings here. No dilapidated miner's cabins, no Victorian houses. The hotels, condos, restaurants, sports stores, and boutiques are all newer structures. The lakeside setting seems perfect for an early settlement, but oddly, there is no trace of the historical past here.

Dillon did not always sit at the edge of the lake. In fact, until the 1960s, there was no Lake Dillon. The story of Dillon is one of development, water rights, and changing times.

The old town, originally situated to the east, was named after an early prospector. The area saw off-and-on gold mining, a little railroading, lumber trading, and much ranching. The first post office opened here in 1883. With the advent of the car came garages and service stations. Roads improved, and more tourists showed up "to breathe the exhilarating Rocky Mountain air," as one advertisement put it. A longtime resident remembers the Dillon of the 1930s: "Ranchers picked up their mail here," he says, "and it was a place for a beer on Saturday night."

trivia

Two historic Georgetown homes, the Bowman-White House and the Hamill House, exemplify the city's Victorian style. Learn more at historic georgetown.org.

But on the other side of the mountains, Denver was growing, and it desperately needed more water. All through the 1940s and early 1950s, the Denver Water Department bought up lands and ranches with water rights. Then, in 1955, Dillon residents were told about the coming storage reservoir. It would flood their town.

After many meetings and complex legal work, the machinery ground into high gear. Dillon had to move. Some people left for warmer climates; others settled in nearby villages. But the citizens decided to create a new Dillon on a hill of pine and evergreen. Here was a chance for a model town.

Down in the valley the old community was dismantled stick by stick. Because the water supply had to be pure, all buildings had to go. Some were cut in half and hauled elsewhere by trucks. Others had to be burned down. The Water Board uprooted telephone lines, removed old pipes, buried the last rusty tin cans. Even the peaceful graveyard, with its rococo stones and metal crosses, had to be shifted to higher ground. The school was moved, and the church found a new home in the reborn Dillon.

Slowly the dam rose until it stood 231 feet high at some points and was capable of backing up 257,000 acre-feet of water. The Roberts Tunnel, more than 23 miles long and costing $50 million, was completed to connect the reservoir with rivers flowing into Denver. Water from thawing snows and the mountain streams steadily accumulated in the reservoir behind the dam.

One August day, the waters rushed over the top and through the "glory hole" spillway into the outlet tunnel. By then nothing was left of the old Dillon townsite. The roads that led to it now lay under about 150 feet of water. The old Dillon was no more.

Among the trees to the west stands the new Dillon. The town officials and the city planners conceived it well. Buildings can be no higher than 30 feet, providing unobstructed views of the lake. Dillon's signs are subdued, modest, and inviting. There is little neon. Only natural materials—the stone and wood of the Rockies, plus glass—are permitted for the houses. The wood may be stained but not painted. The lots and homes are spread out. And timber is cut sparingly, for conservation's sake.

trivia

A mysterious Frenchman named Louis Dupuy originally ran the Hotel de Paris; some Georgetown people say he left a large family in France.

Development continues in Dillon and around the 3,300-acre lake. New shopping areas and businesses appear regularly. The city is currently dealing with the pine beetle infestation that is affecting the entire western US, and many trees are being removed to control the spread of the beetles. Despite the uninvited guests in the surrounding forest, the town and the lakefront remain an enjoyable place to rent a canoe, ride a bike, or walk around and enjoy the local shops and eateries.

The **Dillon Marina** hosts a number of fun community events, including regattas throughout the summer. For details call (970) 468-5100; write 150 Marina Dr., Dillon 80435; or visit townofdillon.com. Free Friday night concerts take place throughout the summer at the Dillon Amphitheater; call (970) 468-2403 for details. Each Friday June to Sept the Dillon Farmers' Market features free entertainment, artisan foods, and other local products. For more information about events and attractions in Dillon during your stay, call (970) 468-2403, visit townofdillon.com, or write Town Office, 275 Lake Dillon Dr., Dillon 80435.

Denver is a mere 70 minutes from Lake Dillon thanks to the time-saving **Eisenhower Tunnel,** which is a story in its own right.

For a hundred years, since the days when railroads were first reaching across the continent, men had worked and dreamed of tunneling through the Continental Divide here at its narrowest point. "Nearly impossible!" a geologist said when a Colorado financier first suggested a long tunnel through the Continental Divide during the 1930s.

"Unpredictable rock!" other geologists warned in 1941. The drilling of a pilot bore already gave a clue to the unstable rock strata of this area. Steel linings buckled in the exploratory shaft. But plans were drawn, and the work began in 1968. For five years tunnel builders, sometimes as many as 1,100 men at a time, battled the mountain some 58 miles west of Denver. Lack of money, politics, explosions, fires, and, most of all, geological problems all thwarted the builders. A tunnel engineer later summed it up better than anyone else. "We were going by the book," he said. "But the damned mountain couldn't read!"

Fortunately, the 8,941-foot-long Eisenhower Tunnel was eventually drilled despite the obstacles. The tunnel makes travel possible in all seasons, and

Georgetown Fishing

The lakes in this area are often crowded during the summer, with the exception of **Silver Dollar Lake.** A somewhat steep, 3-mile round-trip trail leads to the lake, which yields good catches and offers peace and quiet. From Georgetown, head 8.5 miles south on Guanella Pass Road. Turn right at the "Silver Dollar Lake" sign.

saves the motorist 10 miles over the twisting and turning highway that crosses Loveland Pass. Since the tunnel opened in 1973, drivers need no longer expose themselves to the fierce storms and howling winds of the pass. No more jackknifed trucks, stranded cars, or vehicles swept off the highway ledges by avalanches, rockslides, or icy curves taken too fast. One of North America's best-known mountain passes was finally tamed.

The Eisenhower Tunnel is 57 miles west of Denver via I-70. Visit codot. gov/travel/ejmt for more information. After traversing the tunnel, consider a short detour to **Silverthorne,** just 66 miles from Denver, before continuing west. Silverthorne is a worthy year-round destination in Summit County, offering outdoor adventure and a thriving arts and culture scene. The town has a performing arts center, community events, locally owned and operated restaurants and shops. and unparalleled access to the famed fishing waters of the Blue River and surrounding mountains. The town sits between **Eagles Nest Wilderness Area** and **Ptarmigan Peak Wilderness** and within the 2.3 million acres of **White River National Forest.** Eagles Nest is among Colorado's most formidable and rugged areas, encompassing most of the Gore Range and running from 7,850 feet in elevation to well over 13,000 feet, with diverse and spectacular topography.

Ptarmigan Peak Wilderness is 12,760 acres with few trails but an abundance of Rocky Mountain backcountry beauty and solitude.

Eagles Nest Wilderness Area is accessible from Silverthorne to the east and Vail to the west. More than 175 miles of trails enter it, all connecting to the **Gore Range Trail,** which runs the entire north–south length of the area. The trail offers one of Colorado's most challenging and rewarding multiday backpacking treks on the route between Red Buffalo Pass (near Vail) and Eccles Pass (near Frisco). It requires leaving a car at the Meadow Creek/Lily Pad Lake Trailhead in Frisco and the Gore Creek/Deluga Trailhead in Vail. The hike takes two to three days, and backpackers must be well prepared. There are also a multitude of shorter hikes easily accessed from Silverthorne, such as Lily Pad Lake, Angler Mountain Trail, and Willow Falls. For more information contact the Dillon Ranger District, 680 Blue River Pkwy.; (970) 468-5400; fs.usda.gov/main/whiteriver/about-forest/districts. For casual outings, the Blue River Trail in Silverthorne is the perfect paved pathway for family walks or bike rides.

Silverthorne is less than 3 miles from Lake Dillon and just over 10 miles from Breckenridge. The nothing-fancy, affordably priced lodging there makes it an attractive base for exploring Summit County without breaking the bank. Choices include **Quality Inn & Suites Summit County** (530 Silverthorne Ln.; 970-513-1222; choicehotels.com); **Silver Inn** (675 Blue River Pkwy.; 970-513-0104; silverinn.net); and **Bud & Breakfast** at Silverthorne, a marijuana-friendly B&B (358 Lagoon Ln.; 970-368-6757). Lodging here is typically less expensive than other parts of Summit County, making it an attractive base for exploring the county. Several new lodging options opened in the past few years. **Hotel Indigo** (375 Blue River Pkwy.; 970-485-6262; ihg.com) is an upscale lodging option, while **The Pad** (491 Rainbow Dr.; 970-445-7767; thepadlife.com/silverthorne) is Silverthorne's first boutique hotel/hostel property.

Silverthorne also has a burgeoning restaurant scene. From craft beers to authentic ethnic eats, there is plenty to choose from. One to try: **Bluebird Market Hall** (325 Blue River Pkwy.; 303-216-0420; bluebirdmarket.co), Summit County's first food hall.

Year-Round Vacation Areas

Breckenridge is the perfect Colorado frontier town—one of the few that was rebuilt and is now well preserved and thriving.

In 1859, a group of 14 prospectors discovered gold in the Breckenridge area. A town was quickly built by miners who were hopeful that they would strike it rich. One such miner, Tom Groves, walked away a big winner when he discovered "Tom's Baby," a 136-ounce gold nugget. But, like all areas rich in minerals, the mines eventually played out. Breckenridge citizens wouldn't give up, and they found another moneymaker when Summit County's first ski area opened in 1961.

Breckenridge has a Western charm that especially delights European visitors. Here are the earmarks of the old Gold Rush West: fairy-tale Victorian houses with columns, crenellations, and gingerbread trim; the clapboard structures of the miners, beautifully repainted; and store windows filled with antiques. Travelers from the Midwest and East feel the same way; they're walking through a colorful piece of American history. The ski slopes are still named for the old mines in the area: Gold King, Wellington, Bonanza, Cashier, Silverthorne—these were the monikers that excited the gold hunters more than a century ago.

Breckenridge is actually one of Colorado's oldest towns. In August 1859 the first gold seekers came streaming across the Continental Divide to pan gold in the waters of the Blue River. More than $30 million in gold was taken out of the district during its heyday. Later, a silver lode started a second boom. By 1861 some 5,000 people lived in and around Breckenridge. Summit County then extended as far as the Utah line and was one of 17 counties composing the Colorado Territory. It has since been whittled down to 600 square miles. Then, as now, Breckenridge was the county seat. As with other mountain mining towns in Colorado, the precious minerals ran out and mining came to a halt. In the early 1960s, Breckenridge became a year-round resort, at the same time maintaining its century-old status as a former mining community. Development may have brought condos and shopping centers, but it hasn't destroyed the town's historical district. Take a walk along the 6-block stretch of Main Street through the old town for a glimpse back in time. Old storefronts and original brick and wood buildings continue to serve a purpose, housing restaurants, shops, and boutiques.

But there's more. Walk east a couple of blocks from Main Street on Lincoln or Washington or Adams Avenues, and wander the grid of quiet backstreets. Many dozens of old homes sit back among the trees, lovingly restored reminders of the glory mining days of old Breckenridge. Grassy yards, flower gardens, and hummingbirds thrive, and after strolling through this lovely area, you may just be tempted to drop by a real estate office or two.

trivia

In the early 1960s, the original town of Dillon—the whole town!—was moved in order to make way for the Lake Dillon reservoir.

Summer and fall are busy seasons in Breckenridge. Coloradans and out-of-state visitors come here to stay for a few days, renting rooms in nearby condos and lodges. This is a great base for exploring the area south toward Hoosier Pass and beyond to Fairplay. The Blue River runs through town, and several riverfront plaza areas are perfect for sitting under a tree and people-watching. Stop by **Clint's Bakery and Coffee House** at 131 S. Main St. for excellent drinks, baked goods, breakfast and lunch items. Or drop by **Crepes A La Cart,** the outdoor crepes stand at 307 S. Main St. They open at 9 a.m. offering a wide variety of savory lunch and dinner crepes and decadent dessert crepes. There's often a line; meet other travelers and swap stories until your crepe arrives.

Breckenridge in winter is another Colorado favorite. More than 2,908 acres of skiable terrain on 187 trails offer something for every ski level. Snowboarding, snowshoeing, dogsledding, cross-country skiing, and nearby ice fishing are

Safety Tips

In Colorado, state law considers bicycles to be vehicles, and they must obey the same traffic laws as automobiles. Ride single file on the right in the same direction as traffic. Always signal when stopping or turning. When you need to catch your breath, move off the road. It's also good advice to wear a helmet and protective glasses.

all part of the cold-weather scene here. Contact the Breckenridge Ski Resort, 1599 Ski Hill Rd.; (970) 453-5000 or (800) 789-7669; breckenridge.com.

Breckenridge is located 88 miles west of Denver via I-70 and Highway 9. For more information contact the Breckenridge Tourism Office or stop by the Breckenridge Welcome Center at 203 S. Main St. For more information call (877) 864-0868 or visit gobreck.com.

Mining—an important part of Colorado's past—is alive and well and can be glimpsed at the *Country Boy Mine,* 2 miles from downtown Breckenridge. This working mine is one of the few that offers travelers a journey into some of the same places that hard-rock miners went more than 100 years ago when the mine was established. At the Country Boy Mine you can don a hard hat and venture 1,000 feet underground, seeing, feeling, and hearing what actual miner experienced. In Breckenridge turn left (east) on Wellington Road and follow it to a final fork. Turn right, and then drive a mile east on French Gulch Road. Admission costs $35, children 2 and younger free. Open year-round. Call (970) 453-4405 for hours, or visit countryboymine.com.

Vail is probably best known as a world-class ski destination, and that vibe is strong even in summer when the snow retreats to the high peaks. Where else but in Colorado would you expect to find an extensive ski museum? Founded in 1976, the *Colorado Snowsports Museum & Hall of Fame* in *Vail* reaches back to the old miners of the 19th century who raced in the Rockies surrounding their camps, competing against one another on long wooden boards while holding a long staff in one fist for braking. In the museum are photos and artifacts of skiing clergymen like Father John Lewis Dyer, who brought the gospel to Colorado's historic gold towns, as well as the stories of sheepherders and trappers who braved the snows in the 19th century on 9-foot enormous wooden contraptions with crude leather straps holding their boots. Mementos of the first long-ago jumpers will fascinate viewers; photos show them taking off from knolls or flying through the air, equipment sometimes falling off high above the ground. Visitors will learn much about the development of skis, bindings, boots, poles, even the first ski suits, as well as the women's fashions of earlier days, when ladies skied in ankle-length black skirts.

The history of Colorado's famous 10th Mountain Division is well illustrated at the museum; an entire room is devoted to the Mountain Troopers and their initial camps and wartime exploits. A viewing area shows ski videos. Exhibits on avalanche control, up-to-date ski racing, and the history of Vail—it's all here in the center of town. Admission is free, but donations are appreciated. Open daily from 10 a.m. to 6 p.m. Colorado Ski and Snowboard Museum, 231 S. Frontage Rd. East; (970) 476-1876; skimuseum.net. Winter activities range far beyond downhill skiing and snowboarding. Tubing, ski-biking, snowshoeing, kid-size snowmobiling, and cross-country skiing are all available around the resort area. Several restaurants offer romantic, gourmet dinners in the snowy woods; try *Tennessee Pass Cookhouse* (719-486-8114; tennesseepass.com/the-cookhouse) or *Beano's Cabin* (970-754-3463; beavercreek.com/the-mountain/on-mountain-dining/beanos-cabin.aspx). Both are also open in the summer.

Summertime in Vail is a gentle season of greening mountainsides, flowering alpine meadows, and long, warm days. The Vail Farmers' Market and Art Show (Colorado's largest farmers' market) takes place each Sunday from 10 a.m. to 3 p.m., mid-June through late September. Enjoy cool jazz concerts while browsing locally grown produce, fresh baked goods, clothing, jewelry, and handmade items. Golf, kayaking, biking, fishing, and hiking are all popular here in summer. A full calendar of festivals, concerts, and events, many of them free, runs through the summer. For details go to vail.com.

trivia

The utility bill for the Eisenhower Tunnel runs about $80,000 a month—each tunnel (one for eastbound and one for westbound traffic) has 2,000 light fixtures, and each light fixture contains an 8-foot bulb!

After a day of play, take the gondola ride up the mountain after dark and see Vail far below, glittering like a little jewel box.

Two hours west of Denver lie some of the state's most impressive mountains—the *Gore Range.* In Vail itself you'll see Gore Creek, especially in summer. *Gore Mountain,* Gore Wilderness—who in the world was Gore? No, it's not a former vice president. George Gore was one of the more interesting visitors who ever roamed through Colorado. The best place to get acquainted with him might be north of Vail on *Gore Pass,* near Kremmling. Here a bronze plaque is visible beside the highway, at an elevation of 9,000 feet. The words on the bronze give a brief version of his time here:

HERE IN 1854 CROSSED SIR ST. GEORGE GORE. AN IRISH BARONET BENT ON SLAUGHTER OF GAME AND GUIDED BY JIM BRIDGER. FOR THREE YEARS HE SCOURED COLORADO, MONTANA AND WYOMING ACCOMPANIED USUALLY BY FORTY MEN, MANY CARTS, WAGONS, HOUNDS, AND UNEXAMPLED CAMP LUXURIES.

Lord Gore's party, we learn, dispatched "more than 2,000 buffalo, 1,600 elk and deer, and 100 bears," among others. Hunting was nothing new in a land where European trappers and fur traders had already scoured all of Colorado for beaver. But Lord Gore set a record; besides, no one matched his style. The baronet traveled with his retinue of hunters and porters from Ireland; his safari caravan eventually accumulated 112 horses, 21 carts, 30 wagons, and 4 dozen hunting dogs. He roamed the mountains for many months, shooting grizzly bear, pronghorn, and other animals and making elegant camp at night, complete with silver service and rare wines. His Lordship could afford the "unexampled camp luxuries." For one thing, his annual income exceeded $200,000, which was quite a sum during the mid-1850s. For another, the Irish nobleman had a taste for gourmet cuisine and rare wines—and the cooks and servants to attend his needs. Lord Gore had gone to school in Oxford, and his aristocratic tastes included various mansions in Ireland and houses in East Sussex.

Lord Gore's hunt and his exploits are still studied by local children. And thanks to the *Historical Society of Colorado,* future visitors to the region will be reminded of the Irishman by means of the bronze plaque on Gore Pass.

The summit of Gore Pass and the plaque are 17 miles west of Kremmling and can be reached from Denver via US 40. There are picnic grounds on the pass. Return to I-70 by driving south on Highway 9.

Botanists have identified thousands of different flower species in the Rockies. The first sign of spring at lower elevations brings forth a rush of daisies, mountain marigolds, wild sweet peas, fairy trumpets, pink rockhill phlox, and others in a rainbow of hues. Wander up in early summer to Colorado's 8,000- or 9,000-foot levels. Here, almost overnight, you'll see leafy cinquefoils, arnicas,

Rifle Falls State Park

Before you head too much farther west, consider making a side trip to Rifle Falls State Park. Though small, this unique gem of a state park offers visitors the unlikely opportunity to get downright tropical—or close to it! The triple waterfall plummets down 80 feet past limestone cliffs, keeping the lush vegetation moist. Dark, cool caves beckon to curious explorers, and interpretive signs help explain the phenomena. With its $9 daily vehicle pass, the park makes for a worthwhile side trip and a terrific place for a family hike or picnic. Winter activities are also available.

From Aspen, take Highway 82 north about 41 miles. In Glenwood Springs turn left onto 6th Street then left onto North River Drive, following signs to I-70 West. Take I-70 about 25.5 miles to the Rifle exit. Go north on Highway 13 for 4 miles. Turn right on Highway 325 and drive 9.8 miles. Call (970) 625-1607 or write Rifle Falls State Park, 5775 Hwy. 325, Rifle 81650; cpw.state.co.us/placestogo/parks/RifleFalls.

yellow monkey flowers, and the official state flower, the blue Rocky Mountain columbine. (The latter also grows in the foothills.) In July, you'll be welcomed by the star gentians, wood lilies, the mountain aster, and several kinds of larkspur. After the snow has melted in the alpine zone above tree line, the next wave of color arrives, brightening the rocky slopes and high valleys with lavender, crimson, azure, butter yellow, pink, and pure white.

Perhaps the most amazing aspect of these annual displays is the fact that any plant producing such delicate beauty can survive under the freezing winter blizzards, blazing high-altitude sun, blasting winds, and generally harsh climate that occur above timberline. Their existence up here seems miraculous.

In the tundra at high elevations, you'll notice that all the plants are small. Many have short stems or none at all. That helps; the tinier the leaves and lower to the ground they are, the less resistance to the wind. At the same time, roots go deep into the soil, anchoring plants so they don't get ripped away in the stiff gusts. Mountain flowers protect themselves against the elements with protective tiny umbrellas of growth or hairs, or fine layers of woolly matter or waxy leaves that hold in moisture. And many flowers close their petals at night to hold on to the day's warmth.

Colorado is renowned for its wildflowers. Hike just about any place in the mountains from June through August and you will find flowers, often in unlikely places. Different elevations and habitats support entirely different species. The growing season is short, but the state's flora makes up for that brief window of time by putting on one of nature's loveliest of shows. When you're outdoors enjoying the flowers, keep in mind that the vegetation is fragile, often barely holding on under extreme growing conditions. Watch where you're walking and stay on trails. Don't pick wildflowers. They often spread their seeds through their blossoms, so picking the flowers now means there will be fewer flowers next year. Picking flowers is against the law in all national parks, forests, and monuments. And they don't last long, often wilting within an hour. Leave the flowers alive and thriving for everyone to enjoy.

trivia

Gold was first panned in Breckenridge's Blue River in 1859.

At 8,200 feet, the ***Betty Ford Alpine Gardens*** are billed as the world's highest botanic garden, with a lush array of high-elevation perennials, rock gardens, and waterfalls in an already spectacular setting. Open from dawn to dusk, there is no charge to visit the gardens, but donations are accepted. The gardens are located in Ford Park, 522 S. Frontage Rd., Vail; (970) 476-0103; bettyfordalpinegardens.org.

Breckenridge Horseback Riding

Tired of walking? **Breckenridge Stables** offers 90-minute rides along the Breckenridge Trail, which passes some of Colorado's finest scenery. Reserve all rides at least one day in advance. Ride prices are $99 for 90 minutes, with children age 3 or younger paying $50 and doubling up with an adult. Breakfast and dinner rides and lessons are also available. Call (970) 453-4438 or write PO Box 6686, Breckenridge 80424; breckstables.com.

As you continue past Vail and Eagle on I-70 heading west, you'll soon find yourself surrounded by spectacular canyon walls. Welcome to **Glenwood Canyon.** Remarkable for its breathtaking geologic features and lovely scenery, the canyon is rendered even more extraordinary by the fact that the interstate running through it was constructed with a mind to retaining the canyon's wild and natural beauty. Though it's unfortunate a large interstate had to be put in this incredible setting, it is nonetheless encouraging that those in charge of building the road worked hard to make it as environmentally friendly as possible. The interstate swoops and bends with the canyon as it drops deeper into the earth. Between the river and the canyon wall, 16-mile-long **Glenwood Canyon Recreation Trail** parallels the highway. You can catch occasional glimpses of it from the road. Four rest stops along I-70 allow access to the trail within the canyon. The trail starts behind the Yampah Spa and Vapor Caves in Glenwood Springs. This paved trail and the river attract not only hikers and sightseers but also in-line skaters, cyclists, runners, rafters, and kayakers. For more information call (970) 945-6589 or contact Glenwood Springs Chamber Resort Association, 802 Grand Ave.; visitglenwood.com.

One of the jewels of Glenwood Canyon is **Hanging Lake,** an evocative, pristine place, well worth the short but strenuous uphill hike to reach it. Due to overcrowding and the fragility of the lake and trail, permits are required for every hiker. Reservations can be made at visitglenwood.com/hanginglake. The $12 permits include parking. To get there, pull off I-70 when you see the sign; the turnoff is well-marked, but if you're not in the correct lane, you will miss the exit. It's a short hike (only 1.2 miles), but in that distance it climbs 1,020 feet up the mountain. The trail follows Deadhorse Creek past box elders, cottonwoods, and lush fern gardens. Your reward at the top is a spectacular natural lake that was formed long ago when a geological fault caused the hillside to fall away. A nearby stream deposited carbonates over the fault, which hardened and formed a rim. Today the lake is 25 feet deep, crystal clear, and filled with large trout. There is no fishing, so these lunkers have grown uninterrupted by anglers. A boardwalk borders part of the lake, and the mist from the water-falls is cooling in summer.

trivia

Breckenridge features several ghost towns worth checking out: Lincoln City, Swandyke, Dyersville, and others. Breckenridge History offers several guided tours and hikes around Breckenridge, including a Walk Through History Tour and the Tombstone Tales Tour. Visit breckheritage.com or call (970) 453-9767.

Glenwood Springs may be one of the state's more interesting destinations—historically, economically, scenically—yet it never garners the attention accorded to trendy Aspen (41 miles to the southeast), glitzy Vail (59 miles), or cosmopolitan Denver (some 158 miles to the east). The town is the gateway to some of Colorado's most dramatic and most photographed peaks, including the Maroon Bells near Snowmass and lone, spectacular *Mount Sopris,* visible from almost everywhere in the region. The immense *White River National Forest* offers backpackers plenty of wilderness

They Almost Blew It: Vail History

Vail founders never anticipated a success of such magnitude. Although thousands of mountain troopers and skiers passed through the valley during the 1940s and 1950s, none of them saw the potential of Vail Mountain, since the best slopes were out of sight high above the highway. But Peter Seibert, an ex–10th Mountain man and a ski racer, knew a lot about ski areas, and he spent two years hiking, climbing, and skiing all over the Rockies to look for the ideal resort location. One day in 1957, he scaled the Vail Summit with a local prospector who lived in the valley. Upon seeing the bowls and glades and open slopes, Seibert knew he'd found the ideal site. Seibert and some friends invested their savings. But more money was needed.

Unfortunately, at that time Denver's conservative bankers wouldn't gamble on a large new ski area, with Aspen already doing well. All the same, Seibert kept looking for partners. He bought a snowcat and brought visitors to his mountain. He showed films of his powder bowls all over the country and invited prospective investors to ski with him. Eventually he got lucky. A Michigan oilman-skier recognized the potential and found other wealthy backers who spread Seibert's gospel. They raised $5 million, formed Vail Associates, and successfully tapped the Small Business Administration and the no-longer-reluctant Denver bankers. And they sold real estate to precisely the people who had shaken their heads the hardest.

During the summer of 1962, the bulldozers started to dig in. An excellent Milwaukee architect had drawn up the plans and now supervised the frantic building activity. When the dust settled, there stood the first lodges, apartments, malls, homes, and lifts of Vail, Colorado.

Sylvan Lake State Park—Quintessential Colorado

Peaceful and unhurried, **Sylvan Lake State Park** is an alpine retreat down the road from Vail and just south of Eagle. Surrounded by the White River National Forest, Sylvan Lake is a lovely spot for camping, picnicking, or enjoying a quiet lake surrounded by more than 1,500 acres of parkland. Campgrounds, cabins, and yurts are available for overnight stays. For more information contact park headquarters at 10200 Brush Creek Rd., Eagle 81631; (970) 328-2021; or visit cpw.state.co.us/placestogo/parks/SylvanLake.

for roaming around. Anglers find world-class fishing for trout (rainbows and browns) in the surrounding rivers—the Roaring Fork, the Frying Pan, and the Colorado. Rivers attract rafters and kayakers as well; guiding services are available in Glenwood Springs. Hiking is plentiful, and hunters flock to the region for elk, deer, grouse, and waterfowl.

Despite the wealth of outdoor pursuits surrounding the town, the attraction that brings most visitors to the area is the 2-block-long **Glenwood Hot Springs** pool. No matter the season or the weather outside, the therapeutic waters are perfect for easing sore, tired muscles.

The Ute Indians used these springs centuries before the first explorers arrived, claiming they had miraculous healing powers. A famed architect, imported from Vienna, Austria, built the bathhouses here in 1888, and before long assorted American presidents such as Truman, Taft, Hoover, and Teddy Roosevelt came to visit Glenwood's mineral spa and "Natatorium."

Today the recreational swimming pool is kept at 90–93°F (29–32°C); hotter outdoor waters at 104°F (40°C) are also available, fed by more than 3.5 million gallons. The hot springs contain a cornucopia of elements, including magnesium, calcium, sulphates, bicarbonates, phosphates, and silica. Swimmers relish the almost unlimited space in the pool, while those recuperating from injuries enjoy the medical benefits. For additional pampering, the nearby vapor baths feature massages and natural saunas. The pool is open daily, year-round, 8 a.m. to 9 p.m. Rates vary from about $29 to $42 depending on age, season, and time of day or evening. Contact the pool at (970) 947-2955; hotspringspool.com.

While the town's main pool is its best known, **Iron Mountain Hot Springs,** on the banks of the Colorado River, is an inviting option. Its 16 iron-and-mineral-rich soaking pools are fed by 3 springs, and its history dates to 1896 when the West Glenwood Health Spa opened on the property. Today's amenities include a modern bathhouse, the Sopris Café, and a retail shop. The

Vail Day Trip

In Vail you're surrounded by the Rockies, and there are day trip options in every direction. One sure bet is the drive from the top of Vail Pass to the summit of Shrine Pass. The road is open only in summer and has great views of Mount of the Holy Cross. Leave your car and hike around the area for some of the best wildflower displays and scenery in Colorado. Continue about 7 miles to the old mining town of Red Cliff for lunch at **Mango's** (166½ Eagle St.; 970-827-9109; mangosmountaingrill .com). Return on Highway 24, passing an amazing suspension bridge as you make your way to Minturn and back to Vail.

pool opens at 9 a.m. daily year-round and closes at 10 p.m. with a few exceptions. Tickets start at $36..

Glenwood Springs has plenty of lodging, but the most convenient one for soakers is the **Glenwood Hot Springs Lodge.** It's a short walk from the pool to your room. The 107-unit lodge is contemporary and ideally located. Rates are not as high as you might expect. For reservations call (800) 537-7946 or (970) 945-6571. For more information about the pool or lodgings: 415 E. 6th St.; hotspringspool.com. Both the town and the area are blessed with accommodations for every pocketbook. Economy travelers welcome the numerous inexpensive and moderately priced cabins and mom-and-pop motels. Annual festivals, **rodeos,** and mountains all around the town give Glenwood Springs a true Western atmosphere while preserving its small-town feel.

Glenwood can lay claim to another local attraction found nowhere else in the state. **Strawberry Days,** held in June, brings parades, carnivals, top-notch entertainment, an art and crafts market, and sporting events. Strawberry Days, now more than 100 years old, is Colorado's oldest civic celebration, dating back to 1898. Things have changed since the strawberry picnics of those early days, but the town's enthusiasm for this celebration is stronger than ever. The celebration goes for three days, with an estimated 30,000 people showing up to enjoy the party each year. For more information call (970) 945-6589 or visit glenwoodchamber.com/strawberry-days-festival.html.

While you're in Glenwood Springs, take a stroll through the stately **Hotel Colorado,** which graces the National Register of Historic Places. The 128-room hotel, one of the oldest in the state, was modeled after Italy's Villa Medici and boasts a Florentine fountain in a landscaped courtyard. The hotel's renovated lobby is one of the most attractive in the western US. The sparkling chandeliers, fireplaces, oil paintings, fountains, and potted palm trees hark back to the days of royalty and the very wealthy.

The Hotel Colorado was financed by the silver mining of the nearby Aspen region and opened officially on June 10, 1893. The cost was a staggering (at the time) $850,000; some 16 private railroad cars of the industrial barons drew up on a special Glenwood siding. Over time, leading citizens from all over the world registered at the hotel.

trivia

Despite receiving only 9 inches of rainfall and 19 inches of snowfall annually, the area encompassed by the Colorado National Monument was continuously inhabited for thousands of years until 1881. That year, the area's most recent inhabitants, the Utes, were moved by the US military to a Utah reservation. Past inhabitants left evidence of their existence through rock art and other artifacts.

European millionaires arrived in droves to stay and dine here. In 1905 President Theodore Roosevelt brought his own appetite; a typical menu encouraged the presidential visitor and his entourage to consume an eight-course repast: Caviar Canapés, Spring Lamb Consommé, Rothschild Broiled Squab, Veal, Sweetbreads, Fig's Young Turkey, and Roquefort Cheese.

Eventually, Roosevelt—an avid bear hunter—made the hotel his Summer White House, complete with direct telegraph connections to Washington and special couriers bringing international news to the hunting head of state. Other famous guests included the "Unsinkable" Molly Brown, who managed to survive the *Titanic*'s sinking, gangster Al Capone, and President Taft. For more information and reservations contact Hotel Colorado, 526 Pine, Glenwood Springs 81601; (970) 945-6511 or (800) 544-3998; hotelcolorado.com.

Taking It Slow in Aspen

The *Aspen/Snowmass Nordic Trail System* offers cross-country skiers numerous opportunities around the valley. This system is unique because it links two towns (Aspen and Snowmass Village), meandering through meadows, wooded areas, and across three valleys. Choose from 60 kilometers (37 miles) of groomed trails or set off on your own across fresh powder. Two Nordic centers, *Aspen Cross Country Center* (970-925-2145) and *Snowmass Cross Country Center* (970-923-5700), are on the trail network, providing instruction, rentals, snacks, waxing advice, and information on choosing the right trail for your skill level. Directions and information for both centers can be found at aspennordic.com or utemountaineer.com.

A third Nordic center, *Ashcroft Ski Touring* (970-925-1971) is located up the Castle Creek Valley on the Ashcroft Trail System. They offer rentals, instruction, and trail advice, and with 35 kilometers (22 miles) of trail, the center has some of the prettiest routes in the valley. You can also ski or snowshoe into and out of the Pine Creek Cookhouse for a memorable gourmet meal. Visit online at pinecreekcookhouse.com.

For more information about the Glenwood Springs area, contact the Glenwood Springs Chamber Resort Association at (970) 945-6589; glenwoodchamber .com. Glenwood Springs is easily reached from Denver by rental car, bus, or train. Motorists use I-70. The distance from Denver is 158 miles.

Even by Colorado standards, the trip to **Redstone** is long, but it is worth it. The scenery along the way is classic Rockies landscape, and the distance only enhances the charms of the little hamlet of Redstone and its historic inn and castle. The imposing **Redstone Inn** and Tudor clock tower are an unexpected sight in this remote mountain landscape.

The 35 rooms are cozy and unpretentious, although some furnishings are in need of replacement. It's a quirky, one-of-a-kind place, and if you don't need four-star accommodations, this historic hotel in a beautiful setting is a nice escape from the city. The lobby and the restaurant are filled with antiques and have a Victorian atmosphere. The **Crystal River** is quiet and lovely, with fishing and horseback riding available in the warm months. In winter, the inn serves as headquarters for sleigh rides, cross-country skiing, ice climbing, and snowshoeing.

Contact Redstone Inn at 82 Redstone Castle Dr., Redstone 81623; (970) 963-2526; redstoneinn.com. Get to Redstone via I-70 west to Glenwood Springs, then Highway 82 south out of Glenwood toward Aspen; turn right at Carbondale on Highway 133—it's 18 miles to Redstone. For more information about the community and surrounding area, visit redstonecolorado.com.

If you continue along Highway 82 south out of Glenwood, it won't be long until you reach **Aspen.** This pretty town is famous around the world as a mountain retreat for movie stars, music moguls, and the wealthy. The gated communities in the hills above town are where the rich and famous stay and party during ski vacations or summer getaways. It's the best celebrity-spotting place in Colorado.

But Aspen is much more than glitz and glamour, and as you approach the edge of town, you will see why it's become a haven for celebrities. Aspen sits at the upper end of Roaring Fork Valley, surrounded by abundant aspen groves. The Roaring Fork River, a tributary of the Colorado River, runs through town. Mountains and wilderness rise above Aspen on three sides. Nearby Maroon Bells and Maroon Lake are among the most photographed and easily recognizable of Colorado's many natural landmarks. Mention Colorado to someone who's never been here, and the scenery around Aspen is likely the sort of place they have in mind.

Aspen called itself Ute City at first because it was in Ute territory. Silver gave the town its big start back in the early 1880s. Soon after news of the silver discovery broke, prospectors headed up the passes and rushed to Aspen—a

Shrine Ridge Hike

Shrine Ridge is an easy hike that can be accomplished in 2 to 3 hours. Climb through open meadows with abundant wildflowers, then up the steepest part of the trail to the 11,089-foot summit. While atop the mountain, look for "Lord Gore," a man-shaped rock to the northwest. To reach the trailhead, take I-70 to Vail Pass, exit 190. Proceed on Road #709 to Shrine Pass Summit. Turn left here and drive to Shrine Mountain Inn, where you can park.

Vail Hikes

More than 20 scenic trails around Vail take hikers into beautiful backcountry land-scapes. Here are a few of them. Local hotels, sports stores, and residents can direct you to trailheads.

- *Beaver Lake* (good workout with some elevation gain to a pretty mountain lake)
- *Berry Picker* (up Vail Mountain, lots of berries in season; you can hike to top and ride a gondola back down)
- *Booth Creek/Booth Falls* (pleasant hike through aspen groves, colorful in fall)
- *East Vail Hikes* (three trailheads starting at the end of old I-70)
- *Piney Lake* (several trails start from the lake, with a nice picnic spot)

hard, punishing journey, even from nearby Leadville. Some men dropped dead before they could stake their first claim. Western historians still mention the stampede of that winter in 1879. They came on burro, on foot, or on horseback.

Sometimes a man would keel over and die on the Aspen streets. Other prospectors just stuck the body into a snowbank and kept up the frantic search for silver riches. The best years were from 1885 to 1889, when mines galore—with names like the Smuggler or Montezuma—operated above the mountain town. The smelter was booked for weeks, and silver rock would pile up everywhere.

Some miners got rich fast. "The men filled their pockets and fled," wrote one observer of the era. The silver barons built the luxurious Victorian **Hotel Jerome** (330 E. Main St.; 855-923-7640; aubergeresorts.com/hoteljerome) and an opera house. Singers and musicians came from Europe to perform.

The crash came in 1893 and brought lean times. Aspen shriveled from a population of 13,000 to a mere 500. The 1930 census shows a total popula-tion of 705 residents. Many Aspen dwellings stood empty. But several investors saw potential. In the 1940s the rebirth began, and by the early 1950s skiing was well established. Aspen was on its way to a second chance, this time as a world-class ski resort.

Today the town is an eclectic mix of architectural styles: original log cabins, Victorian homes, "mineshaft" condos, and mansions in the hills. Yet despite its flaws, Aspen retains a simplicity that keeps visitors coming back. Aspen summers are a delight, with classical music, lectures, trails for hikers and bikers, rivers for anglers, and an expanded airport for private planes. The ski facilities, with four different ski areas and countless lifts, are all extraordinary, rivaling anything in the Swiss Alps. Restaurants and hotels cater to every budget. And on Red Mountain, where the movie stars live, the parties still go on most every night.

trivia

By the time Glenwood Canyon interstate construction was completed in 1992, more than 150,000 native trees, plants, and shrubs had been replanted in an effort to restore the area. In addition, engineers were careful to plan the route around large old trees instead of chopping them down, and the freshly made rock cuts fit right in with the natural canyon scenery—they had been stained so that they'd appear weathered.

The scene is an early Saturday morning in *Ashcroft,* a remote Colorado ghost town near Aspen. The sun's first rays work their way down nearby Castle Peak and begin spilling across the snowy valley. Nothing stirs in this silent, wintry landscape until a few people assemble down the road from Ashcroft's weathered, abandoned buildings. Several more join them, all carrying snowshoes. By 9 a.m. 40 snowshoers stand ready, almost twice as many as the Colorado Mountain Club

Touring Glenwood Springs

Glenwood Springs is 42 miles northwest of Aspen off Highway 82. "Glenwood," as residents call it, sits in the White River National Forest, which is a 3-hour drive from Denver. Glenwood's two million acres are renowned for all manner of outdoor sports. Flat Tops Wilderness, a huge 117,000-acre plateau north of Glenwood Springs, is a popular destination for anyone seeking quiet and solitude.

Glenwood was named for its hot-spring mineral baths, which are open all year. In the 1880s, silver baron Walter Devereaux decided to convert the springs, which had been used by the Utes for centuries, into a health resort for the rich. He built the 2-block-long swimming pool, intended for the guests of the posh adjacent hotel. By the early 1900s, so many wealthy and famous people came to the spa that a rail siding was installed next to the hotel for private railroad cars. Teddy Roosevelt made Glenwood his "Summer White House" in 1901 and hunted bear in the nearby hills.

The mineral baths and vapor caves are open to visitors. Massages are also available. Locals say the water is a healthy way to ease visitors' aching muscles and stiff joints after days in the nearby wilderness, on long hikes, or on Aspen's ski slopes.

Snowmass Summers

Snowmass summers are mellow. The rocks are warm and meadows fill with wild-flowers: anemones, bluebells, gentian, and Indian paintbrush. Hikers move into the high country. Classes begin at the arts center. Aspen's music festival is only 20 minutes away.

In summer, Snowmass is a center for picnickers, hikers, kayakers, four-wheel enthusiasts, and mountain bikers. Climbers set out for the Maroon Bells. Anglers arm themselves with flies, rods, and nets, and head out for the many trout streams. Horseback riders climb into saddles and disappear into the woods.

Miles of trails, ranging from gentle forest paths to muscle-aching switchbacks, will transport you into an alpine world of mountain blossoms, snowmelt streams, and shady aspen groves.

leader had expected. After a long decline in popularity, snowshoeing is back in fashion, and for several good reasons. Over the last couple of decades the equipment has evolved into lightweight, high-tech gear that makes walking in the snow easy. You don't need lessons; within minutes you will be ready to take off up the trail. And it's excellent exercise. Snowshoeing is really nothing more than winter hiking. You get to enjoy great views, stop whenever you like, and have a solid outdoor workout at a time when others are indoors hiding from Old Man Winter.

On snowshoes you can go just about anywhere, on trail or off, wherever you can find at least a few inches of snow. From the steep winter meadows of the Continental Divide, across the gentle mounds of eastern Colorado, over frozen Lake Dillon, and into the dramatic deep-snow regions above Silverton and Ouray, snowshoers find many hundreds of places to explore. There are no lift lines or tickets to buy. There's no expensive outfit to buy, just standard outdoor winter clothing. Many outdoor shops in Colorado rent snowshoes; cost is around $22 per day for the first day and much less for each additional day. In Denver try REI; the flagship store is at 1416 Platte St.; (303) 756-3100; rei. com/stores/denver.

Summertime in the Colorado mountains is a delight to the ears. Tumbling streams, trilling birdsong, wind whistling down the canyons; it's a daily free concert. But Aspen also happens to be home to a world-famous music festival in a mountain setting unlike any other. Far from any urban center, the music at this altitude seems even more pure and lifting.

The ***Aspen Music Festival and School*** was founded in 1949 with the belief that combining art and nature encourages the growth of the human spirit. This internationally renowned festival presents some of the world's

Choose Your Adventure

Paddle an inflatable kayak on the Colorado. Bike the Glenwood Canyon and Rio Grande trails. Fly fish on the Roaring Fork. Hike throughout the Maroon Bells-Snowmass Wilderness Area. Or take on the extreme whitewater of the Upper Colorado River and Gore Canyon on a multiday trip of Class V adrenalin-packed action. Two good options for these and other outdoor adventures in the area are **Glenwood Adventure Company** ((970) 945-7529 details or glenwoodadventure.com) and. Blazing Adventures Aspen ((970) 923-4544 or blazingadventures.com).

most accomplished classical musicians in a magnificent alpine setting. Over an 8-week period attendees can choose from more than 300 events, including chamber and contemporary music, orchestral concerts, classes, lectures, and kids' programs. Events are held in concert halls, churches, and a permanent tent structure with excellent acoustics. Many events are free, and there's always free seating on the lawn outside the tent. Contact the organization at 225 Music School Rd., Aspen 81611; 970-925-3254/9042; aspenmusicfestival.com. Aspen has other cultural options as well, including the Wheeler-Stallard Museum (620 W. Bleeker St.; 970-925-3721) and the Holden Marolt Ranching and Mining Museum (40180 Hwy. 82; 970-925-3721), both worth a visit.

Nature and the outdoors are among the main reasons people visit Colorado. The first step for many is experiencing the region through road trips, camping, hiking, skiing, rafting, and biking. But many visitors seduced by the grandeur and beauty of the state are curious about the geography, flora, and fauna, and they want to learn more about the ecology and the environment that make the area unique.

The Aspen Center for Environmental Studies (ACES) was formed in 1968 to provide a way for an increasingly urbanized world to rediscover nature. Along with establishing a wildlife preserve in Aspen, the initial focus was to educate schoolchildren about nature and teach environmental responsibility.

Today ACES is an important part of the Aspen community. Thousands of adults and children visit every year to participate in the Naturalist Field School. Instructors from around the country come each summer to teach close to 50 different workshops and courses on the diverse Rocky Mountain ecosystem. Daily courses include hawk, eagle, and owl demonstrations; naturalist-guided walks; a variety of programs for kids; sunset beaver walks;

trivia

Doc Holliday, the famous—or infamous—cowboy, died in Glenwood Springs in 1887; his grave marker epitaph declares only this: HE DIED IN BED.

and campground programs. Course topics include birds, plants, backcountry navigation, families in nature, geology, mushrooms, field journaling, astronomy, and farming.

In the winter, ACES leads snowshoe tours atop Aspen Mountain and Ashcroft ghost town and ski tours at Snowmass. Many Wednesdays at 7:30 p.m. during Potbelly Perspectives, weekly photo presentations by adventurers and biologists transport audiences to faraway lands. For more information and a complete list of courses contact ACES at 100 Puppy Smith St., Aspen 81611; (970) 925-5756; aspennature.org.

Located just 10 miles from Aspen, *Snowmass Village* may not have the instant name recognition enjoyed by its neighbor, but it compensates by offering a wide variety of activities and events throughout the year. You're still deep in the Rockies, so expect to find miles of hiking and mountain biking, fly fishing, rafting, golf, jeep tours, and horseback riding.

But just like Aspen, Snowmass is also a cultural destination. Winter means skiing and other winter sports, but the summer and fall months bring a nonstop selection of unique festivals, concerts, and events. Summer begins with the *Snowmass Rendezvous,* featuring craft beers, tastings, and, of course, music. *Snowmass Rodeo* begins in mid-June and stretches through mid-August. Snowmass Village puts on free music concerts featuring major acts through the summer at Fanny Hill. The *Jazz Aspen Snowmass June Festival* is four nights of some of the best jazz on the planet. *Snowmass Balloon Festival* in September fills the sky for three colorful days with one of the highest-altitude

OTHER ATTRACTIONS WORTH SEEING IN THE CENTRAL MOUNTAINS

ASPEN
Aspen Historical Society Wheeler/
Stallard Museum
(970) 925-3721
aspenhistory.org

Independence Pass
(Hwy. 82; closed in winter)
independencepass.org

DILLON
Copper Mountain Resort
(866) 841-2481
coppercolorado.com

GEORGETOWN
Loveland Ski Area
(800) 736-3754 or
(303) 571-5580
skiloveland.com

GLENWOOD
White River National Forest
(970) 945-2521
fs.usda.gov/whiteriver

IDAHO SPRINGS
Historical Society of Idaho Springs
(303) 567-4382
historicidahosprings.com

Sunlight Mountain Resort

Tired of the crowds at the big resorts? Then maybe it's time to try out Sunlight Mountain Resort. With 72 named trails across 730 skiable acres, plus access to plenty of Nordic trails in the adjacent White River National Forest, this resort offers a great escape. Terrific for families, it's one of Colorado's most affordable mountain resorts and kids 12 and younger ski free. From Glenwood, head south on Highway 117. For more information contact the resort at (970) 945-7491 or (800) 445-7931; sunlight mtn.com. Consider staying at the cozy Sunlight Mountain Inn, 9 miles outside Glenwood Springs (10252 CR 117; 970-945-5225; sunlightmtninn.com).

Ski or Hike Vail—Hut to Hut

For an off-the-beaten-path skiing or hiking experience, try Vail's backcountry hut-to-hut system. The **10th Mountain Division Hut Association** was formed in 1980 to build a backcountry ski hut system in the high mountains between Aspen, Leadville, and Vail. This system of 29 huts connects 350 miles of suggested routes for a true Colorado experience. Distances between huts vary. Now you can reserve the huts for a fee as a takeoff point for day adventures or to ski or hike from hut to hut. These shelters are within the White River and San Isabel National Forests, so stunning vistas are guaranteed. The huts are rugged; bring your own food, water, and sleeping bag. The adventure isn't for everyone, however; in winter the Forest Service advises that the trails require at least intermediate skiing ability. The Hut Association also requires that someone in each group be proficient in backcountry skills, such as avalanche awareness and compass reading. The huts include wood-burning stoves, propane burners, cooking and eating utensils, kitchen supplies, and mattresses and pillows. Reservations are required; call (970) 925-5775 or write 10th Mountain Division Hut Association, 1280 Ute Ave., Ste. 21, Aspen 81611; huts.org.

NOTE: With average elevations of 11,000 feet, you need to prepare for high altitude.

balloon events in the country. *Jazz Aspen Snowmass Labor Day Festival* brings a wide variety of music and headliner performers to the mountain for three days.

In case this partial list isn't enough to entice you to visit Snowmass, there's much more. From late spring through fall, Snowmass hosts bike races, theater, food and wine festivals, and a great July 4th party. But not all visitors come for the festivals and outdoor activities. Some visitors are drawn to Snowmass to follow their muse. Artists come here from around the country and abroad to study at *Anderson Ranch Arts Center,* where dozens of workshops are offered each summer. Classes are available for all age groups and include subjects such as ceramics, painting and drawing, photography, printmaking, furniture design, woodworking, and sculpture. Courses on the 5-acre ranch run from two days to two weeks, giving artists of all levels a place to be inspired, learn new skills, and immerse themselves in the creative process. For more

Versatile Aspen

Most Colorado ski centers consist of dozens of condos, a resort, and a ski hill. By contrast, **Aspen** has four ski areas, and it was a full-fledged town long before skiing arrived. A pedestrian mall and flower boxes and benches invite lingering. Aspen's red, Old West–style brick buildings and Victorian gingerbread homes are periodically restored. The antique cherrywood bars shine, as do the contemporary Tiffany lamps and the stained-glass windows. Aspen outranks most North American ski resorts when it comes to the sheer number and variety of restaurants and nightlife possibilities.

There are close to 80 eating establishments in Aspen ready to satisfy just about any craving. From American to ethnic, gourmet to down home, Aspen has enough bistros, grills, bars, saloons, pubs, subterranean dives, cafeterias, cafes, pastry shops, coffeehouses, and high-end eateries to keep even the most dedicated foodie happy for a long time. It's a cosmopolitan, polyglot, diverse town. Aspen is everything to every level of skier and, happily, to every nonskier as well; the town is ideal for couples or families where one member doesn't ski. Several hundred shops invite browsers; amusements and sports of every kind beckon.

information contact the ranch in Snowmass at 5263 Owl Creek Rd., or PO Box 5598, Snowmass 81615; (970) 923-3181; andersonranch.org. For general information on activities and events at Snowmass call (800) 525-6200 or visit aspen-snowmass.com or gosnowmass.com.

trivia

Legend has it that the teddy bear was born at the Hotel Colorado. One time when frequent visitor President Teddy Roosevelt had a fruitless day of bear hunting, the hotel's maids sewed a stuffed bear in an effort to cheer him up. When he did succeed in hunting down a real bear, his daughter named the bear "Teddy," a name that stuck.

Aspen, Snowmass, and Aspen Highlands have some of the best skiing in the country, including many advanced intermediate and expert runs. The fourth local ski area, little **Buttermilk Mountain,** would at first glance seem to be up against some tough competition. But Buttermilk has carved out a name for itself in two areas. First, it focuses on beginners and skiers who don't need the heart-racing intensity of black diamond slopes. Although Buttermilk has expert runs, it's known as an excellent place for beginners, with an outstanding ski school. The hills are gentle and friendly to those just starting out, or for those who want to take it easy and enjoy the slopes at a mellower pace.

Buttermilk's other specialty is snowboarding. The resort has two separate terrain parks, more than 100 features, a super pipe, and a beginner's pipe, all within the world's longest (2 miles) terrain park. From beginner to Winter X

Games pro, snowboarders of every skill level will find plenty to keep them happy. For more information on Buttermilk skiing, contact Aspen Skiing Company, PO Box 1248, Aspen 81612; (970) 925-1220 or toll-free (800) 525-6200; aspensnowmass.com.

Vail. Aspen. Telluride. Copper. Winter Park. Crested Butte. Snowmass. In the world of skiing, these are household names, spoken in almost reverential tones. Colorado is justifiably famous for its skiing. The snow is light, fluffy, and easy to ski. With so much of the state at high elevations, the region has the terrain, the altitude, and the weather for world-class skiing. And the western landscapes, especially when viewed from the upper slopes, are grandiose.

The state's ski meccas are deserving of their fame. None of Colorado's ski resorts look alike; each has its special character made up of a dozen variables. Century-old mining towns like Breckenridge and Crested Butte have been revived. Aspen is immense and complex. Vail is a giant in every way, an American St. Moritz. Winter Park serves vacationers during the week and Denverites on weekends. Loveland Basin and Keystone yield consistent snow. Uncrowded Telluride has its fast, epic runs nestled in a beautiful box canyon.

If you come to this state anytime between late November and April, you should try to ski, even if you've never done it before. Each resort area offers excellent instruction and beginner slopes. And there are numerous other winter activities, such as cross-country skiing, snowshoeing, sledding and tubing, and sleigh rides. For more information contact Colorado Ski Country USA, 3773 Cherry Creek North Dr., Denver 80209; (303) 837-0793; coloradoski.com.

Grand Junction is at the west end of Colorado, close to the Utah border and the largest city between Salt Lake City and Denver. This is expansive, wide-open country. To the east lies the Grand Mesa, the largest flat-top mountain in the world. To the north are the towering Book Cliffs, the longest continuous cliff face on the planet, stretching for nearly 200 miles. To the west is

Skier's Locomotion up Aspen Mountain

When the **Aspen Skiing Corp.** (now the Aspen Skiing Company) opened its first lifts on Aspen Mountain in 1947, it eliminated one of skiing's biggest drawbacks: climbing the hill.

Skiing 60 years ago was for the truly committed, because if you wanted to enjoy the slopes in winter, you had to hoof it. If skiers were lucky, they could catch a ride with miners up the back of Aspen Mountain.

A year later, you could ascend Aspen Mountain in a single chair. The trip took more than an hour, and you could get a free ticket by helping to "pack" the slopes in the morning. As many as 100 volunteers worked the slopes at the same time.

Rattlesnake Arches, the world's second-largest concentration of arches outside of Arches National Park. There's an entirely different feel here than in the Rocky Mountains or eastern plains. The powerful rivers that course through verdant valleys have sculpted striking mesas, arroyos, plateaus, and pinnacles. The high desert beyond the valley has a stark beauty that for many feels like the true West. The landscape is a collage of mountains, rivers, canyons, lakes, high desert, and lush forests—a complex intersection of many prized ecosystems.

The town was named in 1881 for the nearby confluence of the Grand River and the Gunnison River. When the Grand was renamed the Colorado River in 1921, no one thought to change the name of the city. Historic downtown Grand Junction is a designated park and retains much of its Old West charm with Victorian-era architecture. Coffeehouses, restaurants, and shops invite lingering along the wide sidewalks. The city's downtown streets are home to one of the country's largest sidewalk sculpture galleries with over 115 sculptures and murals collectively named *Art on the Corner.*

One of the *Museums of Western Colorado, Museum of the West* displays the history of the area, beginning with the earliest residents to the pioneers who remain legendary. Displays of prehistoric pottery, Navajo paintings, and rock art vividly evoke the area's rich past. The Old West comes alive with a uranium mine, a stagecoach, a one-room schoolhouse, a firearms exhibit, and the Pastime Saloon. Contact the museum at 462 Ute Ave.; (970) 242-0971; museumofwesternco.com.

Aspen Highlands

Few people know that at one point in mining history—circa 1879 to 1882—Aspen had a nearby competitor named Ashcroft. Located in an adjacent valley, Ashcroft actually boasted several hotels, numerous bars, a jail, and even a newspaper. (The Ashcroft silver riches attracted silver millionaire H. A. W. Tabor and his pretty young bride, Baby Doe.) By 1883, Aspen was famous for its silver wealth, and fortune hunters arrived by the thousands; the inhabitants of Ashcroft, meanwhile, dwindled to about 100 (from 2,600 in its heyday).

And today? Aspen is a successful ski resort, and Ashcroft is a ghost town. A half dozen rickety buildings stand silently below Castle Peak, bleached by sun and wind, pummeled by snow and rain, slowly returning to the earth.

Yet more than 100 years after the silver boom and bust, Ashcroft still holds value. *Ashcroft Ski Touring* offers ski touring and snowshoeing across 35 kilometers of groomed trails, along with rentals, instruction, and advice on where to ski. You reach this quiet area by driving west for half a mile on Highway 82, and then turning on Castle Creek Road. After 12 miles, you see the cross-country trails. Call (970) 925-1044 for more information or visit pinecreekcookhouse.com/ashcroft-adventures.

Aspen Flights

If you're ready to try something totally different, how about taking to the skies on a paraglider?

With no prior experience necessary, you can soar with an experienced certified pilot from near the summit of Aspen Mountain. Scheduled on a daily basis, these summer flights are absolutely unforgettable.

Aspen Paragliding offers an instruction course, including flights, technique, and equipment. For information, call (970) 925-6975 or visit aspenparagliding.com.

Naturalist Nights

Interesting and educational, Naturalist Nights take place every Thursday evening at **Aspen Center for Environmental Studies (ACES)** starting at 6 p.m., Jan through Mar. Naturalist Nights cover a variety of topics, such as "Survival in the Avalanche Zone," "Wolves in the West," and "Birds of the Winter Forest." Admission is free.

Also part of the museum, the **Cross Orchards Living History Farm** re-creates life as it was lived by Grand Valley pioneers in the early 1900s. A country store, blacksmith shop, bunkhouse for workers, and an extensive collection of equipment from the era are part of this 24-acre site. Costumed interpreters add authenticity and explain what life was like for early settlers. The museum is located at 3073 F Rd.; (970) 242-0971.

A third branch of the museum, **Dinosaur Journey** in Fruita, tells the story of the history of ancient dinosaur life in Colorado. This hands-on, interactive museum includes exhibits of actual dinosaur bones, fossils, rocks, minerals, and much more. At Dino Digs, spend the day with a paleontologist working in a real dinosaur quarry, digging for dinosaur bones, turtles, lizards, and mammals in the 150-million-year-old badlands of the Morrison Formation. The digs fill fast and the number of participants is limited, so call ahead for reservations. Contact Dinosaur Journey at (970) 242-0971; museumofwesternco.com/visit/dinosaur-journey.

Grand Junction and the surrounding areas are known for producing some of the best fruit and vegetables in the state. And one of the best places to sample them while enjoying one of the town's signature

trivia

One nugget from the Smuggler Mine in Aspen weighed 1,840 pounds. It was 93 percent pure silver.

events is at the weekly Grand Junction Farmers' Market. Every Thurs mid-June to mid-Sept from 5 to 8:30 p.m., Main Street is closed to car traffic. Farmers, artisans, vendors, musicians, and merchants gather for an evening of socializing, eating, music, and fun. It's a great place to experience a community party, and everyone is welcome. For more information, visit downtowngj.org. Some of the orchards in Grand Junction and Palisade also welcome visitors and offer tours and pick-your-own experiences. It's a tasty way to spend a couple of hours here. For details, visit visitgrandjunction.com/fruit-vegetable-stands or visitpalisade.com.

Travelers with a penchant for sweets should make the pilgrimage to **Enstrom Candies** at 701 Colorado Ave. or 120 W. Park, Ste. 100. Enstrom's has been making candy for more than 50 years, and their almond toffee is an exquisite blend of chocolate, caramel, butter, and nuts that's gained almost mythical status in Colorado and beyond. If you're looking for a Colorado gift for the folks back home, look no further. Stop by in the morning and you can watch candymakers at work pouring molten caramel over layers of chocolate and nuts.

trivia

When the silver boom went bust in the 1890s, Aspen's population plummeted, and the city almost became a ghost town.

And then there's the wine. The eastern section of the **Grand Valley,** stretching from Palisade to Grand Junction, has grown into a productive winery region with more than 30 wineries in and around Palisade. Warm, dry days and cool nights result in a microclimate ideal for wine grapes. Take a day trip from Grand Junction and drive or ebike through the vineyards and peach orchards, stopping for lunch in Palisade. Many wineries offer tours demonstrating how the wine gets from grape to glass.

The **Colorado Mountain Winefest** takes place in mid-September; (970) 464-0111; coloradowinefest.com. For more information and directions to the wineries, contact Grand Valley Winery Association at PO Box 99, Palisade 81526-0099; (970) 464-5867 or (303) 399-7586; winecolorado.org.

Each summer **Two Rivers Winery & Chateau** hosts **Music in the Grapevines,** an outdoor concert series. Guests enjoy a picnic on the grounds and can purchase wine while listening to bluegrass, folk, and jazz. For more information, call (866) 312-9463 or visit tworiverswinery.com.

Each summer, Coloradans also look forward to the Western Slope peach harvest. First come the Elbertas and Red Havens, followed a few weeks later by Suncrest, Sullivan, and Blake. Toward the end of summer the Redskin and Hale arrive. As each variety ripens, peach lovers search fruit markets for the peach of the week. Peach jams, cobblers, and pies show up in restaurants and kitchens.

Palisade celebrates this esteemed fruit with the **Palisade Peach Festival** for three days in mid-August (970-464-7458; palisadepeachfest.com).

Many people drive to the orchards to buy peaches as well as apricots and cherries. Numerous fruit stands also sell local jams, preserves, salsas, and other condiments. For more information on fruit season in the region, contact the Palisade Chamber of Commerce at 319 Main St., 81526; (970) 464-7458; email info@palisadecoc.com or visit palisadecoc.com. Or stop by the Grand Junction Visitor Center at 740 Horizon Dr.; (970) 256-4050.

Travelers in search of deep canyons, red rock walls, and sandstone spires often head to the parks of Utah. But Colorado has its own park, **Colorado National Monument,** where a world of steep plateaus, sheer drop-offs, and craggy rock spires create an evocative landscape. This 31-square-mile monument is easily explored via a 23-mile road that offers numerous overlooks across the high-desert scenery. If you're a road cyclist, it's a great way to absorb the scenery. Thirteen backcountry hiking trails lead into the far reaches of the park.

To reach Colorado National Monument, follow Monument Road out of downtown Grand Junction for 6 miles, which will take you to the entry gate. Fees are $10 per vehicle, $5 per motorcycle or individual biker or hiker. For more information call (970) 858-3617 or write Colorado National Monument, Fruita 81521; nps.gov/colm.

Places to Stay in the Central Mountains

ASPEN

Aspen Mountain Lodge
311 W. Main St.
(970) 925-7650 or
(800) 362-7736
aspenmountainlodge.com
Moderate to Expensive
Comfortable, affordable, and within walking distance to everything in town. On the bus line to the ski resort.

Hotel Jerome
330 E. Main St.
(855) 331-7213
hoteljerome.aubergeresorts.com
Expensive
Luxury historic hotel known for its authentic ambience. The hotel's J-Bar is Aspen's oldest and most famous bar—a place to see and be seen.

Limelight Hotel
335 S. Monarch St.
(970) 925-5120 or
(855) 318-8960
limelightlodge.com
Moderate to Expensive

This contemporary ski lodge located steps from Aspen Mountain and downtown hot spots offers today's technology and environmental focus while honoring its funkier past—and great music is still part of it. Includes nice continental breakfast.

The Little Nell
675 E. Durant Ave.
(970) 920-4600 or
(855) 920-4600
thelittlenell.com
Expensive
Aspen's only ski-in/ski-out hotel, offers recently

renovated rooms, excellent guest service and a wine cellar with 20,000 bottles.

St. Regis Resort
315 E. Dean St.
(970) 920-3300 or
(888) 627-7198
stregisaspen.com
Expensive
Recently renovated luxury hotel located between Aspen Mountain's 2 base ski lifts with high-end amenities in all rooms. The hotel's Remede Spa is one of Aspen's finest.

BAILEY

Glen Isle Resort
573 Old Stagecoach Rd.
(303) 816-0790
glenisleresort.com
Inexpensive to Expensive

BRECKENRIDGE

The Bivouac
9511 Highway 9
(970) 423-6553
thebivvi.com
Inexpensive to Moderate
Hostel-style but with private hotel rooms as well as shared multi-bunk rooms. Rates include complimentary breakfast and Wi-Fi. On one of Breck's free bus routes.

The Lodge at Breckenridge
112 Overlook Dr.
(970) 453-9300 or
(800) 736-1607
thelodgeatbreckenridge
.com
Moderate to Expensive
Boutique hotel with a

mountain cabin feel located 5 minutes from town.

One Ski Hill Place, A RockResort
1521 Ski Hill Rd.
(970) 547-8800
oneskihill.rockresorts.com
Expensive
Ski-in/ski-out luxury lodge with studio to four-bedroom condo units at the base of Peak 8.

River Mountain Lodge
100 South Park Ave.
(970) 453-4711
breckenridge.com
Expensive
European-style lodge steps from historic downtown and across the street from ski area. Free wireless internet, hot tubs, heated pool.

Skiway Lodge
275 Ski Hill Rd.
(970) 453-7573
skiwaylodge.com
Moderate to Expensive
Bavarian-style chalet with 10 guest rooms, all with full baths, 9 with private balconies. Ski-in/ski-out access to the Breck Connect Gondola.

DILLON

Best Western Ptarmigan Lodge
652 Lake Dillon Dr.
(970) 468-2341
bestwestern.com
Inexpensive to Moderate
Affordable ski resort lodging with Jacuzzi and sauna room.

GEORGETOWN

Mad Creek Bed & Breakfast
167 W. Park Ave., Empire
(303) 569-2003 or
(888) 266-1498
madcreekbnb.net
Inexpensive to Moderate
Victorian cottage filled with antiques, featuring full breakfast, afternoon snacks, an outdoor hot tub, and a friendly owner.

Rose Street Bed & Breakfast
200 Rose St.
(303) 569-2222 or
(866) 569-2221
rosestreetbedbreakfast
.com
Moderate
Historic home in Georgetown's Historic Residential District.

GLENWOOD SPRINGS

Glenwood Hot Springs Lodge
(across from Glenwood pool)
415 E. 6th St.
(970) 945-6571 or
(800) 537-7946
hotspringspool.com
Moderate to Expensive
Includes unlimited access to Glenwood Hot Springs Pool and full breakfast.

Hotel Colorado
526 Pine St.
(970) 945-6511 or
(800) 544-3998
hotelcolorado.com
Moderate to Expensive
Historic luxury hotel with well-appointed rooms, free

wireless internet, and spa and massage facilities.

Redstone Inn
82 Redstone Blvd.,
Redstone
(970) 963-2526
redstoneinn.com
Moderate to Expensive
Rustic turn-of-the-20th-century resort with character, charm, and friendly staff in a small mountain village.

GRAND JUNCTION

Two Rivers Winery & Chateau
2087 Broadway
(866) 312-9463 or
(970) 255-1471
tworiverswinery.com
Inexpensive to Moderate
Bed and breakfast in the middle of a vineyard offers upscale lodging, French country chateau decor, and breakfast included.

Hampton Inn Grand Junction
205 Main St.
(970) 243-3222
hamptoninn.com
Inexpensive to Moderate
Located on historic Main Street with free hot breakfast and wireless internet.

Hotel Maverick
840 Kennedy Ave.
(970) 822-4888
Thehotelmaverick.com
Moderate to Expensive
Boutique hotel, hot tub, spacious rooms, complimentary Wi-Fi, Devil's Kitchen restaurant and rooftop patio on-site.

Castle Creek Manor
638 Horizon Dr.
(970) 241-9105
castlecreekmanor.com
Moderate to Expensive
Two miles from downtown, this B&B is a sweet retreat with sweeping views, a full gourmet breakfast, large rooms, and complimentary Wi-Fi. One of the only B&Bs in the area with a liquor licencse.

GRANT

Tumbling River Ranch
3715 CR 62
(303) 838-5981 or
(800) 654-8770
tumblingriver.com
Expensive
Deluxe mountain guest lodge with hiking, horseback riding, fishing, swimming, rafting, and a full dude ranch experience.

IDAHO SPRINGS

Argo Inn and Suites
2622 Colorado Blvd.
(303) 567-4473
argoinnandsuites.com
Inexpensive to Moderate
Located on Clear Creek, clean and comfortable with continental breakfast, free wireless internet, outdoor grills, and fire pit; some rooms with fireplace and private deck.

H & H Motor Lodge
2445 Colorado Blvd.
(303) 567-2838 or
(800) 445-2893
hhlodge.tripod.com
Inexpensive

Clean and affordable lodging.

KEYSTONE

Keystone Lodge & Spa
22101 US 6
(970) 496-4500 or
(877) 317-9435
Keystoneresort.com
Moderate
Views of the mountains and the Snake River, spa, heated pool; a good base for winter or summer activities.

Ski Tip Lodge
764 Montezuma Rd.
(970) 496-4950 or
(877) 317-9435
Keystoneresort.com
Moderate
Cozy alpine B&B with good breakfasts included. AAA Four Diamond Ski Tip Restaurant on-site, and a short shuttle ride away from Keystone ski resort.

SHAWNEE

North Fork Ranch
P.O. Box B
55395 US 285
(303) 838-9873
northforkranch.com
Guest ranch with premier fly fishing and hiking.

SILVERTHORNE

Hampton Inn
117 Meraly Way
(970) 513-4020
Moderate to Expensive
Well located just off I-70, a short drive to Silverthorne and 10 miles to three ski areas, this is just what

you expect from a nice Hampton Inn.

Hotel Indigo
375 Blue River Pkwy.
(970) 485-6262
ihg.com/hotelindigo/hotels/us/en/silverthorne
Expensive
A fitness center, indoor pool, free Wi-Fi, and a nice restaurant on-site a few of the amenities in this 111-room downtown hotel.

The Pad
491 Rainbow Dr.
(970) 445-7767
thepadlife.com/silverthorne
Inexpensive to Moderate
Shared dorms, micro rooms, micro rooms with baths, and a family room are the options here, all aiming to provide economical accommodations for travelers who embrace the spirit of a hostel with amenities. For those wanting a more traditional room, there are private and deluxe private rooms, too. Suites? Sure, in shipping containers.

VAIL

Four Seasons Resort Vail
1 Vail Rd.
(970) 477-8600
fourseasons.com/vail
Expensive
Renowned Four Seasons luxury and service with a European flair at the base of Vail Mountain.

Grand Hyatt Vail
1300 Westhaven Dr.
(970) 476-1234
hyatt.com

Expensive
Ski-in/ski-out lodging set along the banks of Gore Creek offering a pool, spa and complimentary Wi-Fi.

The Sebastian Vail
16 Vail Rd.
(970) 477-8000 or
(800) 354-6908
thesebastianvail.com
Expensive
Stylish, comfortable resort hotel with mountain-view pool in the heart of Vail Village and steps away from Vail Mountain.

Sonnenalp Vail
20 Vail Rd.
(866) 284-4411
sonnenalp.com
Expensive
Luxury accommodations with Old-World ambience, service; among the many amenities are a spa and private 18-hole golf course, plus easy access to Vail Village.

Places to Eat in the Central Mountains

ASPEN

CP Burger
433 E. Durant Ave.
(970) 925-3056
cpburger.com
Inexpensive
Burgers of all kinds, including chicken, tuna, and veggie; salads; fries; and, just outside the doors, a skating rink in winter and mini golf in summer.

Grateful Deli
233 E. Main St.
(970) 925-6647
Inexpensive
Groovy little deli with excellent sandwiches, subs, and paninis—a local favorite.

Hickory House Ribs
730 W. Main St.
(970) 925-2313
hickoryhouseribs.com
Moderate
Extensive menu, the place to go for barbecue in Aspen.

Clark's
517 E. Hyman Ave.
(970) 710-2546
clarksaspen.com
Expensive
Diverse selection of ribs, steak, chicken, fish, soups, stews, chilis, and salads.

Las Montanas
205 S. Mill St.
(970) 429-5255
lasmontanasaspen.com
Expensive
Mexican fare at an elevated level.

Paradise Bakery & Cafe
320 S. Galena St.
(970) 925-7585
paradisebakery.com
Inexpensive
Delicious muffins, croissants, bagels, cookies, and more.

Wild Fig
Mill St.
(970) 925-5160
thewildfig.com
Moderate to Expensive
European-style brasserie serving innovative Mediterranean lunch and dinner.

AVON

Ticino in the Lodge at Avon Center
100 W. Beaver Creek Blvd.
(970) 748-6792
ticinorestaurantavon.com
Inexpensive to Expensive
A gem of an Italian home-style restaurant with pizza and homemade pasta.

BRECKENRIDGE

Blue Moose
540 S. Main St.
(970) 453-4859
Inexpensive to Moderate
Local favorite for tasty, filling breakfasts.

Breckenridge Brewery
600 S. Main St.
(970) 453-1550
breckbrewpub.com
Moderate
Ribs, fish-and-chips, fajitas, and more, along with excellent beer and dramatic mountain views.

Clint's Bakery and Coffee House
131 S. Main St.
(970) 453-2990
Inexpensive to Moderate
The coolest coffeehouse in town, serving fresh pastries, bagels, wraps, and an extensive menu of hot drinks. Free wireless internet for customers.

Crepes A La Cart
307 S. Main St.
crepesalacarts.com
Inexpensive to Moderate
Permanent crepe cart on Main Street offering a variety of savory and sweet crepes.

Giampietro Pasta and Pizzeria
100 N. Main St.
(970) 453-3838
giampietropizza.com
Inexpensive to Moderate
Cozy Italian eatery considered by many locals to have the best pizza in Summit County.

DILLON

Arapahoe Cafe and Pub
626 Lake Dillon Dr.
(970) 468-0873
arapahoecafe.com
Moderate to Expensive
Historic cafe/pub serving tasty breakfast, lunch, and dinner, plus nice wine and creative cocktail lists.

Kemosabe at Silverheels
603 Main St., Frisco
(970) 668-0345
kemosabeatsilverheels.com
Moderate to Expensive
An "American sushi grill," with an east–west vibe and a Colorado-Asian-fusion menu.

EDWARDS

Juniper Restaurant
97 Main St., E101
(970) 926-7001
juniperrestaurant.com
Expensive
Contemporary, seasonal cuisine at one of the best restaurants in the Vail Valley.

GEORGETOWN

The Happy Cooker
412 6th St.
(303) 569-3166
happycookerrestaurant
.com

Inexpensive to Moderate
Home-style American menu of sandwiches, salads, soups, chili, breads, desserts; breakfast and lunch only.

Lucha Cantina at Red Ram
606 6th St.
(303) 569-2300
Inexpensive
luchacantina.com
Homemade, healthy Mexican cuisine, burgers, and a nice tequila selection.

GLENWOOD SPRINGS

Casey Brewing Barrel Cellar
3421 Grand Ave.
(970) 230-9691
caseybrewing.com
Inexpensive
Experience one of Glenwood Springs' celebrated breweries in the taproom or via a curated cellar experience. Casey's has no food of its own, but guests can bring in food from any of the surrounding local restaurants.

Daily Bread Cafe
729 Grand Ave.
(970) 945-6253
dailybreadglenwood.
business.site
Inexpensive to Moderate
Excellent breakfasts, sandwiches, salads, and soups, popular with locals and visitors.

Juicy Lucy's Steakhouse
308 7th St.
(970) 945-4619
juicylucyssteakhouse.com
Moderate to Expensive
Steak, seafood, lamb, pork,

and elk along with daily specials and an expansive list of wines by the glass and bottle.

GRAND JUNCTION

Bin 707 Food Bar
225 N. 5th St., #105
(970) 243-4543
bin707.com
Moderate to Expensive
Grand Junction's most highly rated restaurant has garnered several James Beard Award nominations. The menu features seasonal American cuisine sourced from local, Colorado purveyors.

Dream Cafe
314 Main St.
(970) 424-5353
dreamcafegj.com
Inexpensive to Moderate
Breakfast and brunch; great food with friendly service and a trendy, upbeat atmosphere.

Il Bistro Italiano
400 Main St.
(970) 243-8622
ilbistroitaliano.com
Moderate
Traditional and contemporary from scratch Italian dishes, pastas, pizzas, and small plates, prepared from fresh ingredients.

Main Street Bagels
559 Main St.
(970) 241-2740
gjmainstreetbagels.com
Inexpensive to Moderate
Artisan bakery and espresso cafe with a large patio serving up soups,

salads, hot paninis, and sandwiches.

Pablo's Pizza
319 Main St.
(970) 255-8879
pablospizza.com
Moderate
Creative, award-winning pizza, warm panini sandwiches, and homemade soups. Pleasant patio area.

626 on Rood
626 Rood Ave.
(970) 257-7663
626onrood.com
Moderate to Expensive
Modern American cuisine; highly rated on Trip Advisor, with an extensive wine list.

IDAHO SPRINGS

Beau Jo's Pizza
1517 Miner St.
(303) 567-4376
beaujos.com
Moderate
Legendary among Coloradans for serving some of the best pizza in the state.

Two Brothers Deli
1424 Miner St.
(303) 567-2439
2brosdeli.com
Inexpensive to Moderate
Quality deli with great sandwiches and soups, good service, free Wi-Fi.

MINTURN

The Mexican Bar and Grill
160 Railroad Ave.
(970) 470-4309
themexicanbg.com

Inexpensive to Moderate
Mexican, Tex-Mex, tacos, burrito omelets, and seafood dishes; open for breakfast, lunch, dinner.

RED CLIFF

Mango's Mountain Grill
166½ Eagle St.
(970) 827-9109
mangosmountaingrill.com
Inexpensive to Moderate
Tucked away in a quiet valley with no highway in sight, Mango's is a lively mountain grill with plenty of local color and tasty food.

SILVERTHORNE

Blue Bird Market Hall
325 Blue River Pkwy.
(303) 216-0420
bluebirdmarket.com

Kúcu Tequila Bistro
375 Blue River Pkwy.
(970) 468-5828
kucutequilabistro.com
Inexpensive to Expensive
Open for breakfast, lunch, and dinner, this mountain bistro is located inside Hotel Indigo. The menu is heavy on Mexican staples but nicely augmented by classic American fare and dishes inspired by the ancient people of the plains, plus more than 200 tequilas.

VAIL

Bart & Yeti's
553 E. Lionsheads Circle
(970) 476-2754
Moderate
Homey, economical, and tasty American comfort

food and a focus on sustainability.

Left Bank
183 Gore Creek Dr., #4
(970) 476-3696
leftbankvail.com
Expensive
Traditional French cuisine and an extensive wine list; a Vail Valley favorite for more than 40 years.

Pazzo's Pizzeria
122 E. Meadow Dr.
(970) 476-9026
pazzospizzeria.com
Moderate
Popular pizza palace, service can be variable but pizza is good.

Sweet Basil
193 E. Gore Creek Dr.
(970) 476-0125
sweetbasilvail.com
Expensive
Creative contemporary American cuisine with an extensive wine list; popular with locals and travelers since 1977. All these years later it's still widely celebrated as Vail's top restaurant.

Slope Room
352 E. Meadow Dr.
(888) 794-0410
sloperoom.com
Moderate to Expensive
Alpine bistro focused on creative dishes made with ingredients grown and produced by Rocky Mountain farmers and ranchers. Brunch and dinner served daily.

The Little Diner
616 W. Lionshead Cir.
(970) 476-4279
thelittlediner.com
Moderate
Breakfast is served all day at this breakfast-and-lunch-only eatery.

FOR MORE INFORMATION

ASPEN
Aspen Chamber Resort Association Visitor Center
Corner of Galena St. and Cooper Ave.
(970) 925-1940 or (800) 670-0792
aspenchamber.org

BRECKENRIDGE
Breckenridge Tourism Office
111 Ski Hill Rd., 80424
(888) 251-2417
gobreck.com

GEORGETOWN
Downtown Georgetown Community Center
PO Box 834; 613 6th St., 80444
(303) 569-2888 or (800) 472-8230
georgetowncolorado.com

GLENWOOD SPRINGS
Glenwood Springs Chamber Resort Association
802 Grand Ave., 81601
(970) 945-6589
visitglenwood.com

GRAND JUNCTION
Grand Junction Visitor Center
740 Horizon Dr., 81506
(970) 244-1480
visitgrandjunction.com

IDAHO SPRINGS
Visit Idaho Springs/Visitor Center
2060 Miner St., 80452
(303) 567-4382
visitidahosprings.com

PALISADE
Palisade Chamber of Commerce
305 S. Main St., #102, 81526
(970) 464-7458
visitpalisade.com

VAIL
Vail Resorts Management Company
vail.com

Vail Valley Chamber and Tourism Bureau
100 E. Meadow Dr., 81620
(970) 476-1000 or (800) 653-4523
visitvailvalley.com

Southern Colorado

Colorado Springs & Beyond

Southern Colorado is far from the Front Range, and in many ways it's another world. Too far from Denver for a day trip or short weekend getaway, the area escapes the crowds that can congregate at destinations farther north. No interstates cross the region, which somehow translates to a slower pace of life in this corner of the state. That's all good news for anyone wanting to explore this varied landscape, because many of the state's highlights lie in this area. Mountain ranges such as the Sangre de Cristo, San Juan, La Plata, and San Miguel are home to Colorado's most rugged peaks and largest wilderness tracts. The San Luis Valley and Great Sand Dunes are unexpected and imposing in their vastness. Mining ghost towns, plunging canyons, and alpine meadows jam-packed with wildflowers wait to be explored. Friendly western towns offer a mix of mountain biking, ranching culture, and brewpubs that bring together eclectic communities. The region contains well-pre-served evidence of the ancient Puebloans who lived in the area for centuries before the first Europeans rode up on horseback.

SOUTHERN COLORADO

Dozens of different vacations await visitors to southern Colorado. Take your pick of Victorian mountain towns, red rock canyons, local festivals, alpine ski villages, challenging mountain biking, counterculture communities, ancestral cliff dwellings, rodeo, and some of the best scenery, hiking, camping, skiing, fishing, and other outdoor pursuits to be found on the planet.

The **Devil's Head Lookout Trail,** in the Rampart Range west of the little community of Sedalia (south of Denver) offers a 360-degree view of surrounding Pike National Forest. On clear days you can see mountain peaks over 100 miles away. It got its name from the red rock formations that stick out like two horns. The trail winds through deep pine forests interspersed with aspen, past giant red cliffs. The trail's length—just 1.375 miles—doesn't sound like much; it climbs steeply, though, and includes a 950-foot vertical elevation gain, beginning at 8,800 feet.

Along the way, you get views of **Pikes Peak,** a number of "fourteeners" (peaks over 14,000 feet high), some of the peaks in Rocky Mountain National Park, and the Great Plains. Benches for the tired line the uphill paths. Bring water, since there is none along the trail.

To reach the trailhead, from Denver take Santa Fe (US 85) south to Sedalia (13 miles); turn west toward Deckers (Highway 67) for 10 miles and make another left turn onto the **Rampart Range Road** (Highway 5); go another 8.5 miles until you see the Devil's Head sign. For more information contact the South Platte Ranger District, 30403 Kings Valley Dr., Ste. 2-115; Conifer 80433; (303) 275-5610; fs.usda.gov. If fly fishing calls to you, continue down Highway 67 to the tiny hamlet of Deckers, which is just a historic general store and a place to meet your fishing guide if you book one. The South Platte River here provides abundant food for trout, meaning it's not unusual to catch fish of 15 to 20 inches or more. Stake out a spot anywhere along several miles of river; the fishing is rivaled only by the spectacular landscape.

En route from Denver to Colorado Springs via the interstate, you may see a modest sign that says **"Larkspur."** Few travelers have ever heard of it. Even many Denver residents are unfamiliar with this hamlet.

Yet on weekends from mid-June through July, tiny Larkspur comes alive with a bang. Cannon shots can be heard from afar. When your car draws closer to the hillside, the cannons are followed by medieval trumpets played in unison.

For more than 45 years, the zany, lively **Colorado Renaissance Festival** has entertained summer visitors on a wooded Colorado hillside above Larkspur. Part theater, part learning experience, part petting zoo for children, and part artisans' market, its Renaissance theme begins when you enter the walled compound and you're greeted as "My Lord" or "My Lady." Artisans galore demonstrate their craft: Blacksmiths hammer away, glassblowers regale onlookers with their art, potters shape at their wheels, leatherworkers show their stuff. Bands of costumed musicians wander up the mountainside. Harpists, flutists, bagpipers, and minstrel singers materialize and harmonize.

Several times a day, "King Henry" and his "Court" introduce you to knights jousting on horseback at a gallop, doing tricks with their lances. The stages are busy with storytellers and merrymakers; the pubs dispense barrels of beer and huge turkey legs. Processions of celebrities—Shakespeare, Anne Boleyn—promenade among the visitors, while a few yards away, you can be a medieval archer or knife thrower or dart artist. Encounter the unexpected: Youngsters ride real camels and elephants; jugglers and puppet masters dazzle onlookers. A good time is had by everyone.

There is no charge for parking weekends June through July. To reach Larkspur, take exit 172 from I-25 and follow the signs. Open 10 a.m. to 6:30 p.m. Sat and Sun. Admission costs $28 for adults and teenagers 13 and older and $12 for children 5 to 12; children under 5 are free. Tickets may be cheaper if bought at King Soopers or online. For more information contact the festival at 650 Perry Park Ave., Larkspur 80118; (303) 688-6010; coloradorenaissance.com.

A 10-minute drive south of Larkspur on CR 105 brings you to quiet, photogenic **Palmer Lake.** Almost no travel guide mentions it, and most people bypass it via I-25. Palmer Lake was once a refueling stop for steam railroad engines; now it's almost forgotten. Its colorful history includes gold mines, Indian raids, the occasional scalping, posses hunting murderers, and saloon shootings. Several trailheads in town lead into the hills, and there are good restaurants, shops, and a historical museum. People come here to get away from the city, walk around the lake, or take their young children to the small playground. Traffic is minimal, and it's a fine place to relax. For more information contact the Town Offices at 42 Valley Crescent, Palmer Lake 80133; (719) 481-2953; townofpalmerlake.com. For those who like to hike or bike, the 15-mile **New Santa Fe Regional Trail,** one of the largest continuous trails in El Paso County, begins at **Palmer Lake Recreation Area.** It goes through the town of Monument to the south, ending at the southern boundary of the **US Air Force Academy** (there is no longer public access to the trail from the academy). For more information visit traillink.com.

The Air Force Academy north of Colorado Springs is one of eastern Colorado's most recognized landmarks. Whether you hike, bike, or drive, consider a stop at the academy's visitor center, located at exit 150B off I-25. The stunning **Cadet Chapel** has long drawn visitors interested in architecture or who just want to sit in inspiring surroundings. It was completed in 1963 and is considered to be the architectural centerpiece of the academy's campus with its 17 silver-hued spires that sweep to heights of more than 150 feet. Currently closed as it undergoes an extensive renovation, the chapel is scheduled to reopen in 2023. It is typically open Mon through Sat, 9 a.m. to 5 p.m.; Sun from 1 to 5 p.m. Sunday services are open to all; call (719) 333-2636 for times.

When visiting the academy, ask for a map at the gate. The visitor center is open from 9 a.m. to 5 p.m. daily. For more information call (719) 333-2025 or visit academyadmissions.com/visit-the-academy/self-guided-tours/visitor-center-information.

Continuing south on I-25 from the US Air Force Academy, you'll come to your next stop—the *ProRodeo Hall of Fame and Museum of the American Cowboy,* which presents the West's unique cowboy heritage in a facility that is both entertaining and educational. The cowboy played a vital role in opening the West to the expansion of the 19th century, and his reputation for courage and individualism has become part of our national folklore and culture.

Families with children will enjoy the outdoor corral with its live animals. Inside, dioramas and exhibits display saddles, boots, buckles, spurs, ropes, chaps, branding equipment, and other paraphernalia, all telling the story of rodeo's history in this country. Rodeo as a sport comes alive through the mementos of America's major rodeo champions.

Visitors can learn about such colorful rodeo champs as bull rider Warren G. "Freckles" Brown, reputed to be the oldest man in ProRodeo history to win a riding event. His long career was interrupted by a broken neck, as well as by World War II. With typical spirit during wartime parachute jumps into China, Brown put on a rodeo using army mules and native cattle and declared himself the Orient's all-around champion of 1942.

Over the years, rules and equipment were standardized, judging was streamlined, prize money increased, and the freewheeling entertainment of the 1800s evolved into the modern sport of professional rodeo.

Here the visitor can learn the fine points of saddle bronc riding and how to judge a rider's performance, and can get the jolting sensation—through film with stereo sound—of what it's like to ride a bucking Brahma bull. Other films trace the historical development of rodeo.

The ProRodeo Hall of Fame is located just north of Colorado Springs on I-25 at exit 148. Hours are 9 a.m. to 5 p.m. daily during the summer season, Tues through Sat in winter, except for major holidays. Entrance is $10 for adults, $9 for seniors, $8 for military, and $7 for children 6 to 12. Free for children under 6. Call (719) 528-4764 or write 101 ProRodeo Dr., Colorado Springs 80919; prorodeohalloffame.com.

A definite must-see attraction, the US Olympic & Paralympic Museum celebrates the people, places, history, spirit, and sports of the Olympic and Paralympic games. The downtown facility was voted among the nation's best new attractions and places to visit in 2020. Accessible, engaging, and interactive, the museum's design and exhibitions were created with input from Team USA athletes. Guided tours are offered daily at 11 a.m. and 2 p.m. For more information contact the museum; (719) 497-1234; 200 S. Sierra Madre St.; usopm.org. The wonders of nature blend together at the **Garden of the Gods** in Colorado Springs to create one of the most unusual natural settings in Colorado. Established as a free city park in 1909, the almost 1,370 acres are filled with silent and spectacular red sandstone rock formations, including **Gateway Rocks, Cathedral Spires,** and the **Balanced Rock.** Grasslands meet mountain forests to provide contrasts of scenic beauty. A common resident of the park is the great horned owl, whose keen, light-gathering eyes and superior hearing make it an effective nighttime hunter. Hike, picnic, and horseback ride to fully appreciate the park's natural beauty. But most of all, bring your camera and photograph these wonders (especially at sunset or sunrise, when the low sun accents the naturally colorful red stone).

The park is open daily from November 1 through April 30 from 5 a.m. to 9 p.m. and May 1 through October 31 from 5 a.m. to 11 p.m. **The Garden of the Gods Visitor and Nature Center** is open from 9 a.m. to 5 p.m. in the winter months and 8 a.m. to 7 p.m. Memorial Day weekend through Labor Day weekend. The center offers free color maps of the park and free entrance to the center's extensive exhibits, including two exhibit halls added in 2015. Arrive via exit 146 off I-25. Go west on Garden of the Gods Road and then south on North 30th Street. The visitor center will be on your left at Gateway Road. For more information contact Garden of the Gods Visitor and Nature Center, 1805 N. 30th St., Colorado Springs 80904; (719) 634-6666; gardenofgods.com.

If you want to vacation in luxury, consider the five-star **Broadmoor,** which has 14,110-foot Pikes Peak for a backdrop. The Broadmoor actually began in the 1850s with a Silesian count. He hoped to create another Monte Carlo against the backdrop of Colorado's mountainscape. Eventually, two Philadelphians, Charles Tutt and Spencer Penrose, took over. They'd become rich in Cripple Creek mining and real estate, and as world travelers, they knew what they wanted—a regal, Renaissance-style hotel.

The Broadmoor's doors opened on June 29, 1918; among several notables, the first to register was John D. Rockefeller Jr. Since that day, there has been a stream of industrialists, diplomats, movie moguls, film stars, and titled ladies and gentlemen. They mingle nowadays with anyone who can afford this pricey, year-round retreat. It is among the largest, plushest, and most elegant in Colorado, offering every conceivable amenity. For more information call (855) 634-7111 or (719) 623-5112, or visit broadmoor.com.

The Broadmoor Seven Falls is 10 driving minutes west of the Broadmoor resort. "The Grandest Mile of Scenery in Colorado" lives up to its slogan:

A 1,000-foot-high granite canyon leads to seven waterfalls flanked by healthy forests of juniper, blue spruce, Douglas fir, and ponderosa pine. Not far from the dramatic, perpendicular "pillars of Hercules," you can climb several hundred steep steps to platforms from which you view these scenic wonders.

All visitors must park at the Penrose-Norris Event Center at 1045 Lower Gold Camp Rd.; a shuttle provides transportation to the falls. Hours are 10 a.m. to 6 p.m. weekdays in summer; closed Nov to Mar. Daytime admission ranges from $17 for ages 13 and older to $11 for children 2 to 12. Children under 2 are free. For more information contact Broadmoor Seven Falls at (855) 923-7272; broadmoor.com/adventures/seven-falls.

Located on Cheyenne Mountain just above the Broadmoor resort is the **Cheyenne Mountain Zoo.** With 146 acres and more than 950 animals, the zoo mirrors the natural habitats of animals from Africa, Australia, Asia, and North America. A petting zoo and oversize garden are a delight for kids. To reach the zoo, from I-25 go south on Nevada Avenue. Turn right on Lake Avenue. Turn onto Mirada Road and follow signs to 4250 Cheyenne Mountain Zoo Rd. Admission prices for adults range from $19.75 to $34.75, and children range from $14.75 to $29.75, depending on day and time. Military discounts are available. Children 2 and younger are free. Timed entry reservations are required. For more information call (719) 633-9925 or visit cmzoo.org.

The year was 1806; the discoverer of Colorado Springs' "Great Mountain" was Lieutenant **Zebulon Montgomery Pike.** Neither he nor any of his party got even close to the top, due to bad weather and perhaps a lack of planning. At that time, it certainly wasn't conceivable that one of America's most unusual railroads ever constructed would carry thousands to its summit.

Today you can journey on the country's highest railroad to the apex of famous Pikes Peak. The **Broadmoor Manitou and Pikes Peak Cog Railway,** which is 46,158 feet long, climbs from an elevation of 6,571 feet at the **Manitou Springs** station to one of 14,115 feet at the summit. This is a vertical gain of about 846 feet per mile. The distance is longer than any covered by the famous cogwheel rails in Switzerland.

Along the entire route you'll be treated to a continuous panorama. At the 11,578-foot level, the train emerges from a sea of quaking aspen into the windswept stretches of timberline and climbs into the saddle, where you get an unparalleled view of Manitou Springs and of the Garden of the Gods in the valley below. You also see the vast expanses of the **Great Plains** stretch toward the horizon.

On clear days, you can spot Denver 75 miles to the north of Colorado Springs and the dramatic **Sangre de Cristo Mountains** in southern Colorado. The view to the west is astounding; mile upon mile of snowcapped giants rise into the blue Colorado sky.

The railway gift shop (clothing and curios) is a good place to pick up memorabilia and souvenirs. And although there is a cafe at the top, lines tend to be long. Instead, pick up snacks at the Market at the bottom and eat on the train, or try one of Manitou Springs' restaurants. The Cog Railway runs year-round. Depending on the season, tickets run $58.50 to $68.50 for adults and $48.50 to $58.50 for children 12 and younger. Reservations are highly recommended. The round-trip takes 3 hours and 10 minutes; call for departure times. Take exit 141 (US 24) off I-25. Head west on US 24 for 4 miles to the Manitou Springs exit. Go west on Manitou Avenue for 1.5 miles. Turn left on Ruxton Avenue. The station is three-quarters of a mile up the road. For more information call (800) 745-3773 or (719) 685-5401, or visit cograilway.com.

Back in 1891, the **Cripple Creek** gold strike proved to be the last major gold rush in North America. Within a few years, those mines in the mountains west of Colorado Springs yielded almost a billion dollars' worth of the valuable mineral. By 1900 Cripple Creek had grown to some 50,000 inhabitants. The miners could patronize 75 saloons, 40 grocery stores, 17 churches, and 8 newspapers. Every day a dozen passenger trains steamed into the depot. Eventually, 500 gold mines operated in the area. Some 8,000 men brought on a gambling, carousing, and whoring boom.

Ironically, the man who discovered the first gold vein sold his claim for $500 and proceeded to drink it all away. Colorado Springs owes part of its existence to the prospectors. In time, celebrities came and went. Adventurer Lowell Thomas was born in nearby Victor, now nearly a ghost town. Groucho Marx once drove a grocery wagon in Cripple Creek, and he performed here as well. Jack Dempsey, for a brief bout a miner, trained and boxed in the region. Financier Bernard Baruch worked as a telegrapher here. Teddy Roosevelt, after a Cripple Creek visit, told the world that "the scenery bankrupts the English language." Politicians arrived in droves to see for themselves.

Over the years, gold prices dropped. Production began to slip, and the miners scattered. By 1920 fewer than 5,000 people lived here.

And today? Cripple Creek attracts lots of summer tourists. They come for the narrow-gauge train rides. They pan for gold on Main Street and browse the antiques and souvenir shops housed in historic buildings. They play blackjack, poker, and the slots in more than a dozen casinos. The **Cripple Creek District Museum, Jail Museum,** and **Old Homestead House Museum** (former bordello) offer a glimpse back in time to life during an untamed era. Small cafes serve home-cooked food.

trivia

The Devil's Head Lookout Tower at the end of the Devil's Head Lookout Trail sits atop the highest point in the Rampart Range. It is the last operational lookout on the Front Range.

Each summer the renovated ***Butte Theater*** puts on a full program of summer theater productions. This building, originally constructed in 1896, has had many uses throughout its history. Before its renovation in the late 1990s, the building served as a storage facility for the Cripple Creek Fire Department located below.

Extensive renovations by the city of Cripple Creek restored the theater's splendor. The Butte Theater now seats 174 people and has a 1,350-square-foot stage, state-of-the-art sound equipment and movie projectors, and a snack bar. For more information and performance dates, contact the theater at (719) 689-6402; buttetheater.com.

The old railroad depot has become the ***Cripple Creek District Museum,*** along with an old assay office and the Colorado Trading and Transfer Company building, constructed in 1893. These three buildings are crammed with mementos of the mining age. Superbly maintained, the museum is well worth a visit. Hours are 10 a.m. to 5 p.m. daily mid-May through mid-Oct; Sat and Sun 10

AUTHOR'S FAVORITES IN SOUTHERN COLORADO

Black Canyon of the Gunnison
(970) 641-2337
nps.gov/blca

Cumbres & Toltec Scenic Railroad
(888) 286-2737
cumbrestoltec.com

Durango & Silverton Narrow Gauge Railroad
(970) 247-2733 or (877) 872-4607
durangotrain.com

Flyfishing in Deckers
Hwy. 67 between Sedalia and Woodland Park
discoverdeckers.com/explore-deckers/fishing

Garden of the Gods
(719) 634-6666
gardenofgods.com

Great Sand Dunes National Park
(719) 378-6300 or (719) 378-6399
nps.gov/grsa

The Broadmoor Manitou and Pikes Peak Cog Railway
(719) 685-5401 or (800) 745-3773
cograilway.com

Mesa Verde National Park
(970) 529-4465
nps.gov/meve

Royal Gorge Bridge and Park
(719) 275-7507
royalgorgebridge.com

Town of Salida Downtown and Riverfront
(877) 772-5432 or (719) 539-2068
salida.com or salidachamber.org

Town of Telluride
(888) 605-2578
visittelluride.com

United States Olympic & Paralympic Museum
(719) 497-1234
usopm.org

a.m. to 4 p.m. for the rest of the year. Call (719) 689-2634 or go to visitcripple creek.com. The museum is on Bennett Avenue in Cripple Creek.

Not many visitors venture beyond the town and into the surrounding hills. This leaves plenty of room on the miles of hiking and biking trails leading through stunning scenery in Pike National Forest. Several local outfitters offer horseback riding trips ranging from 1 hour to all day. The mountains are studded with old abandoned mines that can be reached by hiking up old mining roads past rusting machinery and old wooden trestles. View the mines from outside only; they are dangerous and unstable inside, and should not be entered.

The story of the **Mollie Kathleen Gold Mine** is a Cripple Creek legend. Back in 1891, Mollie Kathleen Gortner moved to the area with her family, including her attorney husband, Henry. On an excursion by herself to see a herd of elk (she'd never seen them before), Mollie Kathleen came upon an outcropping of quartz that was veined with gold. Upon attempting to file her claim in town, she was informed that as a woman, she had no right to do so. Not to be deterred, Mollie Kathleen seized the papers and signed them anyway, declaring that the issue could be taken up with her husband if there was a problem. Thus Mollie Kathleen Gortner became the first woman in the area to stake a gold claim. Her mine continued to produce gold uninterrupted for the next 70 years, with the exception of a period of time during World War II when all gold production ceased due to a nationwide ban. Today the gold that came out of the mine would be worth more than $100 million.

The Mollie Kathleen Gold Mine stopped producing long ago, but now visitors can descend 1,000 feet belowground on the country's only historic gold mine tour. Learn about the life and working conditions of the hard rock gold miner. The tour begins with a ride on a skip (elevator) down to the lower levels of the mine. There you can see equipment used to mine at these depths and ride on the last air-powered Tram-Air Locomotive. Appropriate for all ages (there are no steps or ladders to climb), the 40-minute tours of the Mollie Kathleen Gold Mine depart at frequent intervals during the peak season. The mine is open for tours daily from mid-Mar through Oct. Call ahead for times, since they vary depending on the season. Rates are $30 for adults and $18 for children 3 to 12; $2 for ages 2 and under 3. For more information call (719) 689-2466. You can also visit goldminetours.com.

Many people come to Cripple Creek just for gaming at the dozen or more casinos. But regardless of whether you enjoy gambling, the wealth of historical sites and the plentiful outdoor activities are well worth a visit. Cripple Creek is 45 miles west of Colorado Springs. From there it can be reached via US 24 west, then Highway 67. For more information write the Cripple Creek Welcome

Center, PO Box 430, Cripple Creek 80813; call (877) 858-4653, or check out visitcripplecreek.com.

Pueblo, located some 40 miles south of Colorado Springs, hosts the yearly **Colorado State Fair & Exposition,** the largest single event in the state. Every summer, the fair delivers an action-packed 11-day experience for all who visit. Come to see the PRCA Championship Rodeo and stroll the largest carnival and midway in the state. In the agricultural section, view prize lambs, hogs, steers, horses, and other animals. Young animals are available to pet in the children's barnyard. Competition for the best baked goods, jams and preserves, quilting, and scores of exhibits and creative arts displays give visitors literally hundreds of things to see. At night there are performances by some of the nation's top entertainers.

General admission to the state fair is $14 for ages 13 and older; $7 ages 5 to 12; children 4 and younger get in free. Check the fair website for discounted and free days. Hours vary depending on the day and specific section of the fair, with opening ranging from 11 a.m. to 3 p.m. and closing ranging from 11 p.m. to midnight. From I-25, take exit 97A west (Central Avenue). This will take you to Northern Avenue. Follow Northern west; the state fairgrounds will be on your right. Call (719) 561-8484 or (800) 876-4567 for details, or visit colorado statefair.com.

For more information on visiting the Pueblo area, contact the Greater Pueblo Chamber of Commerce, 302 N. Santa Fe Ave., Pueblo 81003; (800) 233-3446 or (719) 542-1704; pueblochamber.org.

trivia

The US Air Force Academy's Cadet Chapel received a 1996 American Institute of Architects award. The chapel conducts services for Protestant, Catholic, Buddhist, Muslim, and Jewish worshippers.

From Pueblo, head west on US 50 to **Cañon City,** known as Colorado's Prison Capitol for the abundance of prisons in the area. One of the nearby attractions is **Shelf Road.** Shelf Road makes up part of the **Gold Belt Tour,** a designated Colorado Scenic Byway. From stunning limestone cliffs that attract rock climbers from all over the world to the sheer drop-offs on the side of the road (hence the name) into lush green valleys, the views and the isolation encountered along Shelf Road are idyllic. Abundant wildlife viewing potential rounds out the area's special charm—possible sightings include mule deer, foxes, hawks, American black bears, and owls.

Some of the driving is on rough roads (it's not for the faint of heart) and should be avoided in wet or icy weather; furthermore, four-wheel drive is recommended for portions of Upper Shelf Road. However, any two-wheel-drive vehicle can navigate the scenic portion of Shelf Road that leads out of Cañon City. The road becomes narrow once it turns to dirt, so drive carefully and slowly, watching for oncoming traffic. Plan ahead where you are going to turn around; a good place is at mile marker 14. The entire Gold Belt Tour encompasses 131 miles of driving and takes roughly 5 hours.

To get there from Cañon City, drive north on Raynolds, and then head north again on Fields after Raynolds swings west. Nine miles along Fields takes you directly to Shelf Road. For more information call (719) 269-8500 or visit co .blm.gov/ccdo/canon.htm.

After a jaunt along Shelf Road, another scenic wonder awaits at the **Royal Gorge Bridge and Park.** The gorge, at 1,200 feet deep, has been compared to the Grand Canyon. With its striking reds, mauves, browns, and yellows, the deep and narrow gorge stopped Lieutenant Zebulon Pike (of Pikes Peak fame) in his tracks back in 1806. He couldn't forge the gorge (and he didn't climb Pikes Peak, either).

In 1929 the Royal Gorge Bridge opened up to traffic after 7 months of construction. The bridge is able to support more than two million pounds. Today people flock from all over to walk across this mighty suspension bridge, allegedly the highest of its kind in the world. In June 2013, a devastating fire destroyed many of the buildings and attractions in the park—but not the famous bridge. The visitor center and other buildings and attractions were rebuilt, including a new high-flying gondola. Sadly, the historic Incline Railway could not be resurrected; however, there's plenty here to keep visitors engaged and on an adrenaline rush, such as the **Royal Rush Skycoaster,** proclaimed the scariest in the world.

The 2,200-foot-long **Aerial Gondola** offers another viewing option as it takes visitors for a ride across this remarkable canyon, 1,200 feet above the Arkansas River. Painted a fiery red, the 35-passenger tram cabin comes with a guide-conductor who assures timid passengers that the tram will not plunge into the Arkansas River, which rages and roars below. Three braking systems and an extra motor guarantee your safety. In the terminals, a total of about 100 tons of concrete and steel anchor the conveyance's enormous cables, providing reassurance with their heftiness. In fact, a helicopter had to string the tram's pilot cable, and more than $350,000 was needed to rig up this tourist attraction.

These days there is much more to the gorge than the aerial tram and visitor center. A roller coaster, carousel, children's play area, zip line, and miniature train are among the options, and of course the bridge itself. Park admission is $32 for adults and teenagers and $27 for children 6 to 12; children 5 and younger are admitted free. Senior and military discounts are available. Park hours vary throughout the year. Admission offers unlimited access to most park attractions, although some attractions are seasonal. The Skycoater and zip line are added-fee attractions. Call for details. The Royal Gorge Bridge and Park is 12 miles west of Cañon City on US 50. Call (719) 275-7507 or visit royalgorgebridge.com. The Cañon City Chamber of Commerce can be reached at 403 Royal Gorge Blvd.; (719) 275-2331 or (800) 876-7922; canoncity.com.

US 50 west from Cañon City takes you to ***Salida.*** There are few more out-doorsy places in Colorado. With the Arkansas River running along the edge of town, and an excellent whitewater course created by the city, Salida is famous for whitewater rafting, kayaking, and fishing. Locals bring their kids to the river to laze on the warm boulders and splash in the shallows. Mountain bikes and road bikes are popular modes of transportation. And the historic district, several blocks of century-old redbrick buildings, is filled with casual cafes and coffeehouses, fine dining, art galleries, a bookstore, and unique boutiques. Stop by the Boathouse, grab a bite to eat, and sit out on the deck overlooking the Arkansas River. The town often shows up on those "Best Places to Live in America" lists. Spend a few hours walking the streets and strolling along the river, and you'll see why.

For more information on Salida visit salida.com or contact the Salida Chamber of Commerce, 406 W. US 50, Salida 81201; (719) 539-2068 or (877) 772-5432; salidachamber.org.

Driving north on Highway 24 from Salida to ***Buena Vista,*** travelers have panoramic views of the ***Collegiate Peaks*** to the west. Nine of the state's 14,000-foot peaks and a handful of 13,000-foot peaks are clustered together in a dramatic backdrop to the valley. Both the Continental Divide Trail and Colorado Trail cross through here, and the area is rich with hiking trails and campgrounds. Anyone interested in climbing some of those fourteeners or just wandering into the backcountry will find a convenient base in Buena Vista. Several motels and a variety of cafes, cantinas, pubs, and coffeehouses make this a popular overnight spot prior to heading into the wilderness.

Each August Buena Vista hosts one of the state's most colorful small-town festivals. ***Gold Rush Days*** combine a celebration of the area's history with contemporary entertainment and a few wacky events thrown into the mix. During the 13.5-mile Pack Burro Race, runners leading burros loaded with mining equipment race along a loop that begins and ends in town. A duck race, crafts and vendors, historical reenactments, storytelling, beer and wine gardens, food, and live entertainment round out the weekend. For more information contact the Chamber of Commerce at (719) 395-6612.

Buena Vista preserves an intriguing bit of Colorado history at the ***Turner Farm and Apple Orchard.*** This early 1900s apple farm has been restored and repurposed as a living museum. Around 50 apple trees, a farmhouse, mother-in-law cabin, homestead cabin, and other buildings give visitors a glimpse into a way of life from another century. On Sunday during the summer a farmers' market is held here. The farm is located at 829 W. Main St. For more information go to buenavistaheritage.org/turner-farm.

Going north on US 285 from the Buena Vista area, the road enters ***South Park,*** a sprawling series of valleys and hills where pronghorn roam the grassy fields and the landscape is largely undeveloped. Up the road is the town of ***Fairplay,*** home to one of Colorado's best-preserved historical sites.

The ***South Park City Museum*** is a restored 1880s mining town with over 40 authentic buildings. As you walk through the streets, you'll pass the saloon, barber shop, dentist office, brewery, chapel, morgue, schoolhouse, doctor's office, narrow-gauge train, and countless other buildings and exhibits. Inside these structures are more than 60,000 artifacts from frontier boomtown life. The museum is open from May 15 to Oct 15. For more information call (719) 836-2387 or visit southparkcity.org.

An easy nearby hike leads to an ancient forest of strangely beautiful trees. The ***Limber Grove Trail*** takes hikers to a stand of thousand-year-old limber pines, twisted and tortured by centuries of wind, rain, snow, and sun. From Fairplay, go south on US 285 1 mile to Fourmile Road, CR 18. Turn west and drive 8 miles to Fourmile Campground. The Limber Grove trailhead is about half a mile farther west on the south side of the road. The trailhead is well marked with good parking. Allow about 2 hours round-trip for this leisurely hike.

trivia

Some of the bristlecone pine trees along the Broadmoor Manitou and Pikes Peak Cog Railway are estimated to be almost 2,000 years old, making them among the oldest living things on Earth.

Continuing north on Highway 24 from Buena Vista to ***Leadville,*** it's time now for a story of love and power, of wealth and poverty, of joys and tragedy, of a Colorado mining town whose fortunes flourished and then vanished. A story so extraordinary that it became the subject of an opera, a play, and many biographies, some good and some bad.

The characters were bigger than life. Begin with Horace Austin Warner Tabor, a onetime Vermont stonecutter, and his straitlaced hardworking wife, Augusta. The couple gave up a Kansas homestead to try their luck first in Denver, then under Pikes Peak, then at Oro City. They arrived in Leadville with a rickety wagon and an old ox during the 1860s, some years after the first gold had been discovered in California Gulch.

The Tabors established themselves as best as they could—Augusta with a tiny rooming house and a small bakery, Horace with a store and later a part-time job as mayor. The Tabors' first break came on April 20, 1878. Two destitute miners, new in town, dropped into Horace's shop. Could he help out with some tools and a basket of groceries? The accommodating mayor agreed to help for a third of whatever minerals they might find. A few days later, some hard digging produced a rich silver vein.

trivia

Mining experts considered Cripple Creek worthless despite frequent reports of gold; still, novice prospectors, mining with pitchforks, eventually developed the "300-million-dollar cow pasture."

The Tabors were launched. By summer that first mine—the Little Pittsburgh—lavished $8,000 a week on its owners. Before long there was $100,000 worth of silver per month; this was followed by other Tabor ventures, all successful. In time, Tabor invested in many mines, controlled a good chunk of the local bank, built the Leadville Opera House, and erected mansions in the mining town and in Denver. He owned a lot of real estate and a hotel. By 1879 Leadville had 17 independent smelters; it took 2,000 lumberjacks to provide enough wood to fire the machinery that processed the silver riches. Thanks to Tabor's new wealth and almost daily discoveries of more ore, the immigrants flooded to Leadville in droves. Celebrities like the "Unsinkable" Molly Brown showed up, as did various Dows, Guggenheims, and Boettchers.

Tabor soon bought an additional mine—the Matchless. He prospered while Leadville grew to a city of 30,000. Oscar Wilde appeared in the famous ***Tabor***

Some Little-Known Facts about Manitou Springs

- It was actually from Manitou Springs' mineral springs that Colorado Springs got its name.
- "Manitou" is a Native American word for "Great Spirit."
- Native Americans attributed supernatural powers to Manitou Springs' waters and temporarily reserved the surrounding area as a sanctuary.

Opera House. The Chicago Symphony Orchestra and the Metropolitan Opera came here, to faraway Colorado. Well-known singers, ballet dancers, actresses, and entertainers arrived to perform.

H. A. W. Tabor became a millionaire many times over. He was a tall man, mustached, kindly, and, as a local historian writes, "outgoing, gregarious, and honest as the falling rain." By contrast, Horace was married to a woman who, although she worked hard, brought Tabor no happiness. She allegedly nagged; she was described as prim and humorless. Perhaps Colorado's richest man thought he deserved better.

Horace Tabor's luck changed one day in 1882. That evening the 50-year-old silver magnate saw Elisabeth Doe-McCourt in the restaurant of Leadville's Clarendon Hotel.

"Baby" Doe was 22—a beauty with shining blue eyes and curly, dark blonde hair. Round-faced and charming, she'd been born into an Irish immigrant family of 14 children. Baby Doe had just emerged from a brief, unhappy marriage with an unsupportive miner in Central City. Recently divorced, she had the good sense to look for a better partner in booming Leadville. She was a respectable young woman. And her search was crowned by success.

What began as a simple flirtation deepened into an abiding love that scandalized people in the Rockies and became the celebrated story of Colorado's opera ***The Ballad of Baby Doe*** by Broadway veterans John Latouche and Douglas Moore.

Horace and Baby Doe were snubbed by Denver high society when Tabor divorced his wife, Augusta, who allegedly received a $500,000 settlement. Tabor soon married his new love. The wedding took place in Washington, DC, in the presence of President Chester Arthur and other dignitaries. Baby Doe received a $90,000 diamond necklace, and she wore a $7,500 gown.

Although young, she actually had greater substance than most of her biographers gave her credit for. She was honest and loyal, helpful to others, and interested in a variety of things. Best of all, she was in love with her much older Colorado husband. Her love was returned.

The Tabors lived the lavish life of luxury to the hilt. Most historians estimate that the Tabors spent some $100 million. Horace Tabor made few new worthwhile investments. For a brief time he was elected to the US Senate.

In 1893 disaster struck Leadville. Silver was replaced by paper money. The nation experienced a financial panic. The Tabors were ruined. The mines began to fail. Real estate was sold to satisfy creditors.

The couple moved to Denver, still in love. Thanks to some contacts, Horace got a postmaster's job for a short time. But the financial plunge must have been too much for him. Soon he was ailing. His final hours came on April 10,

Some Little-Known Facts about Cripple Creek

- In its heyday, the Cripple Creek area produced $25 million in gold in one year.
- Famous Cripple Creek workers included Jack Johnson and Jack Dempsey. Dempsey once fought a bloody, drawn-out battle here in Cripple Creek . . . for 50 dollars.
- Speakeasy hostess "Texas" Guinan started in Cripple Creek. Perhaps this is one of the reasons the city is now best known for its Las Vegas–style gambling.

Take a Ride on the Railroad

For an unusual perspective, explore the area from a car on the **Cripple Creek & Victor Narrow-Gauge Railroad.** It takes about 45 minutes to complete the winding 4-mile ride behind a coal-burning steam locomotive. The train travels through the historic gold mining district, passing abandoned mines, and stopping at several points of interest and photo opportunities. The railroad is open daily from mid-May through the second week of October. Call (719) 689-2640 for departure times. The fare is $17 for adults and teenagers 13 and older, $15 for senior citizens 65 and older, and $12 for children 3 to 12; children 2 and younger ride free; check the railroad's website, cripplecreekrailroad.com, for discount coupons.

1899, at Denver's Windsor Hotel. His wife, Baby Doe, was by his side, holding his hand.

As legend has it, before Horace Tabor died, he once more spoke about his **Matchless Mine** in Leadville. It had long played out after yielding some $1 million during its 14 years of operation. "Hold on to the Matchless," Tabor whispered. "It'll make millions again." His wife nodded.

Baby Doe kept her promise. She moved back to Leadville. Penniless, she lived in a shack beside the mine pit for 36 years. She remained faithful to Tabor.

trivia

The Cripple Creek Mining District, made up of roughly 25 towns in the Cripple Creek area, was once known as "The World's Greatest Gold Camp."

During the winter of 1935, while in her 70s, she shopped at a local grocery for some food. The grocer gave her a ride home in his truck. Baby Doe was dressed in tatters. Her feet were sheathed in sackcloth instead of shoes. The cabin next to the Matchless Mine was squalid, but she kept a rifle in it, protecting her mine.

OTHER ATTRACTIONS WORTH SEEING IN SOUTHERN COLORADO

COLORADO SPRINGS
Old Colorado City
(719) 577-4112
shopoldcoloradocity.com

May Natural History Museum
(719) 576-0450
coloradospringsbugmuseum.com

CAÑON CITY/ROYAL GORGE
Royal Gorge Dinosaur Experience
44895 W. US 50
(719) 275-2726
dinoxp.com

CORTEZ
Trail of the Ancients Scenic Byway
trailoftheancients.com

DELTA COUNTY
Delta County Historical Museum
251 Meeker St., Delta
(970) 874-8721
deltahistorical.org

Visit Delta County
(970) 874-2108
deltacountycolorado.com

Grand Mesa Scenic and Historic Byway
grandmesabyway.com

DURANGO
Purgatory Resort
(970) 247-9000 or (800) 525-0892
purgatory.ski

GUNNISON
Curecanti National Recreation Area and Morrow Point Boat Tour
(970) 641-2337
nps.gov/cure

LEADVILLE
Leadville, Colorado & Southern Railroad Scenic Rides
(719) 486-3936 or (866) 386-3936
leadville-train.com

MANITOU SPRINGS
Cave of the Winds
(719) 685-5444
caveofthewinds.com

MONTROSE
Owl Creek Pass
(970) 497-8558 or (855) 497-8558
visitmontrose.com/outdoors/
wilderness-areas-parks/
owl-creek-pass-silver-jack-reservoir

MT. CRESTED BUTTE
Crested Butte Mountain Resort
(971) 251-7021 or (877) 547-5143
skicb.com

OURAY
Million Dollar Highway
(970) 325-4746 or (800) 228-1876
(Chamber Resort Association)
colorado.com/scenic-historic-byways/
million-dollar-highway

PAGOSA SPRINGS
Navajo State Park
(970) 883-2208 or (970) 883-2628
(marina)
cpw.state.co.us/placestogo/parks/
Navajo

Wolf Creek Pass
(970) 264-2360 (Pagosa Springs Area
Chamber of Commerce)
sangres.com/features/wolfcreekpass.htm

PUEBLO
Nature & Wildlife Discovery Center
(719) 549-2414
hikeandlearn.org

SILVERTON
Silverton Historic District
(970) 387-5654 (Chamber of Commerce)
silvertoncolorado.com

Leadville's altitude is more than 10,000 feet. It gets cold here on winter nights. Baby Doe Tabor was found in her shack on March 7, 1935. She had frozen to death. No one knows how long the body had been there. Ironically, there were some unopened boxes with new blankets sent by some Leadville sympathizers, which the dying woman had refused to use.

trivia

Cripple Creek's Mollie Kathleen Gold Mine, the longest continually operating gold mine tour in the world, boasts the only vertical-shaft gold mine tour in the US.

trivia

Pueblo is known to many as the home of the Federal Citizen Information Center, where Americans can write to "Pueblo, Colorado 81009" for information on thousands of subjects.

The Tabors are buried side by side in Denver. *The Ballad of Baby Doe* was added to the New York City Opera's repertoire shortly after its 1956 debut in Central City. The role of Baby Doe was among the first that Beverly Sills sang for a company she was to head many years later.

And how about the current Leadville? Thanks to the town's solid mining history, there is a 70,000-square-foot **National Mining Hall of Fame & Museum.** This museum should be essential for rockhounds, mining school students, and history buffs. Located in a restored Victorian schoolhouse, the facility retraces the entire Leadville history; you can also view old equipment, assorted rocks and crystals, various artifacts, and dioramas. The Hard Rock Mine is a realistic replica of a hard-rock mine tunnel. Stretching more than 120 feet, the "rock" walls have exposed ore veins. You can also visit the Matchless Mine and Baby Doe's cabin for an additional charge. Admission to the museum is $14 per person. Hours are 9 a.m. to 5 p.m. daily May to Nov; check for times in other seasons. For more information call (719) 486-1229 or visit mininghalloffame.org.

Several other museums in Leadville are also worth visiting. The Heritage Museum displays Victorian furniture, dioramas, and various mining and boomtown paraphernalia as it depicts the Western flavor of Leadville's past. A replica of the Leadville Ice Palace and 10th Mountain Division memorabilia from Camp Hale are also here.

The Matchless Mine and Baby Doe's cabin are the site of the last chapter in the Tabor-Doe saga, and both are open to visitors. The Tabor Opera House on Harrison Avenue was once the largest and grandest opera house west of the Mississippi. The Tabor Home on 5th Street is also open for tours.

The Healy House Museum and Dexter Cabin provide a glimpse of life in a booming silver mining camp. Daniel Healy was an engineer who ran a

Pueblo's El Pueblo History Museum

Designed to be the gateway to the Historic Arkansas Riverwalk of Pueblo (HARP), the El Pueblo History Museum includes a permanent gallery covering the history of Pueblo along with an atrium gallery and a children's gallery. A recreated 1840s adobe trading post, archaeological excavation site, and more, the museum also serves as a central location for tourist information. Contact the museum at (719) 583-0453 for details, or visit historycolorado.org/museums/el-pueblo-history-museum. The museum is located at 301 N. Union St. in Pueblo. Hours are daily 10 a.m. to 4 p.m.

boardinghouse, and James Dexter was a rakish resident who built this luxury cabin as a social club.

More than 70 square blocks of Leadville have been designated a National Historic Landmark District of Victorian architecture, making it one of the largest

TOP ANNUAL EVENTS IN SOUTHERN COLORADO

JANUARY
Ouray Ice Festival
Ouray
(970) 325-4288
ourayicepark.com

Pagosa Springs Winter Fest
(970) 264-2360
pagosachamber.com/winterfest

MARCH
Monte Vista Crane Festival
Monte Vista National Wildlife Refuge
(719) 289-7522
mvcranefest.org

MAY
Music and Blossom Festival
Cañon City
Spring
ccblossomfestival.com

Royal Gorge Rodeo
Cañon City
royalgorgetravel.com/events/
royal-gorge-rodeo

JUNE
Colorado Renaissance Festival
Larkspur
Summer
(303) 688-6010
coloradorenaissance.com

Gunnison River Festival
Gunnison and Altmont
(970) 641-6065
gunnisonriverfestival.com

Telluride Bluegrass Festival
late June
(800) 624-2422
bluegrass.com/telluride

JULY
Cattlemen's Days
Gunnison
mid-July
(970) 596-1413 (tickets)
cattlemensdays.com

Crested Butte Wildflower Festival
(970) 349-2571
crestedbuttewildflowerfestival.com

Paonia Cherry Days Festival
Paonia
early July
paoniacherrydays.com

Pikes Peak or Bust Rodeo
Colorado Springs
Summer
pikespeakorbust.org

AUGUST
Boom Days and Burro Race
Leadville
first full weekend of Aug
leadvilleboomdays.org

Buena Vista Gold Rush Days
Buena Vista
mid-Aug
(719) 395-6612
buenavistacolorado.org/gold-rush-days

Colorado State Fair
Pueblo Fairgrounds
late Aug–early Sept
(719) 561-8484 or (800) 876-4567
coloradostatefair.com

Crested Butte Arts Festival
early Aug
crestedbutteartsfestival.com

Donkey Derby
Cripple Creek
Summer
(719) 270-1999
visitcripplecreek.com/event/
donkey-derby-days

SEPTEMBER
Colorado Springs Labor Day Lift Off
Labor Day weekend
(719) 635-7506
coloradospringslabordayliftoff.com

Telluride Film Festival
(510) 665-9494
telluridefilmfestival.org

OCTOBER
Durango Cowboy Poetry Gathering
Durango
(970) 749-5663 or (970) 946-2460
durangocowboygathering.org

such districts in Colorado. You can enjoy the town's history at any time of year by going on a short historic walking tour through this district. Start your free, self-guided tour at *Ice Palace Park* in the 100 block of West Tenth. Plenty of parking can be found here. The park commemorates the ill-fated Ice Palace, built nearby in 1896. The palace, constructed of 5,000 tons of ice and 307,000 board feet of lumber, lasted only a few months before going under. From the park, you walk southeast to Harrison Avenue, where most of the tour's attractions await your exploration, including the *Heritage Museum,* the *Hyman Block* (where the infamous Doc Holliday shot—but failed to kill—his last victim), the saloon visited by Oscar Wilde, and the *Tabor Opera House.*

For a map of the walking tour, visit leadville.com/walktour or call the Leadville/Lake County Chamber of Commerce at (719) 486-3900 or (888) LEAD-VILLE. For general information about Leadville go to leadville.com. To reach Leadville from Denver, take I-70 west, turning off at Highway 91 (exit 195, Copper Mountain).

Due west of Salida is ***Crested Butte,*** a laid-back mountain town with a scenic ski center. Thirty minutes up the road from Gunnison, Crested Butte is too far from Front Range cities to attract crowds. (Denver is 199 miles to the northeast.) The town is surrounded by almost two million acres of pristine wilderness, giving everyone plenty of elbow room to find his or her own private Eden. Crested Butte has become a major mountain-biking destination with hundreds of miles of trails outside of town. The sport is celebrated during Crested Butte Bike Week each June. An entire week is devoted to racing, guided tours, clinics, and fun competitions like the Chainless World Championships, where spectators have as much fun as riders. A concert at the base of the ski area livens things up. For more information call the Chamber of Commerce at (855) 681-0941 or (970) 349-6438, or visit cbchamber.com.

In a state filled with beautiful mountains, the scenic peaks around Crested Butte rank among the best. The town sits at the end of a long valley, up the road from Gunnison. As the crow flies, it's not far from Aspen, just over the Elk Mountains. And like Aspen, Crested Butte retains some of its mining-town past with restored Victorian houses and buildings.

But the similarities end there. Crested Butte never became a playground for the wealthy and famous. The town is mountain-hip without being pretentious. There may be more bikes than cars here. And some of the locals would probably have fit in just fine back in the old mining days. A marketing campaign for the ski area some years back said it best: "Aspen like it used to be, and Vail like it never was."

trivia

Pueblo was originally a crossroads for travelers, including Spaniards, fur traders, and Native Americans.

trivia

The Royal Gorge Bridge cost more than $10 million to construct.

The skiing here is as good as it gets in Colorado. But summer is a magical time in Crested Butte. One of the state's major festivals is the ***Crested Butte Wildflower Festival.*** The wildflower displays here are among the best in the state. In fact, Crested Butte is recognized by the Colorado legislature as the Official Wildflower Capital of Colorado. All mountain towns have wildflowers, but the climate in this sheltered valley seems to produce more floral quantity and variety than other places around the state. And the festival is scheduled right around the peak wildflower season each summer in mid-July.

Guided hikes and bike rides, 4x4 tours into the backcountry, photography and art classes, home garden tours, medicinal plant classes, wildflower gardening, and birds and butterflies are some of the ways to enjoy the festival. Call (970) 349-2571 for more information, or visit crestedbuttewildflowerfestival.org.

Crested Butte was the site of the first mountain biking in Colorado. In the mid-1970s, after a motorcycle group rode their Harley-Davidsons from Aspen over the rough Pearl Pass jeep road, some "Butte" locals decided to one-up the bikers by doing the same route on bicycles. They hopped on their basic clunkers and rode the 40 miles back over the mountain. With that, a sport was born, and so was the annual Pearl Pass Mountain Bike Tour from Crested Butte to Aspen.

Since then these bikes have evolved from one-speed clunkers into sophisticated machines of lightweight carbon alloy with up to 27 gears. Crested Butte has a wealth of trails available to mountain bikers. Keep in mind that most of these trails are open for public use. Cyclists, hikers, and equestrians share many of the paths through Crested Butte's spectacularly scenic spaces, meaning occasionally you may have to get off your bike and move off the trail to accommodate others. Around the US, failure of cyclists to yield has caused some popular trails to be closed to them. An excellent resource for mountain biking in Crested Butte and the Gunnison Valley is gunnisoncrestedbutte.com/bike, a website with info on the area's more than 750 miles of mountain bike trails.

The **Crested Butte Museum,** housed in an 1883 building formerly used as a gas station and hardware store, has interesting collections and displays depicting early mining, ranching, skiing, and settler life around Crested Butte. Open 10 a.m. to 6 p.m. most days; 331 Elk Ave.; (970) 349-1880; crestedbuttemuseum.com.

Artistic types have been drawn to the area for decades, and as a result, Crested Butte offers a diverse and rich calendar of cultural activities throughout the year. The **Crested Butte Center for the Arts** at 606 6th St. hosts concerts, art displays, classes, films, events, and more. Call (970) 349-7487 or visit crestedbuttearts.org.

The **Crested Butte Mountain Theatre** is located at 403 2nd St. in the 1880s-era Old Town Hall. Since 1972 this group has entertained locals and visitors with live theatrical performances ranging from drama and musicals to comedy and beyond. It's a delightful way to spend an evening. For more information, contact (970) 349-0366; cbmountaintheatre.org.

Three miles up the road from town is ***Crested Butte Mountain Resort,*** another of Colorado's premier ski destinations. The majority of the mountain (57 percent) is for intermediate skiers, with the remaining 43 percent almost equally divided between beginning and advanced runs. There are numerous long, intermediate runs, as well as gentle, rolling meadows with plenty of places to go at your own pace. The trail network is well-planned, and an excellent children's ski school and child-care facility make this an attractive family ski resort.

For many, though, the big draw at Crested Butte is extreme skiing and snowboarding. Both can be found at the Extreme Limits, more than 580 acres of ungroomed, double-black diamond terrain. It's no coincidence that the first ever and longest running extreme skiing competition is held here. Steep bowls, narrow chutes, cliff drops, and through-the-trees skiing await adrenaline junkies who are ready for some of the steepest lift-served runs in North America. Tours are available for expert skiers who want a taste of the mountain's wild side.

For slightly tamer winter fun, there are snowshoe tours, snowcat driving experiences, sleigh ride dinners to Uley's Cabin, and an Adventure Park with lift-served tubing, bungee trampolines, rock climbing, and miniature golf. The Crested Butte Zip Line Tour at the resort is one of the few zip lines in the country that runs in winter as well as spring and fall. As of this writing it's temporarily closed but is expected to reopen. For more information call (877) 547-5143 or visit travelcrestedbutte.com.

Crested Butte's ski season runs from the week of Thanksgiving through early April. The ski slopes are open from 9 a.m. to 4 p.m. daily. Prices vary throughout the season. For more information call (877) 547-5143 or visit skicb.com.

Located at the edge of town, the ***Crested Butte Nordic Center*** is unique. No other cross-country center in Colorado offers in-track skiing so close to a town. An extensive, 55-kilometer network of trails spreads out from three nearby trailheads, making it easy to ski a few morning hours, ski into town for lunch, then take off into the woods again in the afternoon. Choose trails ranging from novice to advanced. The Nordic Center offers lessons, rentals, backcountry tours, ice skating, sledding, snowshoeing, brunch and dinner at the yurt, and many races and events. For information contact (970) 349-1707; cbnordic.org.

When the snow melts and warm weather returns to Crested Butte, the summer season kicks into high gear. Between the Evolution Bike Park, mountain biking and hiking trails, chairlift rides (for hiking, biking, picnics, sightseeing), Adventure Park (minus the tubing in the summer), and the Crested Butte Zip Line Tour, there's no shortage of outdoor activities. Free outdoor concerts happen each Wednesday in July and August at the base of the ski mountain. And in addition to the Wildflower Festival and Bike Week, there's a full schedule of summer festivals, including the Crested Butte Music Festival and the Crested Butte Wine & Food Festival.

Crested Butte is 28 miles north of Gunnison on Highway 135. For more information call (855) 681-0941 or visit cbchamber.com or gunnisonchamber .com. Visitor centers are located in both towns, at 500 E. Tomichi Ave. in Gunnison and 601 Elk Ave. in Crested Butte.

Between Crested Butte and Gunnison, where the East and Taylor Rivers meet to form the Gunnison River, lies the small community of *Almont.* Winter visitors on their way to Crested Butte stop here at places like the Three Rivers Resort & Outfitting for a variety of lodging and outdoor adventure packages. In warm-weather months the area is a good base for nearby camping, canoeing and kayaking, 4x4 driving, hiking, rock climbing, horseback riding, fishing, rafting, and exploring nearby Taylor Canyon. Ranch resorts and riverside cabins offer a quieter, simpler vacation where you can slow down and enjoy the western landscape. The wildflowers along this route are spectacular from late June through mid-Aug. For information visit gunnisoncrestedbutte.com/explore/towns/almont.

Don't overlook *Gunnison* on your way to Crested Butte. With its legacy of ranching and farming, the town and surrounding area are as authentically Western as it gets in Colorado. Cowboy boots and wide-brimmed hats are worn as work clothes. Western State College adds a subtle college-town feel to the community. And nature lovers use Gunnison as a base for excellent nearby fishing, boating, rafting, camping, and mountain biking.

If you want to learn about early life in the area, visit the *Gunnison Pioneer Museum* at 803 E. Tomichi Ave. These 6 acres contain an antique car collection, a narrow-gauge train, two rural schoolhouses, a log cabin chapel, carpenter shop, blacksmith shop, print shop, and displays of pioneer life. Open mid-May through Sept 9 a.m. to 5 p.m. daily; (970) 641-4530.

Tap into the local cultural scene with a visit to the *Gunnison Arts Center* (102 S. Main St.; 970-641-4029; gunnisonartscenter.org). Along with its three gallery exhibit spaces, this community arts center has a busy schedule of performance artists, literary events, movies, music, classes, and a theater. The area attracts artists of all kinds, and the center is a window into that community.

The *Gunnison Valley Observatory* houses the largest public telescope in Colorado. Located off Gold Basin Road at the base of "W" Mountain, on CR 38, the observatory houses a 30-inch reflector telescope, taking advantage of the unpolluted atmosphere here to scan the skies. The observatory is open to

Some Little-Known Facts about Leadville

As the highest incorporated city in the US, Leadville is just below the timberline.

Legend says that in the old days, a barrel of Leadville whiskey was worth as much as $1,500.

Tents were once pitched along the main street, and it was boasted that each was "the best hotel in town."

"Unsinkable" Molly Brown made her fortune here; also David May, Charles Boettcher, Charles Dow, and Meyer Guggenheim.

visitors every Friday and Saturday evening in summer. For more information call (970) 642-1111 or visit gunnisonobservatory.org.

For those who enjoy whitewater sports and for those who enjoy watching them, **Gunnison Whitewater Park** is a pleasant place to spend a few hours. A series of rock structures along a several-hundred-foot section of the Gunnison River creates a paddling playground for kayaking, canoeing, and rafting. A walking path and picnic area offer good vantage points to watch the action. For more information, visit gunnisoncrestedbutte.com/visit/trip-planning/things-to-do/boating.

Hartman Rocks Recreational Area, located just 5 minutes from downtown Gunnison, has more than 20 trails on 8,000 acres of public land. This network of trails welcomes hiking, singletrack and doubletrack mountain biking, rock climbing, and horseback riding. In winter the area is popular for cross-country skiing and snowshoeing. The routes pass through rolling hills of sagebrush with granite rock outcrops and occasional cottonwood groves. To get there, drive west on US 50 about 1.5 miles from downtown, and turn left (south) on Gold Basin Road (City Road 38 just before the twin bridges). Go for about 2.2 miles and turn right for Hartman Rocks.

Nine miles west of Gunnison along US 50 is **Curecanti National Recreation Area,** a series of three reservoirs set in a starkly beautiful volcanic landscape. One of them, Blue Mesa Reservoir, is the largest body of water in the state, and from its depths have come several state-record lake trout. Swimming, camping, boat rentals, sailboarding, and other activities are available.

Continuing along US 50, an hour out of Gunnison you will come to the dramatic **Black Canyon of the Gunnison National Park,** which became a national park in 1999. In the sunlight, the massive black granite towers, pillars, and stone blocks turn mauve. In all, the Black Canyon of the Gunnison National

Farmers' Markets

In southwestern Colorado farmers' markets are a friendly introduction to the community. Locals gather to peruse fresh produce, cheeses, jams, and meats, browse locally made products, and enjoy a hot drink and fresh pastry while socializing with neighbors and listening to live music. Markets are open from June through Oct. Start with these:

Cortez, Saturday 7:30 to 11:30 a.m.; cortezfarmmarket.com

Dolores, Wednesday 4 to 7 p.m.; mesaverdecountry.com/see-do/
agricultural-adventures/farmers'-markets

Durango, Saturday 8 a.m. to noon; durangofarmersmarket.com

Mancos, Thursday 4 to 7 p.m.; mesaverdecountry.com/see-do/
agricultural-adventures/farmers'-markets

Park comprises some 30,385 acres. Carved by the river, the canyon measures 53 miles long and 2,722 feet from the rim to the bottom at its deepest point.

There are three roads in the park: East Portal, North Rim, and South Rim. Each offers spectacular views, but only East Portal allows access to the bottom by car. The South Rim Visitor Center offers exhibits detailing the geology and history of the canyon. This is a good place to learn about the scenic overlooks along each drive, and to find out about the hiking trails, from easy to moderate, leading to different vistas. The area can be hot in summer, so come prepared with water and a hat. Two campgrounds offer tent and RV camping, but vehicles more than 35 feet long are discouraged. The closest lodging outside the park is in Montrose, 15 miles southwest.

Rock climbing in the canyon is considered one of Colorado's best big-wall destinations and is only for experienced climbers. Some routes can take several days to complete, requiring climbers to overnight on narrow ledges or in hammocks slung from the rock wall.

The national park is open year-round. The entrance fee is $30 per vehicle for a seven-day pass and includes all passengers in a private, noncommercial vehicle; ages 16 and younger are free. The North and South Rim stations are open daily, but access is limited in winter. The campground is open all year, although two of the three loops are closed in winter. To get to the South Rim take US 50 from Montrose for 15 miles to Highway 347. The visitor center is at the South Rim. The North Rim is 11 miles south of Crawford via US 92 and North Rim Road, which is closed during winter. Contact Park Headquarters, 102 Elk Creek, Gunnison 81230; (970) 641-2337; nps.gov/blca.

Nearby **Montrose** is a convenient base for exploring the Black Canyon of the Gunnison and surrounding public lands. Almost 300 miles from Denver, this city on the Western Slope is a mecca for outdoor activities ranging from hiking and camping to mountain biking, cross-country skiing, and snowmobiling. The historic downtown, Museum of the Mountain West, Montrose County Historical Museum, and Ute Indian Museum all offer insights into life in the Old West.

North of Montrose, the town of **Delta** has many buildings on the National Historic Register. Visit the **Fort Uncompahgre Interpretive Center on the Old Spanish Trail** at pretty **Confluence Park** to see a reconstruction of the original trading post used by trappers, traders, and Native Americans. More than 200 years old, the **Ute Council Tree** at the entrance to Delta is a majestic cottonwood where Chief Ouray met with white settlers in an effort to keep peace with the Utes. The **Delta County Historical Museum** in the old firehouse recounts the cultural heritage and natural history of the area. When you need a break from history, head to some of Delta County's 13 wineries and 5 tasting rooms. Visit deltacounty.com.

trivia

Leadville, at 10,152 feet above sea level, is North America's highest incorporated city.

Leadville Visit

While in Leadville, well-conditioned adventurers won't want to miss a chance to hike Colorado's highest mountain, **Mount Elbert** (14,433 feet).

Depending on time and ability, hikers can choose one of the mountain's two main trails:

North Mount Elbert Trail is a 5-mile hike to the summit. From 6th Street in Leadville, head south on US 24 for about 4 miles. Go west on Highway 300 for three-quarters of a mile, and then south (left) on Lake CR 11 for 1.25 miles. Head west (right) on FR 110 for 5 miles, which will take you to the parking area at Halfmoon Campground.

South Mount Elbert Trail can be serene; it is seldom crowded. It is 5.5 miles to the summit, with a trailhead near Lakeview Campground. Go south on US 24, and then head west on Highway 82 for about 3.5 miles. Go north on Lake CR 24 for just over a mile to reach the parking area, just north of the campground.

With a 4,500-foot elevation gain, both trails should be attempted only by hikers who are in good shape and are knowledgeable about safety in hiking.

Southwestern Colorado

As you drive toward the southwestern corner of Colorado from the northeast, you have the chance to visit one of the most geologically unique areas on the continent. ***Great Sand Dunes National Park & Preserve*** is on the short list of "don't miss" places that both residents and visitors return to year after year, and for good reason. These dunes, the tallest in North America, at 750 feet high, run 8 miles in length at their longest point, covering 30 square miles in the main dune field.

The 150,000-acre park offers hiking, overnight camping, and birding here and in nearby wetlands such as in the San Luis State Wildlife Area. But most visitors come to climb the dunes. There are few experiences that can compare with being on them. Climb to the top of a ridge and take in the view of golden sandy waves stretching for miles to the distant Sangre de Cristo Mountains, then drop into a trough until you are in a valley surrounded by towering hills of sand. Stop and listen to the silence broken only by the wind as it pushes thousands of the tiny grains. Climb back several ridges into the dunes and you will be alone.

For more information contact the San Isabel National Forest, Leadville Ranger District, 810 Front St., Leadville 80461; (719) 486-0749; fs.usda.gov/psicc. Most visitors come during the hot months of July and August. Make sure you wear shoes to climb the dunes during this season—the sand can reach temperatures of 140°F. Save the bare feet for wading across the soft, water-cooled sand of ***Medano Creek.*** Flowing at the base of the dunes during the spring snowmelt, Medano Creek is one of the few places in the world to experience "surge flow," where creek water comes in rhythmic waves. The best times to experience surge flow depend on annual snow levels. The creek often begins flowing in March and may last until July or longer after a heavy-snowfall winter. After dry winters the creek may not even reach the main parking area.

Great Sand Dunes National Park & Preserve is located on Highway 150 in the south-central part of the state, just 16 miles off US 160, the main east–west highway through southern Colorado. Individuals age 17 or older pay a $3 entry fee. The site is open daily. The visitor center is also open daily except for federal holidays. Visitor center hours are 9 a.m. to 6 p.m. in summer and 9 a.m. to 4:30 p.m. or 5 p.m., as staffing permits, the rest of the year. The 88-site campground is available on a first-come, first-served basis, and fills up fast on summer weekends. Campers should come prepared to face gnats and hungry mosquitoes in late spring and early summer. For more information contact Great Sand Dunes National Park, 11999 Hwy. 150, Mosca 81146; (719) 378-6395; nps.gov/grsa.

Thirty-eight miles southwest of the park is ***Alamosa,*** a good overnight base for exploring the sand dunes. Each spring the town fills with birders

Southwest Colorado Overview

In the San Juan Range of southwest Colorado, piñons and junipers yield to spruce and aspen as you go up in elevation. The weather in towns like Durango and Cortez is remarkably mild year-round, despite copious snowfall in the heights. The mountains are always cooler than the lower, drier elevations, but usually comfortably so, especially in summer when days are short-sleeves warm, and a light blanket is de rigueur for sleeping at night.

As is common throughout Colorado, summer is the main tourist season in southwest Colorado, followed by the ski months of winter. **Caution:** Skiing through waist-deep, soft powder in the high, dry air on a typical sunny winter day may be addictive. The sun always comes out after a storm, so skiers sans jackets by noon are another common sight.

Colorado's legendary outdoor world has much to do with its geography. The state has 1,143 mountains rising to an altitude of at least 10,000 feet above sea level—and 1,000 are 2 miles high or more. Fifty-four often snow-crowned peaks towering above 14,000 feet give the state more than six times the mountain area of Switzerland. For more information on hiking and climbing the mountains, contact the Colorado Fourteeners Initiative at (303) 278-7650; 14ers.org.

eager to see the sandhill cranes and thousands of ducks and other waterfowl that stop at the Alamosa and Monte Vista National Wildlife Refuges, just southeast and northwest of town, respectively. The birds are celebrated during the *Monte Vista Crane Festival* (mvcranefest.org) in March. The *Luther Bean Museum and Art Gallery* (719-587-7151; adams.edu/lutherbean) in Richardson Hall at the Adams State College displays Native American and Hispanic pottery and textiles, European porcelain and furniture, and a changing exhibit of regional arts and crafts.

Twenty-six miles east of Alamosa on US 160 is *Fort Garland Museum Cultural Center* in a compound built in 1858 to protect settlers from Ute Indian resistance. Frontier scout Kit Carson was a post commander here, and the famous Buffalo Soldiers were stationed here from 1876 to 1879. The fort has been restored, and its rich history is depicted in the parade grounds, adobe buildings, and displays. The folk art and culture of southern Colorado's Hispanic community are also highlighted. The museum is open year-round; daily from 9 a.m. to 5 p.m., but check before going. For more information call (719) 379-3512 or visit historycolorado.org/museums.

trivia

Two thousand miles of trout-fishing streams and Colorado's largest lake are within driving range of Gunnison—excellent fishing!

Drive south from Fort Garland on Highway 159 for 16 miles and you'll come to **San Luis,** established in 1851 and the state's oldest town. The local Hispanic population worships at the original Sangre de Cristo Parish church. Of special interest to visitors and a famous Catholic pilgrimage site are the **Stations of the Cross,** a set of 15 bronze sculptures on the **Hill of Piety and Mercy** in town, representing the last hours in the life of Christ. The life-like statues line a cactus-strewn path leading up the hill to the domed, adobe **Chapel of All Saints.** The short but steep walk is peaceful, the sculptures are exquisite, and the surrounding scenery of juniper, piñon, and yucca is typical of the area. For more information drop by the visitor center at 408 Main St. or call (719) 672-3002.

From San Luis, drive west for 31 miles on Highway 142 to the village of **Manassa,** the home of 19th-century boxing champion Jack Dempsey. A small museum containing artifacts from his career is housed in the cabin where Dempsey was born.

When Highway 142 ends 3 miles farther west at Highway 285, turn left and travel south for 7 miles to Antonito. By now you're just a few miles from the New Mexico border. You're also at the start of one of America's most scenic narrow-gauge rail trips. The **Cumbres & Toltec Scenic Railroad** travels between Antonito and Chama, New Mexico, encountering tunnels, loops, trestles, gorges, rivers, forests, meadows, and spectacular scenery as it crosses the state border 11 times. This is the country's highest and longest coal-fired, steam-operated, narrow-gauge railroad, combining a great train ride with a truly historic artifact of the Old West. In 2012, the railroad was awarded National Historic Landmark designation. For more information call (888) 286-2737 or visit cumbrestoltec.com.

If you're traveling north from Alamosa, drive 13 miles north on Highway 17 to Mosca for one of Colorado's more unexpected wildlife encounters. The **Colorado Gators Reptile Park** (719-378-2612; coloradogators.com) is a working

Florissant Fossil Beds National Monument

One of the richest and most diverse fossil deposits in the world lies in this grassy mountain valley. Once a primeval rain forest, the area was covered by volcanic ash 30–40 million years ago, perfectly preserving insects, plants, and redwood stumps up to 14 feet wide. The visitor center with exhibits and a brief film is a good first stop before exploring the monument. There are 14 miles of trails and hourly ranger talks at the amphitheater during the summer. The monument is 2 miles south of the town of Florissant. For directions and more information, contact (719) 748-3253; nps.gov/flfo.

Highway of the Fourteeners

From Buena Vista, this 19-mile stretch of US 24 along the Collegiate Peaks Scenic Byway offers dramatic, close-up views of 10 of Colorado's 14,000-foot mountains. Nowhere else in the US will you see so many high peaks in one place. Allow about 30 minutes for the drive, more if you stop for photos.

tilapia fish farm and reptile sanctuary, and they serve as an animal rescue facility for unwanted or abused reptile pets. The geothermal pools here attract a variety of bird species, making it a popular spot for birders.

Located a few miles east of Highway 17 and nestled against the edge of the San Isabel National Forest just north of Great Sand Dunes National Park is a town unlike any other in Colorado. Formerly a small mining burg, **Crestone** and the surrounding area have developed into a spiritual and New Age center with representatives of a variety of world religions. Several Tibetan centers, a Zen Buddhist center, Hindu temple, Carmelite monastery, and a regular schedule of New Age events bring spiritual pilgrims to Crestone. Ecotourists come to hike the adjacent mountains. The town is popular with day-trippers, who visit the temples, wander around the few shops, browse the Saturday market, and walk through the village. While some visitors are quickly bored, others are content to slow down and embrace the quirky ambience of this tiny village.

Farther west on scenic US 160 and south of Wolf Creek Pass is **Pagosa Springs.** Named for the Ute word *Pagosa,* meaning "boiling water," Pagosa Springs has a continual supply of natural geothermal energy. Many a weary traveler has stopped for a day or more to soak in these healing waters at The Springs Resort and Spa and to enjoy nearby San Juan National Forest and Weminuche Wilderness. Nearby stables rent horses and lead trips. Fishing, mountain biking, and hiking are all options.

Another water wonder near Pagosa is **Treasure Falls.** This is the longest waterfall in the entire San Juan National Forest. The short hike is a perfect place to break up a long drive and stretch the legs. To get there, follow US 160 east for 15 miles toward scenic Wolf Creek summit. The parking lot and trailhead are on the right (east) side of the road. A short quarter-mile well-worn trail climbs 300 feet up the canyon through dense pine and oak forest to Colorado's mini-version of Niagara. For more information write to Pagosa Ranger District, 180 Pagosa St., PO Box 310, Pagosa Springs 81147; (970) 264-2268; fs.usda.gov/sanjuan.

To the west of Pagosa Springs stands a man-made wonder built a thousand years ago. The stone ruins of **Chimney Rock** were home to the ancestors of

Bureau of Land Management & US Forest Service

The Bureau of Land Management (BLM) administers millions of acres of public lands around the country, including 8.4 million acres in Colorado, while the US Forest Service (USFS) manages 14.3 million acres in the state. State offices for both organizations can direct you to specific regional and local offices, many of which are listed throughout this book as well. For more information, look on the USFS website—fs .usda.gov—or contact the USFS Rocky Mountain Regional Office at (303) 275-5350. For information about BLM lands in Colorado, visit co.blm.gov/index.htm or contact the BLM Colorado state office at (303) 239-3600.

the modern **Pueblo Indians** and are of great spiritual significance to these tribes. More than 200 homes and ceremonial buildings were constructed around the area, and archaeologists have found hundreds of individual sites. Named for the towering twin spires of natural stone that dominate the landscape, Chimney Rock provides expansive views to the far distance. Although Chimney Rock is a national monument, it's actually part of the US Forest Service. Chimney Rock is located 17 miles west of Pagosa Springs via US 160, and then southwest on Highway 151.

For information on activities led by guides and outfitters, visit recreation. gov/ticket/facility/234787. Interpretive programs at the monument provide insight into the rich history and culture of the area. For more information contact Chimney Rock Interpretive Association, PO Box 1662, Pagosa Springs 81147; (970) 883-2455 (May 15 through Sept 30) or (970) 731-7133 (off-season, Oct 1 through May 14); chimneyrockco.org. For more information about the Pagosa Springs area write to Pagosa Springs Area Chamber of Commerce, 105 Hot Springs Blvd., Pagosa Springs 81147; (970) 264-2360; pagosachamber.com.

Another 17 miles south past Chimney Rock on Highway 151, **Navajo State Park** is Colorado's version of Lake Powell. Sprawling Navajo Reservoir is surrounded by piñon and juniper hillsides that look more like New Mexico than Colorado. That's no surprise, since the reservoir extends 35 miles across the state line. Boating, fishing, hiking, biking, and camping keep visitors busy during the day, while quiet nights under starry skies promise a good night's sleep. For more information call (970) 883-2208 or visit cpw.state.co.us/placestogo/parks/Navajo.

The chute opens, and the cowboy holds on to the horse's riggings with one hand. The horse rears wildly, resenting the man on his back, hooves flailing in all directions, a bucking, pitching, twisting, snorting, wild-eyed animal. The cowboy's hat flies off and lands in the dust. He has been on the horse for

5 seconds now, and he still hangs on. Leaning back until his shoulder blades graze the animals back, the man's outstretched arm hits the horse's flank. Six seconds now. Seven. Eight.

The buzzer sounds and the cowboy jumps safely to the ground. Eight seconds of bareback riding can seem like 8 hours. In the early days of rodeo, the rider stayed in the saddle "until the horse was rode or the cowboy throwed." Today, the saddle bronc rider must stay aboard 8 seconds, while at the same time not disqualifying himself in any number of ways. It takes a tough person to ride at the rodeo.

These Western riding competitions are an important income source for some Colorado cowboys. Rodeo began in the 1700s with the vaqueros, Spanish cattlemen in the American West. In the 1800s, American cowboys would hold informal riding, roping, and cattle driving competitions. The sport caught on and became commercialized with the early efforts of entrepreneurs such as Buffalo Bill Cody and Will Rogers. By the 1970s rodeo turned professional, and today it is a big business, earning the top performers a comfortable living.

Every summer Colorado towns such as Leadville, Brush, Walden, Steamboat Springs, La Junta, Las Animas, Durango, Gunnison, Kiowa, Kremmling, Salida, and others are part of the rodeo circuit for a few days. Each offers a standard mix of bull riding, steer wrestling, bareback, team roping, and other events that compose this slice of true Americana. As you drive around the state, ask locally; there's bound to be a rodeo not too far away. For more information contact the ***Colorado Pro Rodeo Association*** at (719) 647-2828; colorado prorodeo.com.

Durango lies in the Animas River Valley against a backdrop of the San Juan Mountains. It's the largest town in southern Colorado, but with only 16,000 people, you'll quickly fall under its small-town charm. The lovingly preserved historic downtown area is filled with restaurants, art galleries, coffeehouses, and shops. Wander south from the intersection of 13th Avenue and Main past elegant buildings from the 1800s, then head east to 3rd Avenue, where an eclectic

Gunnison County Facts

- Gunnison County is part of two byways: West Elk Loop Scenic & Historic Byway and Silver Thread Scenic & Historic Byway.

- Crested Butte has the largest aspen grove in the US; see it when traveling over Kebler Pass, a gravel road that is closed in winter.

- Crested Butte is one of the birthplaces of mountain biking along with Marin County, California.

Colorful Locals

In the early days in Durango, there was a rowdy local set that went by the name of the Stockton-Eskridge Gang. These boys and a group of local vigilantes once fought an hour-long gun battle on the main street through town.

In 1885, locals set out on an expedition to New Mexico. Their goal? To "dig up Aztecs." Included in the supplies were five cases of tobacco, three cases of beer, 10 gallons of "heavy liquids," four burro-loads of "the stuff that busted Parliament," seven reels of fuse, soap, cigars, one fish line, rubber boots, bread, lard, and a pound of bacon.

Newspaperman Dave Day, the witty, often profane editor of the *Durango Democrat* in the 1890s, once had 42 libel suits pending against him.

In 1922 William Wood, city editor for the *Durango Herald,* was shot dead in front of the barber shop by Rod Day (son of former editor Dave Day), editor of the *Durango Democrat,* after a long squabble that started over Prohibition and reached a peak over the printing of a scandal. Never mind that the two papers merged six years later. Ah, the good old days.

mix of period homes and mansions line the street. With more restaurants per capita than San Francisco, the town takes pride in cuisines ranging from French and American Southwestern to sushi and Himalayan. Four brewpubs keep the town supplied with handcrafted, award-winning beers. The **Rocky Mountain Chocolate Factory** is based here, sending premium chocolate candies across the US and Canada. Held every Saturday morning from spring through fall, the **Durango Farmers' Market** is one of the best in the state.

But as inviting as the culinary scene may be, there's much more to do and see in the area. Start with a walk along the 7-mile-long Animas River Trail that goes through town and watch rafters, kayakers, and canoeists navigate the rapids. A 2-mile stretch of the Animas south of downtown has a Gold Medal designation water for fishing. Outside of town, more than 350 miles of trails await hikers, horseback riders, mountain bikers, wildflower enthusiasts, and anyone who enjoys stunning outdoor scenery.

With its mild climate and close proximity to some of the state's most stunning scenery, Durango is also known for the many festivals that fill the calendar. Ranging from bike races, river fests, and bluegrass gatherings to celebrations of beer, coffee, film, and motorcycles, the town is host to a wide variety of local festivals and community parties that welcome visitors. For a complete list go to durango.org.

Durango is the departure point for the **Durango & Silverton Narrow Gauge Railroad,** a heritage railway that takes passengers on a 45-mile, 7-hour

St. Elmo

Far up a dirt road, deep in the mountains of Chaffee County, lies the ghost of St. Elmo. This weathered ghost town, where creaking wooden sidewalks meander past splintered wooden buildings with false fronts, is among Colorado's best preserved.

Once a rollicking mining town, St. Elmo sits quietly in a wooded valley, home to hummingbirds and chipmunks. From Buena Vista take US 24 south for 8 miles to Nathrop, then CR 162 west for 16 miles. For more information see st-elmo.com.

round-trip to the historic mining town of **Silverton.** These steam-powered trains date back to the 1920s and before, and the nicely restored coaches and open-air cars allow you to enjoy the changing scenery. It's easily one of the classic Colorado sightseeing journeys. The train has both summer and winter schedules, as well as special event trains, with a range of prices depending on the class and several departures a day in summer. For more information contact the railroad at 479 Main Ave., Durango 81301; (970) 247-2733 or (877) 872-4607; durangotrain.com.

trivia

In December 1999, the city of Pueblo was astonished to find 17 trees on its Historic Arkansas Riverwalk of Pueblo (HARP) destroyed within a matter of days. The culprit? A Colorado beaver whom officials affectionately deemed "Bandit" before they relocated the creature to a place a little farther out of town

While traveling on the train, a number of guests get off at a stop partway to Silverton in order to experience one of Colorado's more thrilling activities. **Soaring Tree Top Adventures** is the largest canopy tour zip line course in the world, and the only way to get here is via the train. With 27 spans and more than 1.5 miles of zip line, the course takes guests through old-growth forests and over the Animas River on this daylong experience. The train ride, zip line experience, and a gourmet lunch are included in the price. Soaring Tree Top Adventures is open

Eat a Peach

Each summer from July through October, local farmers offer apples, cherries, peaches, pears, and apricots, often organically grown, at numerous roadside stands across Delta County. Delta and the nearby towns of Cedaredge and Paonia each host farmers' markets through the summer.

Agritourism

The Ancestral Puebloans of Mesa Verde were the first farmers in southwestern Colorado, laying the foundation for today's farmers and ranchers. These days the region produces a delectable variety of edibles, and visitors can choose from a wide range of activities to experience the agricultural products produced nearby, including farm and ranch visits and stays, farmers' markets, and restaurants. Here are a few to get you started:

Farm and Ranch Stays:

Canyon of the Ancients Guest Ranch, Cortez; (970) 565-4288; canyonoftheancients.com
Circle K Guest Ranch, Dolores; (970) 562-3826 or (800) 477-6381; ckranch.com
Majestic Dude Ranch, Mancos; (970) 533-7900; majesticduderanch.com

Farm and Ranch Visits:

Gunnison River Farms; Austin; (970) 835-3962
Jumpin' Goat Dairy, Buena Vista; (719) 395-4646; jumpingoodgoats.com
Mountain Goat Lodge, Salida; (719) 539-7173; mountaingoatlodge.com
Zapaata Ranch, The Nature Conservancy, Mosca; (719) 378-2356; ranchlands.com

Locally Produced Food Sources:

Carver Brewing Co., Durango; (970) 259-2545; carverbrewing.com
Dolores River Brewery, Dolores; (970) 882-4677; doloresriverbrewery.com
The Farm Bistro, Cortez; (970) 565-3834; thefarmbistrocortez.com
J. Fargo's Family Dining & Microbrewery, Cortez; (970) 564-0242; jfargos.com
Metate Room, Mesa Verde NP; (970) 529-4422; visitmesaverde.com

from mid-May through mid-Oct. For more information call (970) 769-2357 or visit soaringcolorado.com.

Anyone interested in experiencing an authentic Western rodeo should head to **La Plata County Fairgrounds** in Durango. Each summer the fairgrounds hosts a series of rodeos where spectators enjoy a variety of events, including bareback riding, saddle bronc riding, barrel racing, and the most dangerous sport in the world, bull riding. For information on summertime rodeos, contact Visit Durango at (800) 525-8855; durango.org.

Located 18 miles north of Durango on US 550, the year-round **Purgatory Resort** remains a secret to many Coloradans. This remote oasis has everything—nature, atmosphere, and amenities. In the summer months, guided horseback expeditions depart each day from the stables, bringing you into the one-million-acre San Juan National Forest. Fishing, river rafting, jeep tours into the high country, mountain biking, golfing, an alpine slide, and a day camp for kids are just a few of the activities. In winter, the resort is one of the state's classic ski mountains, with 88 trails, 5 terrain parks, 1,360 skiable acres, and an average of 240 inches of snowfall each year. As you ski around the mountain, you're surrounded by the spectacular scenery of the rugged San Juans. Other fun winter activities include snow tubing, Nordic skiing, snowshoeing, dogsledding, zip-lining, backcountry skiing, and snowmobiling. For more information contact Purgatory Resort, 1 Skier Place, Durango 81301; (970) 247-9000 or (800) 525-0892; purgatory.ski. For more information about Durango and surrounding areas contact Visit Durango at (800) 525-8855; durango.org.

Located 25 miles southeast of Durango in Ignacio, the **Southern Ute Cultural Center and Museum** depicts the history and culture of the Ute people through their eyes. Early rock art, a re-created camp scene, and the tumultuous time of reservations and boarding schools are a few of the subjects covered here. Priceless artifacts, permanent exhibits, a museum store offering Native American art and crafts, and a changing temporary gallery round out the center's offerings. Admission is $7 for adults, $4 for seniors, and $3 for children 3 to 14. Children under 3 are free. For more information call (970) 563-9583 or visit southernutemuseum.org.

Just 35 miles west of Durango is **Mesa Verde National Park.** With more than 4,700 archaeological sites in the park, this is an extraordinary place, made even better by the restraint with which the National Park Service has limited development. Aside from the narrow road, the museum and visitor center, a small restaurant and shop, and trails leading to the cliff dwellings, almost nothing here hints at the 21st century. Ravens and vultures drift across the ridges. Coyotes yip and howl on moonless nights. The fragrance of piñon and juniper sweetens the dry mesa air after a summer squall. The only things missing are the hundreds of people who called this place home some 800 years ago.

Mesa Verde is best known for its Ancestral Puebloan cliff dwellings. A UNESCO World Heritage Site, these structures represent an astonishing culture that thrived for 700 years in this harsh land. A good place to begin your visit is at the **Chapin Mesa Archeological Museum,** where you can see baskets, pottery, agricultural tools, and exhibits describing these first residents. At Far View Visitor Center you can purchase tickets for ranger-guided tours of the three main cliff dwelling areas. Self-guided tours to two of the cliff dwellings as well as several hiking trails are available for further exploration. Drive across Wetherill Mesa through the ponderosa, spruce, and juniper, stopping to explore the mesa-top sites and admire the views from various overlooks. Dawn and dusk offer quiet moments when the cliffs are bathed in warm, golden light.

Devote at least a full day to the park, two if possible. It is an 8-hour drive southwest of Denver and is about an hour and a half west of Durango on US

160, midway between Mancos and Cortez. About 500,000 visitors come here each year, with most of them visiting during the summer months. The park is open all year, with some activities closed during winter.

Mesa Verde National Park is open daily year-round. The park entry fee is $30 per vehicle in the summer season, $20 the rest of the year. The Mesa Verde Visitor and Research Center is open year-round; hours depend on the season. For park information call (970) 529-4465 or visit nps.gov/meve/index.htm. Camping is available at Morefield Campground, 4 miles inside the park, on a first-come, first-served basis. The campground is never full. Lodging is available at Far View Lodge. For more information call (800) 449-2288 or (970) 564-4300, or visit visitmesaverde.com.

When visiting Mesa Verde you're not far from the Four Corners area, where Colorado, Utah, New Mexico, and Arizona meet. The sky seems even bluer here against the red rock buttes, mesas, and canyons. Mesa Verde was the major population center for the Ancestral Puebloan people, but there were many communities scattered for hundreds of miles across the four-state area of Colorado, Utah, New Mexico, and Arizona. The remains of many are hidden in remote areas and can only be reached on foot. But others are vehicle accessible, and exploring them will increase your fascination for the culture that flourished here long ago.

A quieter, less known site west of Cortez is ***Hovenweep National Monument.*** Six Puebloan-era villages lie in a landscape of arroyos, mesas, and sage, straddling the Colorado-Utah border. With artistic skill that would rival a stonemason's today, ancient Pueblo Indians built these towers in several configurations. Round, square, and oval structures dot the canyon edge. Each rock was trimmed to fit exactly with its neighbor, and the lines of the buildings are straight and almost smooth. Small peepholes and keyhole entrances could have provided views of a possible enemy approaching or just been a way to keep an eye on the rest of the community. Hiking and interpretive trails link most structures. These towers and buildings were constructed around the same time as Mesa Verde, but the monument's solitude and fewer visitors make for a very different experience from the better-known park to the east. Allow at least a half day to explore the monument.

The ranger station is open year-round and operates a bookstore and a small museum. Bring your own food; there is none available. A small campground with picnic tables and water offers overnight stays. Hovenweek National Monument does not charge an entry fee. Call for directions; the only paved entrance is from Utah. Hovenweep is open year-round. The visitor center is open from 8 a.m. to 6 p.m. daily Apr through Sept and 8 a.m. to 5 p.m. the rest of the year (closed Thanksgiving, Christmas, and New Year's Day). For more information call (970) 562-4282 or visit nps.gov/hove/index.htm.

Telluride

Telluride is renowned for its breathtaking alpine beauty, but many people don't realize that the town lies in the center of the greatest diversity of geology and archaeology in the nation. This area, known as the **Grand Circle,** encompasses four states, numerous state and national parks, and a variety of topography from the Rocky Mountains to the Painted Desert.

For those with an interest in Native American culture, the city of **Cortez** is the gateway to both the **Southern Ute** and **Ute Mountain Ute Indian Reservations.** The **Ute Mountain Utes** are one of seven original Ute bands that once inhabited the entire state of Colorado. The Ute Mountain Tribal Park, set in a classic Southwestern landscape of mesas and canyons, contains an impressive collection of Ancestral Puebloan cliff dwellings, ruins, **petroglyphs,** and pictographs. Access is restricted to tours with Ute guides, who provide interpretation of the culture and history of these homelands.

The half-day tour visits petroglyphs, pictographs, scenic landmarks, and some surface archaeological sites. All sites on this tour are within easy walking distance of the gravel road. The full-day tour is more strenuous, including climbs up rock faces via a series of ladders and a 3-mile walk on unpaved trails. The reward is a visit to four well-preserved cliff dwellings.

Tours begin at the visitor center/museum, 20 miles south of Cortez at Highway Junction 160/491. For more information contact the Ute Mountain Tribal Park, PO Box 109, Towaoc 81334; (970) 565-9653; utemountaintribalpark.info/index.html.

trivia

For amateur geologists, most sand at Colorado's Great Sand Dunes is between 0.2 and 0.3 mm in diameter, composed of 51.7 percent volcanic rock fragments, 29.1 percent quartz, 8.9 percent feldspar, 2.5 percent sandstone, 0.7 percent magnetite, 3.4 percent other minerals, and 3.7 percent other rocks.

Highway 550 from Durango to Ouray passes though some of the state's most stunning mountain scenery. Climbing over Red Mountain Pass, the road switchbacks down into **Ouray,** often referred to as "The Switzerland of America." As you drive into town and gaze up at the soaring mountain peaks on all sides, you'll understand why. Nestled in a narrow river valley, the town is also blessed with hot springs. The **Ouray Hot Springs and Pool** (1220 Main St.; 970-325-7073) has a large pool partitioned into different sections, each with a different temperature. Every area comes with views of the surrounding peaks. The **Wiesbaden Hot Springs** (625 5th St.; 970-325-4347; wiesbadenhotsprings

Hot Springs

Set along the banks of the San Juan River, Pagosa Springs offers numerous thera-peutic, mineral-rich pools for soaking weary muscles after a long day of skiing, backpacking, golfing, or driving. Two spas in the middle of town offer day rates and overnight accommodations. For more information, call (970) 264-2360 or go to pagosachamber.com.

.com) is a small natural hot springs spa and lodge with an outdoor swimming pool, private outdoor spa with soaking pool, and vapor cave.

Ouray is also known for the many jeep trails in the mountains surrounding town. Four-wheel-drive routes such as Imogene, Engineer, and Black Bear Passes are so popular that during the colorful autumn foliage season traffic jams sometimes develop. You don't need to be an off-road expert to enjoy these high-altitude trips; several companies in town offer tours into the back-country to experience some of Colorado's most dramatic mountain terrain. When the tour is over, return to town for an ice-cream cone while browsing the many boutiques, galleries, and restaurants along Main Street.

At the edge of town, **_Box Canyon Waterfall & Park_** (30 Box Canyon Rd.; 970-325-7080) has several short trails leading into a deep box canyon carved out of limestone by Canyon Creek. It's a nice place to picnic, and exhib-its at the visitor center explain the geology, wildlife, and history of the area.

Down the road in Ridgeway, **_Orvis Hot Springs_** (1585 CR 3; 970-626-5324; orvishotsprings.com) is a clothing-optional natural hot springs resort with four outdoor soaking pools, an indoor pool, and two private tubs. Lodging is also available here, and room guests have access to the pools all night. One of the valley's many pleasures is lying in the hot pools at night under a sky filled with sparkling stars.

Whenever the Rio Grande Southern rolled into the **_Telluride_** station back in the boomtown days of the early 1900s, legend has it that the conduc-tor would yell, "To hell you ride!" reminding passengers of the jarring, dusty journey they'd just completed. These days most people arriving at this former gold-mining town think they've pulled into paradise. Nestled in a box canyon where waterfalls roar down from surrounding peaks, Telluride sparkles as one of Colorado's crown jewels.

The town has two personas. In winter, heavy snowfall makes it a deep-powder ski destination. But when the snows melt each spring, wild-flowers bloom, hummingbirds return, and Telluride becomes a sun-drenched alpine village where festivals, fun, and a funky mountain atmosphere drive away winter's chill.

At less than a mile long, the place is made for walking. Victorian buildings line Main Street. While the brothels and gambling dens are gone and the saloons have lost their rough edges, the town offers delights and distractions those miners never imagined. Throughout the summer, festivals celebrate everything from jazz, blues, and bluegrass to wine, film, and mushrooms.

Colorful shops, cafe bakeries, galleries, and bookstores provide plenty of low-volume entertainment. But sometimes paradise means nothing more than a morning latte and a comfortable bench along Main Street to watch the local color and wonder whether it's true that there are more dogs than residents in Telluride.

With rugged mountains on all sides, there are plenty of reasons to leave the pavement. The *San Miguel River Trail* follows the river for 2.7 easy miles.

Bridal Veil Falls, the tallest free-falling waterfall in Colorado, can be reached via a steeper hike of 1.8 miles. For an easier route and a panoramic view, ride the free 12-minute gondola from town up to *Mountain Village,* Telluride's upscale sister hamlet. Once there, ogle the sky-high real estate, or take off on one of many hiking and biking trails that start here.

Telluride's gold-rush era left numerous high country roads, and today those tracks lead to weathered mining ruins. Local companies offer jeep tours to Tomboy and Alta ghost towns, Imogene and Ophir Passes, and points beyond.

Experienced 4x4 enthusiasts can buy a detailed map and take off on their own past flower-filled meadows to panoramic vistas. For more information call (888) 605-2578 or check out telluride.com.

trivia

Although Pagosa Springs water is used primarily for bathing, some of the hotter springs, at 153°F, are used for energy to heat houses and buildings.

The name says "bluegrass," but don't let that fool you. The famous *Telluride Bluegrass Festival* may be one of the country's most progressive bluegrass gatherings, but expect to hear folk, rock, blues, country, pop, Celtic, world beat, and just about everything in between. Set in the box canyon amid soaring mountains, the four-day event takes place at one of the most spectacular locations in America. When it's time for a break from the music, Telluride is a short stroll away, where eclectic eateries, galleries, coffeehouses, quirky shops, and bars await in the Victorian-era historic district. As a true Colorado tradition with stunning scenery, superb music, and plenty of friendly folks, this festival is a national treasure. Call (800) 624-2422 or visit bluegrass.com/telluride.

Places to Stay in Southern Colorado

ALAMOSA

Hampton Inn Alamosa
710 Mariposa St.
(719) 480-6023
hilton.com/en/hotels/
alscohx-hampton-
alamosa-co
Moderate
Modern, clean, with free
Wi-Fi and breakfast.

Holiday Inn Express & Suites
3418 Mariposa
(719) 589-4026
Moderate
Newer hotel with upgraded
rooms, free wireless
internet, and breakfast.
Pets allowed.

ALMONT

Almont Resort
10209 N. Hwy. 135
(970) 641-4009
almontresort.com
Moderate to Expensive
Historic lodge and cabins
at the headwaters of the
Gunnison River offering
fishing, horseback riding,
rafting, skiing, mountain
biking, and more on 90
acres.

Harmel's on the Taylor
6748 CR 742
(970) 641-1740 or
(800) 235-3402
harmels.com
Moderate to Expensive
Ranch resort at the
confluence of 3 rivers

offering rafting, fly fishing,
horseback riding, and
gourmet meals.

Three Rivers Resort
130 CR 742
(970) 641-1303 or
(888) 761-FISH
3riversresort.com
Inexpensive
Cabins on the Taylor
River with fishing, rafting,
kayaking, and mountain
relaxation.

BUENA VISTA

Best Western Vista Inn
733 US 24 North
(800) 809-3495 or
(719) 395-8009
bestwestern.com/vista
innbuenavista
Moderate
Breakfast included, friendly
staff, free high-speed
internet, dependable
Best Western amenities,
and pool.

Cottonwood Springs Hot Springs Inn & Spa
18999 CR 306, 5.5 miles
west of Buena Vista
(719) 395-6434
cottonwood-hot-springs
.com
Inexpensive to Moderate
Lodge and cabin room
rates include use of hot
springs pools.

Surf Chateau
1028 Wave St.
(719) 966-7048
surfchateau.com
Expensive
Overlooking the Arkansas
River, this design-centric
hotel offers upscale
hospitality and outdoor

adventures just beyond the
doors.

CAÑON CITY

America's Best Value Inn & Suites Cañon City
1925 Fremont Dr.
(719) 275-3377
americasbestvalueinn.com
Inexpensive
Affordable, hot tub and
pool, complimentary
wireless internet.

Parkview Inn Motel
231 Royal Gorge Blvd.
(719) 275-0624
parkviewinnmotel.com
Inexpensive
Located across from
the Royal Gorge Route
Railroad, this place is clean,
quiet, and a good value,
with free wireless internet
and friendly owners.

Royal Gorge Cabins at Echo Canyon
45054 W. US 50
(800) 748-2953
royalgorgecabins.com
Expensive
Across the road from Echo
Canyon River Expeditions,
these luxury cabins meld
upscale lodging with
outdoor adventure for
singles, couples, and
families. Glamping tents are
available, too. Royal Gorge
Bridge & Park and Royal
Gorge Dinosaur Experience
are a short drive away.

COLORADO SPRINGS

Antlers Hilton Colorado Springs
4 S. Cascade Ave.
(719) 955-5600

antlers.com
Moderate
Four-diamond hotel in downtown within walking distance to restaurants, shops, museums, and clubs, with complimentary wireless internet, guest access to a fully equipped health club, and it's dog-friendly.

The Broadmoor
1 Lake Ave.
(719) 623-5112 or
(855) 634-7711
broadmoor.com
Expensive
Among Colorado's top resort hotels, historic, luxurious, with a championship golf course and a choice location nestled against the foothills of the Rockies.

Holden House 1902 Bed & Breakfast Inn
1102 W. Pikes Peak
(719) 471-3980 or
(888) 565-3980
holdenhouse.com
Moderate
Long-established B&B with 6 guest suites on a residential street, free wireless internet, and afternoon wine social.

Kinship Landing
415 S. Nevada Ave.
(719) 203-9309
kinshiplanding.com
Inexpensive to Expensive
Locally owned, sustainably run hotel near downtown with private rooms, dorm-style rooms, and even camping decks for added adventure.

Mining Exchange
8 S. Nevada Ave.
(719) 323-2000
wyndhamhotels.com/
wyndham-grand/colorado-
springs-colorado/
the-mining-exchange-a-
wyndham-grand-hotel
Expensive
Historic hotel, beautifully renovated in the heart of downtown Colorado Springs. Relax in overstuffed sofas and chairs to people-watch.

Old Town Guesthouse Bed & Breakfast
115 S. 26th St.
(719) 632-9194 or
(888) 375-4210
oldtown-guesthouse.com
Moderate
Clean and contemporary lodging in a centrally located historic building, with an evening wine/beer reception.

Rodeway Inn & Suites Garden of the Gods
1623 S. Nevada Ave.
(719) 623-2300
rodewayinn.com, then enter "Colorado Springs" in search field.
Inexpensive to Moderate
Affordable, free wireless internet, pet-friendly.

CORTEZ

Best Western Turquoise Inn and Suites
535 E. Main St.
(970) 565-3778 or
(800) 547-3376
bestwestern.com
Moderate
Spacious, clean rooms

in a pet-friendly inn, with outdoor heated pool and complimentary hot breakfast.

Holiday Inn Express Mesa Verde–Cortez
2121 E. Main St.
(970) 565-6000 or
(888) HOLIDAY
igh.com/holidayinnexpress/
hotels
Moderate
Clean, comfortable, and friendly, with on-site restaurant serving Southwestern cuisine.

CRAWFORD

Smith Fork Ranch
45362 Needle Rock Rd.
(970) 921-3454
smithforkranch.com
Expensive
All-inclusive luxury guest ranch in Gunnison National Park with gourmet cuisine amid mountains, rivers, lakes, and stunning views.

CRESTED BUTTE

Cristiana Guesthaus
621 Maroon Ave.
(888) 606-5326 or
(970) 349-5326
cristianaguesthaus.com
Moderate
Cozy bed-and-breakfast lodge located 1 block from shops and restaurants in the main business district.

Elk Mountain Lodge
129 Gothic Ave.
(970) 349-7533 or
(800) 374-6521
elkmountainlodge.com
Moderate
Historic hotel, completely

renovated, includes full breakfast, wireless internet, indoor hot tub, bar, and sunroom.

Old Town Inn
708 6th St.
(888) 349-6184
oldtowninn.net
Moderate
Good-value lodging with hearty continental breakfast, an outdoor hot tub; close to historic downtown shops and restaurants. Free wireless internet, pet-friendly.

Purple Mountain Lodge Bed and Breakfast
714 Gothic Ave.
(970) 349-5888
purplemountainlodge.com
Moderate to Expensive
Quiet 6-room B&B, with hot tub and day spa. Staff happily offers recommendations on local activities. No children under 12.

CRIPPLE CREEK

Carr Manor
350 E. Carr Ave.
(719) 689-3709
carrmanor.com
Moderate to Expensive
Luxury historic inn with full breakfast, evening coffee, tea, and cookies, free Wi-Fi, and 14 uniquely decorated rooms.

Gold King Mountain Inn
601 E. Galena Ave.
(719) 689-2600 or
(800) 445-3607
playwildwood.com/hotel
Moderate
Part of Wildwood Casino,

so discount packages are available for breakfast, dinner, and casino gaming.

Imperial Casino Hotel
123 N. 3rd St.
(719) 689-2561
imperialhotelrestaurant.com
Moderate
Restored historic Victorian hotel and restaurant with authentic Old West atmosphere.

J.P. McGill's Hotel and Casino
232 Bennett Ave.
(719) 689-2446 or
(800) 635-5825
triplecrowncasinos.com
Moderate
Located above the casino floors, this place was nicely remodeled, with free Wi-Fi and plush pillow-top mattresses.

DELTA COUNTY

The Bross Hotel B&B
312 Onarga Ave. (Paonia)
(970) 527-6776
brosshotel.com
Moderate
Turn-of-the-20th-century 10-room hotel richly appointed with period antiques and remodeled with modern amenities. Full breakfast, expansive views from guest rooms.

The Cedaredge Lodge
810 N. Grand Mesa Dr.
(Hwy. 65), Cedaredge
(970) 856-3728
thecedarlodge.com
Inexpensive to Moderate
Relaxing, cozy lodge with hot tub, loaner bikes, an outdoor cooking space,

massage service, and creekside lounging areas.

DURANGO

Antlers on the Creek Bed & Breakfast
999 Lightner Creek Rd.
(970) 259-1565
facebook.com/
antlersonthecreek
Moderate to Expensive
Luxury mountain B&B with 7 rooms. Rates include breakfast, complimentary Wi-Fi, and a complimentary happy hour.

Bear Paw Lodge at Vallecito Lake
18011 CR 501 (Bayfield)
(970) 884-2508
bearpawlodge.com
Moderate
Affordable seasonal cabins on a scenic lake in the San Juan National Forest with easy access to fishing and hiking.

General Palmer Hotel
567 Main Ave.
(970) 247-4747 or
(800) 523-3358
generalpalmerhotel.com
Moderate
Victorian-style hotel blending antique furnishings with modern amenities.

Purgatory Resort
1 Skier Place
(970) 247-9000 or
(800) 525-0892
purgatory.ski
Expensive
Located at Purgatory ski area; wide variety of year-round outdoor activities.

Rochester Hotel
726 E. 2nd Ave.
(970) 764-0035
rochesterhotel.com
Expensive
Boutique hotel located
in a quiet area 1 block
from Main Street galleries,
shops, restaurants,
museums.

Siesta Motel
3475 Main Ave.
(970) 247-0741 or
(877) 314-0741
durangosiestamotel.com
Inexpensive to Moderate
Family owned and
operated offering free WiFi,
picnic area, grills, and a
welcome to dogs.

The Strater Hotel
699 Main Ave.
(970) 247-4431 or
(800) 247-4431
strater.com
Moderate to Expensive
Beautifully restored historic
downtown hotel with
adjoining eating options
at Diamond Belle Saloon,
Office Spiritorium, and
Mahogany Grille.

GREAT SAND DUNES

Great Sand Dunes Lodge
7900 Hwy. 150 North
(Mosca)
(719) 378-2900
gsdlodge.com
Inexpensive to Moderate
Conveniently located by
park entrance, with heated
indoor pool and free
wireless internet.

GUNNISON

**Holiday Inn Express &
Suites**
910 E. Tomichi Ave.
(970) 641-1228 or
(888) 5465-4329
hiexpress.com
Moderate
Dependable Holiday
Inn standards, with
free breakfast, a fitness
center, heated indoor
pool and whirlpool, and
complimentary wireless
internet.

Inn at Tomichi Village
41883 US 50
(970) 641-1131
theinntv.com
Inexpensive to Moderate
Nicely appointed rooms
in a boutique hotel offer a
slew of amenities including
large flat-screen TVs,
complimentary breakfast,
indoor pool and hot tub,
and one of Gunnison's best
new restaurants.

Island Acres Resort Motel
38339 W. US 50
(970) 641-1442
islandacresresort.com
Inexpensive
Cabin-like motel units in
a relaxed atmosphere
on 3 acres filled with
large cottonwood trees.
Individually decorated
rooms combine 1950s
charm with Gunnison's
history. Green motel facility,
pet-friendly.

Lost Canyon Resort
8264 Hwy. 135
(970) 641-0181
facebook.com/
people/Lost-Canyon-

Resort/100069905544194
Inexpensive to Moderate
Quiet, rustic cabins on
the Gunnison River, fully
supplied with bedding,
linens, and kitchen utensils.
Free wireless internet,
pet-friendly.

LEADVILLE

Delaware Hotel
700 Harrison Ave.
(719) 486-1418
delawarehotel.com
Moderate to Expensive
Historic hotel with a ghost
or two. Bought in 2021,
the new owners are making
improvements large and
small.

**Grand West Village
Resort**
999 Grand West Dr.
(800) 691-3999 or
(719) 486-0702
grandwest.com
Expensive
Lodge-style condominiums
with fully equipped
kitchens, fireplaces, and
laundry.

MANITOU SPRINGS

El Colorado Lodge
23 Manitou Ave.
(719) 685-5485 or
(800) 782-2246
el-colorado-lodge.com
Inexpensive to Moderate
Historic lodge with
Southwestern-style adobe
cabins, heated swimming
pool, hot tub, outdoor
recreation.

**Red Crags
Bed-and-Breakfast Inn**
302 El Paso Blvd.

(719) 685-4515 or
(800) 685-4515
redcrags.com
Moderate
Historic Victorian mansion
B&B located on a bluff
with expansive views of
Manitou Valley. All room
have king beds, most have
fireplaces. Outdoor Jacuzzi,
private picnic area, and
barbecue pit.

Rocky Mountain Lodge and Cabins
4680 Hagerman Ave.,
Cascade
(719) 684-2521
rockymountainlodge.com
Moderate
Six bedrooms, separate
cottage and cabin lodging,
a great room with massive
fireplace, an outdoor
hot tub, and gourmet
breakfast.

The Cliff House
306 Canon Ave.
(719) 785-1000
thecliffhouse.com
Expensive
Historic hotel, beautifully
restored in the heart of
downtown Manitou Springs
within easy walk of local
hot spots.

Town-N-Country Cottages
123 Crystal Park Rd.
(719) 685-5427 or
(800) 366-3509
townncountryc.com
Moderate
Quaint cottages in a quiet,
tree-filled setting, with a
heated pool and hot tub.

MESA VERDE

Far View Lodge
At Navajo Hill; in the park
15 miles from entrance
(800) 449-2288
visitmesaverde.com/
lodging-camping/far-view-
lodge
Inexpensive to Moderate
Open Apr to Oct.
Breathtaking views, private
balcony with all rooms,
Western decor, excellent
dining at adjacent Metate
Room. Book in advance.

MONTROSE

Black Canyon Motel
1605 E. Main St.
(970) 249-3495 or
(800) 348-3495
blackcanyonmotel.com
Inexpensive to Moderate
Complimentary breakfast,
pool and hot tub, grassy
picnic area.

Country Lodge
1624 E. Main St.
(970) 249-4567
countrylodgecolorado.com
Inexpensive
Individually decorated
rooms, hot tub, pool and
gardens, wireless internet.

Red Arrow Inn & Suites
1702 E. Main St.
(970) 249-9641
redarrowinnsuites.com
Moderate
Nice complimentary
breakfast, spacious rooms
and friendly staff.

MT. CRESTED BUTTE

Crested Butte Mountain Resort
(877) 547-5143

skicb.com
The go-to source for
lodging on the mountain
and around Mt. Crested
Butte.

Elevation Hotel & Spa
500 Gothic Rd.
(970) 251-3000
elevationresort.com
Expensive
Luxury ski-in/ski-out resort
property combines cozy ski
lodge feel with hip urban
decor.

Grand Lodge Crested Butte
6 Emmons Rd.
(877) 547-5143
skicb.com/plan-your-trip/
stay/crested-butte-lodging.
aspx
Moderate
Full-service affordable and
pet-friendly hotel close
to ski lifts, with spacious
rooms, heated indoor and
outdoor pools, hot tub.

Lodge at Mountaineer Square
620 Gothic Rd.
(877) 547-5143
skicb.com/Plan-Your-
Trip/stay/details/
The-Lodge-at-Mountaineer-
Square?location=569191
Moderate
Luxury ski resort
accommodations 50 yards
from slopes for winter or
summer.

Nordic Inn
14 Treasury Rd.
(970) 349-5542 or
(800) 542-7669
nordicinncb.com
Inexpensive to Moderate
Family-owned lodge

with outdoor hot tub, free wireless internet, a fireplace in the lobby, and continental breakfast.

West Wall Lodge
14 Hunter Hill Rd.
(877) 547-5143
westwalllodge.com
Expensive
Luxury condos.

OURAY

St. Elmo Hotel
426 Main St.
(970) 325-4951
stelmohotel.com
Moderate to Expensive
Historic hotel lovingly restored with turn-of-the-20th-century furnishings, sauna, and hot tub. Breakfast included.

Timber Ridge Lodge
1550 Main St.
(970) 325-4856
timberridgelodgeouray.com
Inexpensive to Moderate
Near downtown and Ouray hot springs, with free Wi-Fi. Pets allowed.

Twin Peaks Lodge & Hot Springs
125 3rd Ave.
(970) 325-4427 or
(877) 863-6478
twinpeakslodging.com
Moderate
Hot springs soaking pool, full hot breakfast, pet-friendly, and 4-wheel drive Jeeps available for rent on property (reserve before arrival if possible).

Wiesbaden Hot Springs Spa & Lodging
625 5th St.

(970) 325-4347
wiesbadenhotsprings.com
Moderate
Rooms include access to hot springs, vapor cave, outdoor pool, and discounts on spa services.

PAGOSA SPRINGS

The Springs Resort & Spa
323 Hot Springs Blvd.
(800) 225-0934
pagosahotsprings.com
Expensive
All rooms come with 24-hour complimentary access to the soaking pools on arrival and departure days.

Club Wyndham Pagosa
42 Pinon Causeway
(970) 731-8000
clubwyndham.com
Inexpensive to Moderate
One- and two-bedroom fully furnished condos with kitchen, washer, dryer, and free wireless internet.

PUEBLO

Days Inn by Wyndham
4201 N. Elizabeth
(719) 543-8031
wyndhamhotels.com/days-inn
Inexpensive to Moderate
Affordable, with continental breakfast and free wireless internet.

Santa Fe Inn & Suites
730 N. Santa Fe Ave.
(719) 543-6530
santafeinnpueblo.com
Inexpensive
Complimentary breakfast, newly remodeled rooms,

seasonal pool, free wireless internet, pet-friendly.

RIDGWAY

Chipeta Solar Springs Resort & Spa
304 S. Lena St.
(800) 633-5868
chipeta.com
Moderate to Expensive
Adobe-style boutique resort retreat with unique rooms, hot pools, spa, yoga and fitness center, and Four Corners Cafe.

SALIDA

Amigo Motor Lodge
7350 US 50
(855) 729-0465
amigomotorlodge.com
Moderate
Accommodations include traditional motor lodge guest rooms done up with Southwest flair and impeccably designed Airstream trailors, for a nostalgic yet thoroughly modern and hip aesthetic.

Blue Coyote Ranch
6720 CR 104
(719) 539-2002
bluecoyoteranch.com
Moderate to Expensive
A converted Tudor mansion offers traditional inn rooms; cabins tucked into the pines sleep 6. Innkeepers are around if you need them, but this is mostly a self-service model.

Woodland Motel
903 W. 1st St.
(719) 539-4980
woodlandmotel.net
Inexpensive to Moderate

Close to downtown historic district, clean, pet-friendly accommodations with free wireless internet. Some units have kitchens.

TELLURIDE

Hotel Columbia
301 W. San Juan Ave.
(970) 728-0660 or
(877) 686-4834
hotelcolumbiatelluride.com
Expensive
Modern boutique hotel offering luxury accommodations with excellent hospitality, good location across the street from main ski resort gondola, and excellent complimentary European-style hot breakfast.

Lumiere with Inspirato
118 Lost Creek Ln.
(970) 369-0400
lumierewithinspirato.com
Expensive
Luxury boutique hotel with plush furnishings, designer decor, and free wireless internet.

Mountain Lodge
457 Mountain Village Blvd.
(970) 369-5000
mountainlodgetelluride.com
Moderate to Expensive
Upscale hotel suites and condo rentals at the ski slope, with an outdoor deck with a heated pool and Jacuzzi, concierge services, and free wireless internet.

New Sheridan
231 W. Colorado Ave.
(970) 728-4351 or

(800) 200-1891
newsheridan.com
Moderate
Telluride's newest "old" hotel with rich historic ambience and renovated guest rooms; home to the New Sheridan Bar and Chop House restaurant.

Places to Eat in Southern Colorado

ALAMOSA

Calvillo's Mexican Restaurant
400 Main St.
(719) 587-5500
calvillosmexicanrestaurant.
wordpress.com/menu
Inexpensive to Moderate
Authentic Mexican cuisine and occasional mariachi music at this local favorite.

Milagro's Coffeehouse
529 Main St.
(719) 589-9299
milagroscoffeehouse.org
Inexpensive
Friendly local coffeehouse with all proceeds going to a local shelter. Excellent coffee, breakfast, and pastries.

San Luis Valley Brewing Co.
631 Main St.
(719) 587-2337
slvbrewco.com
Inexpensive to Moderate
Good selection of handcrafted beers and a diverse menu of quality

pub entrees, salads, and appetizers.

ALMONT

Almont Resort
10209 Hwy. 135
(970) 641-4009
almontresort.com
Inexpensive to Moderate
Two dining rooms offering fireside dining and homemade food in a friendly atmosphere.

Three Rivers Resort Smokehouse
(seasonal)
130 CR 742
(970) 641-1303 or
(888) 761-3474
3riversresort.com
Moderate
Breakfast, lunch, and dinner served indoors or on the outside patio.

BUENA VISTA

Asian Palate
328 E. Main St.
theasianpalate.com
Moderate
Full sushi bar, Thai and Asian cuisine. Free wireless internet.

Brown Dog Coffee Company
713 US 24
(719) 395-2634
browndogcoffee.com
Inexpensive
Local coffeehouse with good coffee and teas, kombucha, and more.

Eddyline Restaurant at South Main
926 South Main
(719) 966-6000

eddylinebrewing.com
Moderate
Buena Vista's premier brewery runs an excellent restaurant with salads, pastas, burgers, and more. Eddyline's excellent beers are available, but so too are wines, whiskey, and other spirits.

CAÑON CITY/ROYAL GORGE

8 Mile Bar & Grill
45000 W. US 50
(800) 755-3746
raftecho.com/8-mile-bar-grill
Moderate
Echo Canyon River Expeditions' casual eatery raises the bar on rafting company restaurants by miles. The food is excellent, the menu diverse, the beverage options expansive.

Canon City Queen Anne
813 Macon Ave.
(719) 275-5354
thecanoncityqueenanne.com
Expensive
Reservations are a must. High tea—scones and Devonshire cream— is combined with a multicourse dinner, including soup, salad, entree (steak, salmon, prime rib and more), sides and dessert.

Le Petit Chablis Restaurant & Bakery
512 Royal Gorge Blvd.
(719) 269-3333
lepetitchablis.com

Expensive
Homemade breads and pastries along with classic French cuisine and New Orleans–inspired dishes.

Pizza Madness
509 Main St.
(719) 276-3088
mypizzamadness.com
Inexpensive to Moderate
Award-winning, handcrafted pizza, fresh salads, calzones, fresh baked sandwiches, and microbrews.

COLORADO SPRINGS

Carlos Bistro
1025 S. 21st St.
(719) 471-2905
carlosbistrocos.com
Expensive
Italian/Mediterranean bistro with excellent food and service, praised by locals.

Edelweiss
34 E. Ramona Ave.
(719) 633-2220
edelweissrest.com
Inexpensive to Moderate
Authentic Old World German dishes including schnitzel, bratwurst, and sauerbraten along with traditional continental fare.

Four by Brother Luck
321 N. Tejon St.
(719) 434-2741
fourbybrotherluck.com
Moderate to Expensive
Local celebrity chef Brother Luck "Beat Bobby Flay," was a finalist on *Chopped*, and was a favorite on *Top Chef*. Four celebrates the four main providers who

supply their ingredients; the hunter, the gatherer, the fisherman, and the farmer.

Golden Bee at the Broadmoor
1 Lake Ave.
(719) 577-5776
broadmoor.com
Moderate to Expensive
British pub offers freshly prepared pub food paired with English and Irish draft beers. Nightly entertainment includes sing-alongs 9 p.m. to midnight.

La Baguette French Bistro
4440 N. Chestnut St.
(719) 599-0686
labaguettefrenchbistro.com
Inexpensive
European deli and bakery.

La Casita Mexican Grill
(3 locations)
3725 E. Woodmen Rd.
(719) 536-0375
4295 N. Nevada Ave.
(719) 599-7829
306 S. 8th St.
(719) 633-9616
Inexpensive to Moderate
Award-winning, made-from-scratch Mexican food using fresh ingredients.

Marigold Cafe & Bakery
4605 Centennial Blvd.
(719) 599-4776
marigoldcafeandbakery.com
Moderate
French bistro–inspired menu coupled with an in-house bakery make this a local favorite.

CORTEZ

Metate Room
(Mesa Verde National Park)
(602) 331-5210 or
(800) 449-2288
nps.gov/meve/planyour
visit/restaurants.htm
Moderate to Expensive
Award-winning restaurant
serving contemporary
cuisine inspired by
Ancestral Puebloan
regional heritage foods and
flavorings.

Silver Bean Coffee Shop
410 W. Main St.
(970) 946-4404
Inexpensive
Tastefully kitschy roadside
attraction and coffee shop
in an Airstream trailer.

CRESTED BUTTE

Camp 4 Coffee
402½ Elk St.
(also a location in Crested
Butte South)
(970) 349-5258
camp4coffee.com
Inexpensive
Coffee, smoothies,
and more.

Marchitelli's Gourmet Noodle
411 3rd St.
(970) 349-7401
marchitellisgourmetnoodle.
com
Moderate to Expensive
Wide variety of Italian
pastas and entrees.

Pitas in Paradise
302 Elk Ave.
(970) 349-0897
pitasinparadise.com
Inexpensive
Mediterranean-style cafe
with gyros, rice bowls,
salads, milk shakes, and a
wide range of pitas.

Secret Stash
303 Elk Ave.
(970) 349-6245
secretstash.com
Moderate
Gourmet pizzeria, exotic
specialty drinks, and cool
local ambience.

The Slogar
517 2nd St.
(970) 349-5765
slogarcb.com
Moderate
A longtime favorite in
town, new owners bought
The Slogar in 2018. Not
to worry, the fab fried
chicken is still a staple,
along with steak, ribs, and
a vegetarian option for
a main course, and you
still get a first course and
a dessert, too. The wine
and cocktail programs
have been improved and
expanded, and most
everything is made from
scratch.

Soupcon Bistro
127A Elk Ave.
(970) 349-5448
soupconcb.com
Expensive
Four-course tasting menu
is an extravaganza of
tastes and textures with
French and American
inspiration.

CRIPPLE CREEK

Maggie's
300 E. Bennett Ave.
(719) 689-3977
Inexpensive
American fare in a
family-friendly setting.

DURANGO

Carver Brewing Co.
1022 Main Ave.
(970) 259-2545
carverbrewing.com
Moderate
A popular local spot for
breakfast, lunch, and
dinner in a friendly brewpub
atmosphere with a sunny
outdoor patio.

Chimayo Stone-Fired Kitchen
862 Main Ave.
(970) 259-2749
chimayodurango.com
Moderate to Expensive
Shared plates, stone-fired
pizzas, Mexican, fish and
veggies dishes.

636 Main Ave
636 Main Ave.
(970) 385-1810
636mainave.com
Moderate to Expensive
Excellent contemporary
American cuisine with lots
of meat and fish dishes
combining intriguing flavors
and accompaniments.
Some vegetarian options
and an expansive
specialty martini menu
for the sophisticated or
adventurous.

Seasons Rotisserie & Grill
764 Main Ave.
(970) 382-9790
seasonsofdurango.com
Moderate to Expensive
Wood-burning grill
is the centerpiece of
this restaurant serving
simple dishes with fresh

ingredients. Extensive cheese and salumi selections.

Steamworks Brewing Company
801 E. 2nd Ave.
(970) 259-9200 or
(877) 372-9200
steamworksbrewing.com
Inexpensive to Moderate
Gastropub fare includes regionally raised meats, sustainable seafood, salads, pizza, Southwestern-style dishes, and vegetarian entrees.

FAIRPLAY

Millonzi's Restaurant
501 Front St.
(719) 836-9501
millonzisrestaurant.com
Moderate
Wide range of Italian favorites and a nicely affordable wine list.

GUNNISON

Blackstock Bistro
122 W. Tomichi Ave.
(970) 641-4394
blackstockbistro.com
Moderate to Expensive
The menu is divided into Big Plates and Small Plates, plus Maishu Ramen. The drink menu includes martinis and other cocktails along with beer and wine.

Garlic Mike's
2674 Hwy. 135
(970) 641-2493
garlicmikes.com
Moderate to Expensive
Longtime favorite for

Italian food in a friendly atmosphere.

High Alpine Brewing Co.
111 N. Main St.
(970) 642-4500
highalpinebrewing.com
Moderate
High Alpine specializes in passionately crafted beer, as well as a nice cocktail list. The compact menu features mainly appetizers, salads, and creative pizzas.

The Dive Gunnison
213 W. Tomichi Ave.
(970) 641-1375
thedivegunnison.com
Inexpensive to Moderate
The menu emphasizes pub food with some elevated options such as coconut curry mussels and steak frites.

LEADVILLE

City on a Hill Coffee & Espresso
508 Harrison Ave.
(719) 486-0797
cityonahillcoffee.com
Inexpensive
Good coffee, breakfast burritos, baked goods, and free Wi-Fi.

High Mountain Pies
115 W. 4th St.
(719) 486-5555
hmpies.com
Inexpensive
Gourmet pizzas, barbecue, and sandwiches.

Quincy's Steakhouse
416 Harrison Ave.
(719) 486-9765
quincyssteakandspirits.com
Moderate to Expensive

Affordable steaks and prime rib.

MANITOU SPRINGS

Adam's Mountain Cafe
26 Manitou Ave.
(719) 685-1430
adamsmountain.com
Inexpensive to Moderate
Largely organic offering, with many vegetarian and vegan entrees, prepared with fresh, quality ingredients.

The Briarhurst Manor
404 Manitou Ave.
(719) 685-1864 or
(877) 685-1448
briarhurst.com
Expensive
Fine dining with classic American cuisine of steaks, lamb, game, chicken.

Sahara Cafe
954 Manitou Ave.
(719) 685-2303
thesaharacafe.com
Inexpensive to Moderate
Highly rated Middle Eastern cuisine including gyros, shawarmas, falafel, and mezze plates.

MT. CRESTED BUTTE

Butte 66 Roadhouse BBQ
10 Crested Butte Way
(970) 349-2999
Inexpensive to Moderate
Popular slopeside bar and eatery offering pubgrub, draft beer, and a deck for awesome views.

Iron Horse Tap
The Plaza
(970) 349-7300
ironhorsetapcb.com

Inexpensive to Moderate
Popcorn chicken, fries,
organic salads, and
a selection of pizzas,
including a custom option
for vegans, vegetarians,
and those wanting to skip
the gluten.

OURAY

Bon Ton Restaurant
426 Main St.
(970) 325-4419
bontonrestaurant.com
Moderate to Expensive
Upscale casual Italian
cuisine at one of the area's
finest restaurants.

Ouray Brewery
607 Main St.
(970) 325-7388
ouraybrewery.com
Inexpensive
Tasty pub fare and
handcrafted beers in a
friendly local setting.

PAGOSA SPRINGS

Alley House Grille
214 Pagosa St.
(970) 264-0999
alleyhousegrille.com
Moderate to Expensive
Elegant but casual
atmosphere serving global/
Colorado fusion cuisine in a
restored cottage.

Chavalo's Taqueria
301 N. Pagosa Blvd., #B-2
(970) 731-2501
chavolospagosasprings.
com
Inexpensive
Authentic Mexican food
and good margaritas; a
local favorite.

Pagosa Baking Company
238 Pagosa St.
(970) 264-9348
pagosabakingcompany
.com
Inexpensive
Open for breakfast and
lunch, the menu includes
breakfast burritos, quiche,
sandwiches, wraps, and
salads, and there's an
entire menu devoted to
"sensitivities" featuring
gluten-free, lactose-free,
and vegan items.

Pagosa Brewing & Grill
118 N. Pagosa Blvd.
(970) 731-2739
pagosabrewing.com
Inexpensive
Gastropub cuisine: burgers,
tacos, pizza, salmon,
soups, and of course,
good beer.

PUEBLO

Cactus Flower Restaurant
4610 N. Elizabeth St.
(719) 545-8218
cactusflowerrestaurant.com
Moderate
Diverse Mexican cuisine
prepared with fresh
ingredients.

Papa Jose's Union Cafe
320 S. Union Ave.
(719) 545-7476
restaurantwebexpert.com/
PapaJoses
Inexpensive
Family-owned Mexican
restaurant; a local favorite,
with fresh ingredients and
good service.

SALIDA

Café Dawn
122 E. 1st St.
(719) 539-5105
cafe-dawn.com
Inexpensive
Tasty drinks and all-natural
Colorado products in
historic downtown setting.

TELLURIDE

Allreds
Top of St. Sophia Gondola
(970) 728-7474
tellurideskiresort.com/
dine/#Allred's%20
Restaurant
Expensive
Eclectic menu of steak,
seafood, chicken,
pasta, and lamb, with a
panoramic mountain view
from the dining room.

Baked in Telluride
127 S. Fir St.
(970) 728-4775
bakedintel.com
Inexpensive
A Telluride favorite for 30
years serving breakfast,
lunch, dinner; pizza, soup,
salads, sandwiches, and
numerous baked goods are
available.

Brown Dog Pizza
110 E. Colorado Ave.
(970) 728-8046
browndogpizza.com
Moderate
Menu features a long list
of traditional and creative
pizzas, plus sandwiches
and salads.

La Marmotte
150 W. San Juan Ave.
(970) 728-6232
lamarmotte.com

Moderate to Expensive
Elegant French bistro
fare with sunny patios, a
quaint dining room, and a
separate bar.

La Piazza Del Villaggio
117 Lost Creek Ln.,
Mountain Village
(970) 728-8283
telluridepizzeria.com
ristorante.com

Moderate to Expensive
The menus of La Pizzaria
and La Piazza have been
combined—pizza and fine
dining on one menu, lots of
choices. Still all Italian.

**Oak, The New Fat Alley
BBQ**
250 San Juan Ave.
(970) 728-3985
oakstelluride.com

Moderate
Beer, bourbon and BBQ—
what's not to like? But also
burgers, salmon, gumbo,
and veggie options, among
other tantalizing dishes.

FOR MORE INFORMATION

ALAMOSA
**Alamosa Convention and Visitors
Bureau**
610 State Ave., 81101
(800) 258-7597
alamosachamber.com/
alamosa-county-marketing-district

CAÑON CITY
Cañon City Chamber of Commerce
403 Royal Gorge Blvd., 81212
(719) 275-2331 or (800) 876-7922
canoncitychamber.com

COLORADO SPRINGS
**Colorado Springs Convention and
Visitors Bureau**
515 S. Cascade Ave., 80903
(719) 635-7506 or (800) 888-4748
visitcos.com

CRESTED BUTTE
**Crested Butte/Mt. Crested Butte
Chamber of Commerce**
601 Elk Ave., 81224
(970) 349-6438
(855) 681-0941
cbchamber.com

CRIPPLE CREEK
Cripple Creek Heritage Center
9283 South Hwy. 67
(719) 689-3315
visitcripplecreek.com

DELTA
Delta Area Chamber of Commerce
301 Main St., 81416
(970) 874-8616
deltacolorado.org

DURANGO
Durango Area Tourism Office
802 Main Ave.
(970) 247-3500 or (800) 525-8855
durango.org

GUNNISON
**Gunnison Country Chamber of
Commerce**
500 E. Tomichi Ave.
(970) 641-1501
gunnisonchamber.com

LEADVILLE
**Leadville/Lake County Chamber of
Commerce**
809 Harrison Ave.
PO Box 861, 80461
(719) 486-3900
leadvilleusachamber.com

MANITOU SPRINGS
**Manitou Springs Chamber of
Commerce & Visitors Bureau**
354 Manitou Ave., 80829
(719) 685-5089
manitousprings.org

MESA VERDE AREA

Cortez Area Chamber of Commerce
20 W. Main St., 81321
(970) 565-3414
cortezchamber.com

Mesa Verde Country Visitor Information Bureau
(970) 565-4048
mesaverdecountry.com

Mesa Verde National Park
PO Box 8, Mesa Verde 81330
(970) 529-4465
nps.gov/meve

MONTROSE

Greater Montrose Chamber of Commerce
1245 E. Main St., 81401
(970) 765-0914
greatermontrosechamber.com

MOSCA

Great Sand Dunes National Park & Preserve
11999 Hwy. 150, 81146
(719) 378-6395
nps.gov/grsa

PAGOSA SPRINGS

Pagosa Springs Area Chamber of Commerce
105 Hot Springs Blvd.
(970) 264-2360
pagosachamber.com

PIKES PEAK REGION

Pikes Peak Region Attractions
1763 S. 8th St., Ste. 2
(719) 685-5894
pikes-peak.com

PUEBLO

Greater Pueblo Chamber of Commerce
302 N. Santa Fe Ave., 81003
(800) 233-3446 or (719) 542-1704
pueblochamber.org

SALIDA

Salida Chamber of Commerce
406 W. US 50, 81201
(877) 772-5432 or (719) 539-2068
salidachamber.org

TELLURIDE

Telluride Tourism Board
226 W. Colorado Ave.
(888) 605-2578
visittelluride.com

Denver & the Plains

Denver Metropolitan Area

With its former folksy label of Cow Town long retired, **Denver** is renowned as a hip, sophisticated city at the edge of the Rocky Mountains. A vibrant cultural scene, 300 days of sunshine each year, and easy access to some of the country's prettiest land-scapes make the Mile High City one of the most enticing destina-tions in the American West.

Although the presence of the National Western Stock Show every January fills the streets with Stetson hats and cowboy boots, few would deny that Denver has become an excit-ing cultural center. With the nation's second-largest theatrical venue, a sizzling culinary scene, diverse music and nightlife choices, world-class museums, numerous brewpubs, seven major-league sports teams, and one of the largest bike trail systems in the country, that historical moniker of Cow Town no longer fits.

Long before the cows and the city culture arrived, Native American tribes lived here at the junction of Cherry Creek and the South Platte River. Utes, Cheyenne, Arapaho, and Chero-kee hunted the plains and traveled into the mountains each

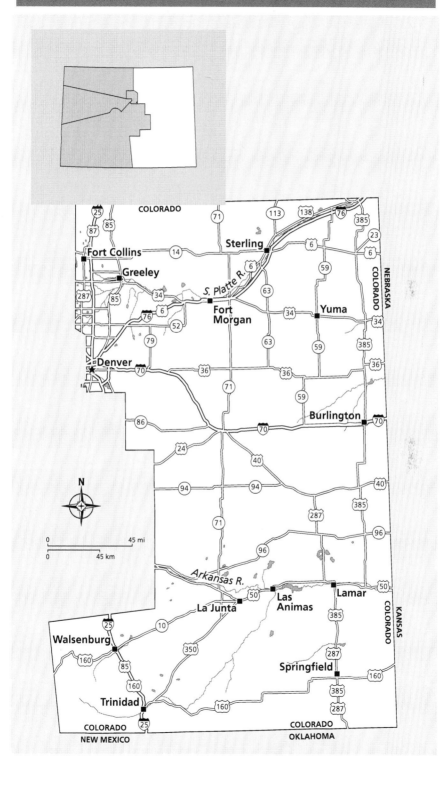

summer in search of game. Trappers and explorers wandered through in the 1800s, but overall this prairie wilderness was a quiet place. In July of 1858 an event took place near the mouth of Little Dry Creek that would change the landscape and its native people forever. Gold was discovered.

From 1859 to 1861, around 100,000 gold seekers streamed into the region, lured by exaggerated tales back east of riches waiting to be found. Within 18 years Denver was the capital of the nation's 38th state, and 35,000 people lived here. Not much gold was discovered in the local streams, but in the nearby mountain towns of Central City and Black Hawk, large deposits were uncovered. Denver became a supply center, and much of the money earned in the mining camps made its way back to town. Gold brought more fortune hunters from all over North America, but most of them did not strike it rich. Still, they flocked to the area.

By 1890 over 100,000 people called Denver home. Silver had been discovered in the previous decade, and a new era of opulence arrived. Corruption was common as city officials and police partnered with underworld figures such as Soapy Smith and Lou Blonger to profit from gambling, con games, and other illegal enterprises. Miners returning from the fields found bawdy houses along Market Street catering to every budget and desire. The street had originally been named Halliday Street to honor one of Denver's founders, but it was so covered with bordellos and gambling halls, the family asked them to take their name off the street and it was changed to Market Street. Hustlers were waiting at gambling tables to separate the miners from their hard-earned gold. Denver's vice district during these early days was second only to those of San Francisco's Barbary Coast and New Orleans's Storyville.

According to local historian Richard Grant, "The silver barons built elaborate mansions on Capitol Hill. Gamblers, drifters and gunmen flooded the saloons and gaming halls on Larimer and Market Streets. Bat Masterson tended bar here, Soapy Smith ran the West's largest gang of thieves, crooks and con artists, and anyone who was anyone in the 'Old West' paid at least a visit to Denver's mud-filled, honky-tonk streets."

Colorado moved forward into the 20th century, and as the gold and silver petered out, ranching, farming, and manufacturing replaced mining. By 1910 the city had become the commercial and industrial center of the Rocky Mountain region, with a large cattle market and the largest sheep market in the world. By 1940, 322,000 people lived here. Denver was on its way to becoming the city it is today.

As Denver modernized, old edifices were torn down and replaced with new structures. Unfortunately, some of the classic architectural gems, the Tabor Grand Opera House and the Windsor Hotel among them, were razed to make way for modern glass-and-steel skyscrapers. But quite a few of the

Victorian buildings still exist. The historic **Brown Palace Hotel** (321 17th St.; 303-297-3111; brownpalace.com) and **The Oxford Hotel** (1600 17th St.; 303-628-5400; theoxfordhotel.com) are alive and well. It is well worth the effort to stop in at the Brown Palace for afternoon tea or a drink in the Ship Tavern. One of the city's pleasures is to relax in the expansive, beautifully detailed atrium while sipping tea and listening to harp or piano music.

History lovers will enjoy the **Molly Brown House Museum,** where Colorado's past is well-preserved. After she became wealthy, the "Unsinkable" Molly Brown lived her flamboyant life in this 1889 mansion of native Colorado lava stone. Following Molly's death in 1932, the building served as a rooming house. It was remodeled or divided at the whim of each successive owner. Rescued in 1971 by Historic Denver Inc., the mansion was decorated as Molly herself had done, using old photographs she had taken of her home's interior. The Molly Brown House has been restored to its former opulence. It is located at 1340 Pennsylvania St.; (303) 832-4092; mollybrown.org. Admission is $16 for adults and teenagers, $14 for senior citizens 65 and older, and $12 for children 6 to 18; children 5 or younger free. Open year-round Tues through Sun from 10 a.m. to 4 p.m.; closed Mon and major holidays. Guided tours in the mornings; explore on your own all day.

Colorado's **Governor's Mansion** (also known as the **Cheesman-Boettcher Mansion**), a redbrick colonial building with white stone trim, was built by one of the state's distinguished pioneer families, the Cheesmans. (Cheesman Park is named for them.) The mansion has been the executive residence of the state's governor since 1960. Furnished with luxurious art, antiques, and furniture, the house is available for limited tours. It is located at 400 E. 8th St. in Denver. For information about tours, email info@grpfund.org.

The **Byers-Evans House,** a mansion at 1310 Bannock St. built in 1883, has been restored to its original grandeur. Admission and a guided tour cost $8 for adults, $6 for seniors and students, and free for ages 18 and younger. Hours are 10:30 a.m. to 3:30 p.m. Mon, Thurs, Fri, and Sat; 1 to 3:30 p.m. Sun. For more information contact the Byers-Evans House at (303) 620-4933 or visit historycolorado.org.

Probably the best place in the city to learn about the area's history and prehistory is the nearby **History Colorado Center** at 1200 Broadway. The museum is open daily 10 a.m. to 5 p.m. Admission is $15 for adults, free for children 18 and younger. For more information contact the History Colorado Center at (303) 447-8679 or visit historycolorado.org.

The most sumptuous of all the historic buildings in this part of Denver is the castle-like **Capitol Hill Mansion,** an impeccable, deluxe bed-and-breakfast at 1207 Pennsylvania. The mansion, a landmark listed in the National Register of

Explore Denver on Two Wheels

For a truly green tour of the Mile High City, explore Denver's 850 miles of off-road, paved, and packed-earth bike paths on your own bike or one of the many bikes and scooters you can rent on demand on Denver streets via an app.

Historic Places, is not far from the Governor's Mansion and the Molly Brown House. The 1891 furniture is hand-carved oak and maple, and original Colorado landscape paintings enhance the interiors. Some rooms come with four-posters and mountain-viewing balconies. Fresh flowers, high-speed internet, afternoon wine socials, and gourmet breakfast are included with all rooms. For more information contact the Capitol Hill Mansion at (303) 839-5221; capitolhillmansion.com.

The undisputed spot where Denver's history, heritage, and evolution as a hip and sophisticated urban center of the 21st century converge is **Union Station,** part of the landscape since 1881. The original building burned down in 1894, and the next structures went through several transformations until 1914. For 100 years the building remained pretty much as it was, at first a glorious representative of Beaux Arts architecture and the golden age of train travel, and then a dismal, underused facility in need of repair. Dana Crawford, urban preservationist, visionary and developer, became the driving force behind the station's meticulous renovation and renewal, just as she had for Larimer Square and much of LoDo. In July 2015 Union Station reopened. The transportation hub for the metro RTD bus and light-rail system and Amtrak station connecting rail passengers to San Francisco and Chicago, Union Station is also a central gathering spot for locals and visitors with four restaurants, outposts of a few local retailers, a boutique hotel (named for Crawford), and two bars. It hosts events throughout the year, including July 4 and New Year's Eve celebrations.

Careful attention was paid to the building's history, with many original architectural details painstakingly preserved and new details added that reflect its connection to trains. Look up at the massive chandeliers and wall sconces; can you tell which are original? It's the sconces, but the chandeliers were created to reflect similar details. Also note the flower-motif molding. Once hidden by layers of dreary brown paint, this lovely detail featuring the columbine, Colorado's state flower, was discovered and preserved to beautiful effect.

Drop into **The Terminal Bar** for happy hour—it's located at the former ticket window—to try one of the many Colorado beers on tap, or make a reservation for **Cooper Lounge** on the mezzanine, where a nice wine list, craft cocktails, and artisanal cheese plates await. Restaurants include options from two of Denver's top chefs, Jen Jasinski, whose ***Stoic & Genuine*** serves utterly fresh seafood flown in daily, and Alex Seidel of Fruition fame, whose ***Mercantile Dining & Provision*** is the ultimate farm-to-table choice, as Seidel has his own Colorado farm from which many menu items come. Patrons can sit down for casual/fine dining or grab something to take along from Mercantile's market side. For a behind-the-scenes look at the station, sign up for a tour, offered most Fridays at 2 p.m. through the Crawford Hotel. The $20 fee benefits a local nonprofit and includes a voucher for a beverage at The Terminal Bar. For details call (720) 460-3700 or visit thecrawfordhotel.com/tours.

If there is one thing Denver does well (after more than 130 years of practice), it is the saloon. The first permanent structure in Denver was a saloon, and today there are sports bars, art bars, blues bars, fern bars, outdoor cafe bars, English pubs, "Old West" saloons, rock bars, city-overlook bars, country-and-western bars, art deco bars, and even bars that don't serve alcohol. Denver, and the state in general, leads the nation in beer brewing, and the city's craft microbreweries rank among the best in the country.

In addition to an abundance of saloons, Denver has more sporting goods stores and ski shops per capita than almost any other population center in the world and a corresponding number of recreation facilities such as free outdoor tennis courts, city golf courses, and ball fields.

Denver is also a serious year-round spectator sports town with seven major-league teams. Four facilities—***Coors Field, Empower Field at Mile High, Ball Arena,*** and ***Dick's Sporting Goods Park***—offer comfortable venues for watching professional baseball, football, basketball, ice hockey, soccer, and lacrosse. Fans flock to cheer on the Rockies, Broncos, Nuggets, Avalanche, Rapids, Mammoth, and Outlaws teams as they battle their lower-altitude competitors.

All these recreational choices may mislead visitors into thinking that Denver is all ball games and bars. But there is much more to the Mile High City than nightlife and sports. In fact, no other city between Chicago and the West Coast can match Denver's eclectic cultural landscape. Just one example is the architecturally striking ***Hamilton Building*** at ***Denver Art Museum,*** on 13th Avenue between Bannock and Broadway. Designed by internationally known architect Daniel Libeskind, the playful, dreamlike geometry of the titanium-clad structure has changed the city's skyline. Constructed at a cost of more than $100 million, the building more than doubled the museum size. Contemporary and modern, Western and Native American, Asian, and European collections, as well as temporary exhibits and a spectacular rooftop sculpture garden, offer something for everyone. Now the original building has also been renovated and it, too, is architecturally stunning.

The museum is open daily 10 a.m. to 5 p.m. and until 9 p.m. on Tuesdays. Admission for Colorado residents is $10 for adults and $8 for seniors (65 and over) and college students. Colorado residents can enjoy the museum for free the first Saturday of each month. Admission for nonresidents is $13 for adults, $10 for seniors and students. All children 18 and younger are free. For more information contact (720) 865-5000; denverartmuseum.org.

The somewhat quirky **Kirkland Museum of Fine & Decorative Art** is one of the most interesting museums in Denver's museum district, aka the Golden Triangle. The Kirkland houses an extensive and fascinating collection of 20th-century decorative arts ranging from art nouveau and Bauhaus through modern and pop art, and includes the original studio of Denver artist Vance Kirkland. The gift shop is excellent. To learn more visit kirkland museum.org.

Also part of Denver's burgeoning Cultural Arts District, the **Clyfford Still Museum** is devoted to the works of one of the most important painters of the 20th century. Representing over 90 percent of the artist's lifetime output, much of this work has been hidden from public view for 30 years but is now permanently displayed here. The museum is located at 1250 Bannock St. Open Wed through Sun 10 a.m. to 5 p.m. Admission is $10 for adults, $8 for seniors, and no charge for ages 17 and under; (720) 354-4880; clyffordstillmuseum.org.

Another worthwhile stop on Denver's culture circuit is the **Museum of Contemporary Art** near Riverfront Park, which presents an eclectic mix of modern art, photography, and new media. Instead of permanent collections, the MCA rotates traveling exhibitions through its five gallery spaces, offering new art installations on a continual basis. The rooftop MCA Cafe & Bar is a relaxing place for lunch with free Wi-Fi and great views of downtown. Hours are noon to 7 p.m. Tues through Thurs, Fri noon to 9 p.m., and 10 a.m. to 5 p.m. Sat and Sun. Admission is $10 for adults; $7 for college students, teachers, and seniors; visitors 18 and under are free. Located at 1485 Delgany St.; (303) 298-7554; mcadenver.org.

Denver's penchant for culture is evident across the city. Visitors can take in a play at the boldly designed **Denver Center Theatre,** part of the **Denver Performing Arts Complex** (DPAC), which is the setting for a wide variety of theater productions. DPAC, at 1101 13th St., is home to two production companies—Denver Center Theatre Company and Denver Center Productions (DCP). Among its many roles, DCP is responsible for importing touring Broadway shows and a variety of world-class entertainment.

Next door to DPAC is the nearly 2,700-seat **Boettcher Concert Hall,** where music lovers enjoy the offerings of the **Colorado Symphony Orchestra** and

Civic Center Eats

Every Thursday from May to September, more than 20 local food trucks roll into the main esplanade at the Civic Center, and diners select from hundreds of gourmet lunch items between 11 a.m. and 2 p.m. From here you're within sight of the Capitol, the Denver Art Museum, and the Denver Public Library. Enjoy live music and great views while connecting with the local lunchtime scene.

other performers. For information call (303) 268-3639 or visit coloradosymphony .org. The season runs from September through May. Boettcher Concert Hall is located at 14th and Curtis Streets in Denver. Culturally, with its theaters, art cinemas, ballets, and classical music, the city has come of age.

Denver is a more interesting and diverse city thanks to the many ethnic groups living here. The longtime Hispanic population contributes a rich and proud heritage. With nearly a third of Denver's residents having Latino ancestry, the city offers a wide range of Hispanic culture in the form of restaurants, music, stores, and events such as the annual Cinco de Mayo celebration, the largest one in the country. Federal Boulevard north from Alameda has hundreds of businesses catering to the Hispanic market.

A sizable Vietnamese population has introduced the city to the pleasures of this delightful Asian cuisine, and the 8-block stretch of South Federal Boulevard from Alameda Boulevard to Mississippi Street has dozens of restaurants, shops, cafes, and markets, including Chinese and Thai restaurants. Japanese people have long been a part of Denver's ethnic mix, and the downtown Sakura Square with its local Buddhist temple, as well as numerous area sushi restaurants, bring a taste of Japan to the city. The Korean population is substantial, especially in the suburb of Aurora. The area around South Havana Street and South Peoria Street by Parker Road has dozens of excellent Korean restaurants, as well as stores and businesses.

Over the last few decades Denver has evolved from a meat and potatoes town into a center for innovative and exciting cuisine. The city's culinary scene keeps expanding, with a wide range of tantalizing fare from around the globe.

Denver Restaurant Week, typically in February, is a 10-day celebration of culinary Denver. More than 150 restaurants across the city offer a multicourse dinner for a fixed price, typically $30 or $60 per person (not including tax or gratuity). This fun event is a great way to enjoy excellent dining while sampling the many gastronomic destinations of the city. For more information go to denverrestaurantweek.com.

Some of these restaurants are familiar locations set in popular art and entertainment districts, while others are hidden off the beaten path in suburban strip malls and small neighborhoods. Hungry people can find American comfort food, Indian, Ethiopian, Nepalese, Middle Eastern, Korean, Vietnamese, Chinese, Thai, Moroccan, Greek, Armenian, Hungarian, German, Italian, Swiss, French, and, of course, Mexican fare. Attempting to include the hundreds of good ones would require an entire dining guide. They are all worth exploring.

Of the many superb Asian restaurants, **ChoLon Modern Asian Bistro** (1555 Blake St.; 303-353-5223; cholon.com/denver) consistently delivers creative, memorable entrees. A longtime Cherry Creek favorite is **Cherry Cricket** (2641 E. 2nd Ave.; 303-322-7666; cherrycricket.com), known for legendary burgers and a friendly neighborhood bar atmosphere.

Denver's LoDo (Lower Downtown) district brims with outstanding dining spots. **Rioja** (1431 Larimer St.; 303-820-2282) is the flagship restaurant of one of Denver's best-known chefs, Jen Jasinski, a James Beard Foundation award winner. Rioja is Mediterranean-inspired but successfully ventures into a variety of unexpected ingredients and flavors. **Ultreia** and **Stoic & Genuine** are Jasinki's eateries in Union Station. Among the best of the city's upscale Mexican restaurants is **Tamayo** (1400 Larimer St.; 720-946-1433; richardsandoval.com/Tamayo). Its rooftop patio has a great view of the mountains. **Le Roux** (1510 16th St.; 720-845-1673; lerouxdenver.com) offers French dishes in an utterly romantic setting. Many hot dog aficionados claim the best they've ever tasted came from **Biker Jim's Gourmet Dogs Cart** (16th and Arapahoe on the 16th Street Mall; 720-746-9355; bikerjimsdogs.com). The charismatic hot dog hero offers a multitude of exotic entrees: elk, antelope, buffalo, reindeer and wild boar brats, and more.

Another thriving restaurant scene is west of downtown in the Highlands neighborhood, both lower and upper. **Avanti Food & Bar** (3200 Pecos St.; 720-269-4778; avantifandb.com) brings together the food truck and restaurant scene in one space, with seven mini restaurants housed in industrial containers around a central eating area and two bars. Among the choices are excellent South American arepas (similar to empanadas), "Mexiterranean bites," Japanese-inspired cuisine, and Middle Eastern shawarmas. **Cafe Brazil** (4408 Lowell Blvd.; 303-480-1877; cafebrazildenver.com), a neighborhood hot spot that has built a cultlike following over the years, offers all things Brazil, with bold flavors and delicious seafood. **Postino** (2715 17th St.; 303-433-6363; postinowinecafe.com) is part of the culinary "less-is-more" scene. Its offerings are limited—the focus is small plates and wine—but what it offers, including one of the best patios in the Highlands, is very well done. Brunch is tasty, too. Housed in an old service station that's been converted into one of Denver's hottest restaurants, **Root Down** (1600 W. 33rd. Ave.; 303-993-4200; rootdowndenver.com) is another example of the city's culinary prowess. With great views of downtown and a menu that also uses locally grown and organic ingredients whenever possible, this hip neighborhood hot spot serves up creative American and global cuisine for carnivores, vegetarians, and everyone in between.

Also in LoHi, **Linger** (2030 W. 30th Ave.; 303-993-3120; lingerdenver .com) and El Five (2930 Umatilla St; 303-524-9193; elfivedenver.com), sister restaurants to Root Down, serve international fare, tapas, and small plates in wonderfully eclectic dining spaces with, yes, more sweeping views of the city skyline. For dessert go to **Little Man Ice Cream** (2620 16th St.; 303-455-3811; littlemanicecream.com). In the summer the scene on the patio is like a town square with couples, families, and neighbors gathering under the towering steel milk can for some of the finest ice cream in town.

Over on South Federal Boulevard, among the many dozens of Vietnamese restaurants lining the street, **New Saigon** (630 S. Federal Blvd.; 303-936-4954; newsaigon.com) has been consistently good for many years. Overlook the often curt waitstaff; the food is worth the trip. Denver's growing RiNo (River North) district, historically Five Points, just north of LoDo and an easy bike ride via the South Platte River Greenway Trail, embraces culinary arts as well as every other type of art. A one-stop shop for food, wine, and craft beer is **The Source** (3550 Brighton Blvd.; 720-443-1135; thesourcedenver.com), a collective-space concept. Fifteen merchants include Temaki Den, sibling of South Pearl's uber popular Sushi Den, is one of the best Japanese restaurants in Denver. It's pricey but worth every penny. Adjacent is The Source Hotel, which also houses excellent restaurants and bars. The downside is parking, which is now almost exclusively available in an expensive garage.

Denver's reputation as a cow town may be a thing of the past, but each January the city embraces its Western heritage with the world's largest stock show. Of the numerous annual events that take place in Denver, the **National Western Stock Show, Rodeo, and Horse Show** is the biggest and longest— a two-week happening that brings rodeo, horse shows, livestock competition, and a range of entertainment showcasing the Western lifestyle. The National Western was born in a circus tent in 1906, and has long been housed in the National Western Complex. In 2015, Denver voters approved a major new Denver Western Center to replace the aging complex, ensure the future of the Stock Show, house a new vet school in conjuction with Colorado State University, and make Denver an equestrian center for major international horse shows. What won't change is wide appeal of the stock show, including what may be its most unusual and beloved component, the annual appearance of the grand-champion steer in the lobby of the Brown Palace Hotel during tea, red-carpet walk and all (make reservations well in advance to be among those enjoying traditional afternoon tea with a distinctly Western twist).

More than just entertainment, the National Western remains an important stock show for ranchers. You can view more than 15,000 live, scrubbed, and brushed Herefords, Angus, Simmentals, Shorthorns, Longhorns, Arabian horses, Morgan horses, draft horses, miniature horses, ewes, and lambs, all in their neat pens. Some 600,000 visitors flock to the arenas to buy, sell, learn, and socialize. Millions of dollars exchange hands here.

General admission tickets cost about the same as for a movie; event tickets are additional. For more information call (303) 297-1166 or visit national western.com.

Got a carnivorous hankering? The **Buckhorn Exchange** is allegedly Colorado's oldest restaurant (it celebrated its centennial in 1993). It is certainly one of the most original.

Moreover, it's a saloon, a magnet for celebrities and tourists, and a one-of-a-kind eatery. In addition to beef and buffalo, the Buckhorn Exchange serves elk, ostrich, yak, rattlesnake, Rocky Mountain oysters, alligator, quail, and duck. The downstairs restaurant-museum is cluttered with more than 500 taxidermy pieces, including pronghorn, deer, bear, wolverine, mountain goat, moose, weasel, zebra, and birds of all kinds. More than a hundred rifles, pistols, and other weapons are on display. The saloon is upstairs, complete with a giant oak bar that was shipped here by oxcart.

The **Buckhorn Exchange** was begun in 1893 by owner Henry H. Zietz, a cowboy and scout with Buffalo Bill; personal bodyguard of Leadville's silver millionaire Horace Tabor; and hunting guide of President Theodore Roosevelt, who arrived in his private train in front of the Buckhorn. The restaurant's official history relates that Henry Zietz "catered to cattlemen, miners, railroad builders, Indian chiefs, silver barons, roustabouts, gamblers, the great and the near-great." In December 1900 a masked gunman rode up to the restaurant, waved a .45, and demanded all money and valuables to be placed on the bar, "and be quick about it!" When the gunman rode away at a gallop,

trivia

Denver has 300 days of sunshine annually—more hours of sun each year than San Diego, California, and Tampa, Florida!

he found himself pursued by Zietz's rifle-raising customers, who "handily dispatched the miscreant to greener pastures." The Buckhorn's redbrick building is at 1000 Osage St., 5 blocks west of Santa Fe Boulevard. Dinner is served Mon to Thurs from 5 p.m. to 9 p.m.; Fri, Sat, and Sun 4:30 to 9:30 p.m. For information or reservations call (303) 534-9505 or visit buckhorn.com.

AUTHOR'S FAVORITES IN DENVER & THE PLAINS

Bent's Old Fort
(719) 383-5010
nps.gov/beol

Brown Palace Hotel
(800) 321-2599 or (303) 297-3111
brownpalace.com

Clyfford Still Museum
(720) 354-4880
clyffordstillmuseum.org

Confluence Park and **Denver Bike Paths**
South Platte River at downtown REI store
denver.org/things-to-do/
sports-recreation/bike-trails

Denver Art Museum
(720) 865-5000
denverartmuseum.org

Denver Botanic Gardens
(720) 865-3500
botanicgardens.org

Denver Center for the Performing Arts
(303) 893-4100
denvercenter.org

Denver Museum of Nature & Science
(303) 370-6000
dmns.org

South Platte River Greenway Trail and 36+-mile biking/walking path
Along the South Platte River, extends from Brighton to Chatfield State Park
denver.org/things-to-do/
sports-recreation/bike-trails

Kirkland Museum of Fine & Decorative Art
(303) 832-8576
kirklandmuseum.org

Larimer Square
larimersquare.com

Tattered Cover Book Store (LoDo)
(303) 436-1070 or
(800) 833-9327
tatteredcover.com

Washington Park
(303) 698-4930
denver.org/neighborhoods/
washington-park

Larimer Square is a carefully renovated, 18th-century downtown oasis with a national reputation. In 1858, Denver's founder, General William E. Larimer, erected the city's first building here, a modest log cabin. Apparently the general had an odd sense of humor; the doors were coffin lids. As the city grew, Larimer Street became one of the most famous thoroughfares in the West. Saloons, gambling houses, and brothels catered to a steady stream of customers. It was a wild place during a boom time. The restaurants, hotels, and theaters of its heyday were renowned. Stories of what happened when the famous, infamous, and desperados of the West met made good newspaper copy. And tales of what went on behind closed doors in the neighborhood shocked a nation. Gambling and boozing were rampant.

As the years passed, Denver gradually moved uptown, and the blocks around Larimer Street became a skid row area. Thanks to the gin mills and

A Stroll Along the South Platte River

Early pioneers deemed the South Platte River "too thick to drink, too thin to plow." As Denver grew, the local river became a dumping ground—polluted, abused, and neglected. In 1974 a major clean-up effort began, and today it's a 30-mile greenway of parks, trails, trees, and wildlife habitat. The *South Platte River Greenway Trail* is a paved riverside path shared by walkers, bicyclists, birders, skaters, and joggers. Whitewater boat chutes provide thrills for kayakers and fun for spectators during spring snowmelt. Any stretch is pleasant, but some favorites are the urban section heading upriver from the confluence with Cherry Creek (by the downtown REI flagship store), and the section heading upriver from the crossing at Alameda Avenue to the trail end just north of Chatfield State Park. For more information contact Visit Denver, The Convention & Visitors Bureau; (303) 892-1505 or (800) 233-6837; denver .org/things-to-do/sports-recreation.

flophouses, the handsome Victorian buildings were forgotten, although amid the grime and dirt, their architectural beauty remained. Razing was a frequent threat.

More than 100 years later, a group of Colorado businesspeople joined forces to restore the old buildings and preserve at least a portion of Denver's Victorian heritage. The excitement that once was historic Larimer Street soon returned, and today the entire lower downtown area, known as *LoDo,* is the city's hip epicenter anchored by Union Station. Dozens of restaurants, cafes, bars, coffeehouses, boutiques, businesses, and hotels fill the district, with many residing in renovated buildings well over a century old. For authentic Western wear, go to *Rockmount Ranch Wear* (1626 Wazee St.; 303-295-9126), an iconic Denver business offering Western shirts, skirts, belts, hats, and much more. A few blocks away on McGregor Square, the *Tattered Cover* is one of the best bookstores in the country. At the northern edge of LoDo and directly across from Tattered Cover is *Coors Field,* home to the Rockies baseball team. On Friday and Saturday nights LoDo buzzes with energy as thousands of people come in search of good food, drink, and fun. Popular watering holes, especially for millennials, include *View House Eatery Bar & Rooftop* on Market Street. At other times of day or evening, LoDo is good for strolling and discovering the charms of this historic area. One of the most popular spots to watch sports is in *McGregor Square,* between 19th and 20th Streets and Wynkoop and Wazee Streets. The 60' × 20' outdoor screen draws large crowds on game days and when major sporting events are in play. While there, grab a bite at *The Original* or *Carmine's on McGregor.*

Larimer Square and nearby streets contain outstanding examples of early Denver Victorian architecture, complete with gaslights, handwrought

TOP ANNUAL EVENTS IN DENVER & THE PLAINS

First Friday Art Walks
Santa Fe Drive Art District
First Fri of each month
artdistrictonsantafe.com

JANUARY
National Western Stock Show, Rodeo, and Horse Show
National Western Complex in Denver
early to mid-Jan
(888) 551-5004 (tickets)
nationalwestern.com

MARCH
Denver March Powwow
Denver Coliseum
(303) 934-8045
denvermarchpowwow.org

MAY
Cinco de Mayo "Celebrate Culture" Festival
Civic Center Park
On or about May 5
(303) 534-8342
cincodemayodenver.com

Red Rocks Amphitheatre Summer Concerts
May through Aug
(720) 865-2494
redrocksonline.com

JUNE
Denver People's Fair
Civic Center Park
(303) 777-6887
facebook.com/denverpeoplesfair/

Cherry Blossom Festival
Sakura Square
June or July
(303) 951-4486
cherryblossomdenver.org

Denver Botanic Gardens Summer Concert Series
June through Aug
(720) 865-3500
concerts.botanicgardens.org

Greeley Stampede and Rodeo
Greeley
late June through early July
(970) 356-7787
greeleystampede.org

Pridefest
Civic Center Park
(303) 733-7743
glbtcolorado.org/pridefest

JULY
Cherry Creek Arts Festival
Cherry Creek
early July
(303) 355-2787
cherrycreekartsfestival.org

Colorado Dragon Boat Festival
Lakewood
late July
info@cdbf.org
cdbf.org

AUGUST
Larimer County Fair and Rodeo
Loveland
early Aug
(970) 619-4009
larimercountyfair.org

SEPTEMBER
Denver Chalk Art Festival
Golden Triangle Neighborhood
(303) 840-0045
denverchalk.art

OCTOBER
Denver Zombie Crawl
Skyline Park to 16th Street
Mallregistration@denverzombiecrawl.com
eyeheartbrains.com

Great American Beer Festival
Colorado Convention Center
(303) 447-0816
greatamericanbeerfestival.com

DECEMBER
New Year's Eve Downtown Fireworks
16th Street Mall
December 31
(303) 892-1505
milehighholidays.com

Zoo Lights
Denver Zoo
nightly in Dec
(720) 337-1400
denverzoo.org/events/zoolights

leaded-glass windows, stairways, historic markers, restored cornices, and benches for relaxing and watching the world go by. In the restaurants and shops, you'll find Tiffany lamps, cherrywood bars, rosewood paneling, old wallpapers, and lead or pressed-tin ceilings. Sadly, a number of historic buildings were lost during the urban renewal development of the 1960s and 1970s, but of the ones that remain, some date back to the 1880s and 1890s. Larimer Square is now a Landmark Preservation District, and it's listed in the National Register of Historic Places. For more information call (720) 805-1973 or visit larimersquare.com.

Among the historic district's many old buildings, **The Oxford Hotel** has been a part of Denver's colorful story since it became the city's first hotel in 1891. Today this luxury hotel is across the street from Union Station and within a short walk of Coors Field. The hotel's legendary Cruise Room Martini Bar opened the day after Prohibition was repealed in 1933. Fashioned after one of the lounges on the *Queen Mary,* its art deco decor remains the same as on the day it opened, with beautifully preserved chrome and neon reflecting on wood panels. A free jukebox and an extensive menu of martinis and classic cocktails make this a popular port of call during a night out in LoDo. Find it at 1600 17th St.; (303) 628-5400; theoxfordhotel.com.

Designed by renowned architect I. M. Pei, Denver's mile-long **16th Street Mall** offers shops, restaurants, people-watching, street entertainers, and the free MallRide that gives explorers easy access to all that Denver offers between Civic Center Park and Union Station. Three pedestrian bridges at the west end of the mall connect to the Highlands neighborhood, which has the massive REI flagship store, excellent restaurants, hip bars, and coffee shops. For more information contact **Visit Denver, The Convention and Visitors Bureau** at (800) 233-6837 or (303) 892-1505; denver.org.

From its international debut in 1892 up to the present, Denver's **Brown Palace Hotel** has lived up to its motto, "Where the World Registers." Indeed, this historic hotel is a classic. Nearly every US president since Theodore

Arkansas Valley Fair

Billed as the oldest continuous fair in Colorado, the *Arkansas Valley Fair* in Rocky Ford is a five-day celebration each August featuring parades, music, entertainment, horse races, livestock shows, and the best cantaloupes in the world. Find out more at (719) 254-7723; arkvalleyfair.com.

Roosevelt has spent time here. Winston Churchill, Elvis Presley, and the Beatles all slept here—though not on the same night.

"The Brown," as Denverites have nicknamed it, is a remarkable example of Victorian architecture. Upon entering the hotel lobby, your eyes are drawn upward past six tiers of wrought-iron balconies to the stained-glass cathedral ceiling. The decorative stone on the pillars is Mexican onyx. Changing displays of historical memorabilia decorate the luxurious lobby. Old guest registers, menus, and photographs take you back to relive the role the Brown Palace played in the history of Denver.

The hotel is named for its builder, Henry Cordes Brown. As Brown watched 19th-century Denver grow, he saw the need for a fine hostelry for visiting Easterners who came to do business with Colorado mining companies and railroads. The builder envisioned this hotel to rise from a triangular plot of land he owned near the center of the city.

A prominent Denver architect, Frank E. Edbrooke, designed the building in the spirit of the Italian Renaissance. Because of the geometric pattern of Brown's land, the edifice took on an unusual shape. Edbrooke gave the building a tri-frontage and then planned it so that each room faced a street. Without any interior rooms, every guest could have a view, plus morning or afternoon sunshine. The contractors constructed this soon-to-be famous landmark from Colorado red granite and warm brown Arizona sandstone.

Completed in 1892 at a cost of $1 million, the 10-story building had 400 rooms. Fireplaces were standard for each room, as well as bathroom taps yielding artesian water straight from the hotel's wells (as they still do today). The finest achievements in steam heating and electricity were incorporated into the structure, while linens, china, glassware, and silver came from the finest craftsmen. The Brown was also noted as the second fireproof edifice in the country. Denver society was formally introduced to the Brown Palace soon after its opening when the Tabors threw a fancy ball. In the years since, the Brown has hosted thousands of such glittering evenings.

Today the Brown Palace Hotel is listed in the National Register of Historic Places. Even in modern times it continues to provide guests with historical

Melon Capital of the World

Located 11 miles northwest of La Junta, tiny **Rocky Ford** is famous around the state for honeydew, watermelon, and especially cantaloupe. Each August harvesting begins, and numerous roadside stands offer some of the best melons in the county.

authenticity, Victorian charm, and good service. The original decor has been preserved, especially in the restaurants, and walking through the hotel doors feels like stepping back in time. On many Friday and Saturday nights local regulars come into the large atrium to sing along with the piano player. The Brown Palace Hotel is at 321 17th St.; (303) 297-3111 or (800) 321-2599; marriott.com/en-us/hotels/denak-the-brown-palace-hotel-and-spa-autograph-collection.

Since Denver's first house was built in the 1850s, the city has expanded into a variety of unique neighborhoods, each with its own flavor. These are places where locals go to relax over a meal, meet friends, and enjoy city life. There are dozens of interesting neighborhoods to explore around Denver, some sprawling for blocks and others no more than a couple of cafes, a bar, a bookstore, and a coffee shop tucked away in a leafy backstreet. Here are a few places to begin.

The **Uptown** neighborhood just east of downtown is a mix of Victorian and Queen Anne homes with great views of the city skyline. **Restaurant Row** along 17th Avenue is lined with cafes, bistros, taco bars, coffeehouses, and a variety of popular nightclubs—almost all with outdoor patios. Try Hamburger Mary's for a bit of local color. East Colfax Avenue in the Capitol Hill neighborhood has some of the city's best music venues (Fillmore, Ogden, and Bluebird Theater), as well as numerous restaurants and independent stores, including the **Tattered Cover Book Store** and **Twist & Shout,** Denver's go-to for vinyl and every other version of recorded music. Cherry Creek North, running about 8 blocks long by 3 blocks wide, is the upscale dining and shopping district. For

trivia

In the 1860s, as Denver competed with other mining towns for the status of being Colorado's premier city, Denver was made up of nothing but crude cabins and one saloon—Colorado's first.

trivia

Every year since 2000 the Denver Public Library has been recognized by Hennen's American Public Library Ratings as one of the top libraries in America for population centers with more than 500,000 people.

Denver & Beer

Denver is a beer lover's bonanza. Brewing more beer than any other city in the US, Denver has a wide selection of microbreweries, brewpubs, and beer cafes—one for every 1,200 citizens, which is 76 times the national average. Here are a few places to begin your own beer pilgrimage:

Black Shirt Brewing Co., 3719 Walnut St.; (303) 993-2799; blackshirtbrewingco .com

Call to Arms Brewing Company, 4526 Tennyson St.; (720) 328-8528; calltoarms brewing.com

Cerebral Brewing, 1477 Monroe St.; (303) 927-7365; cerebralbrewing.com

Denver Beer (Taproom), 1695 Platte St.; (303) 433-2739

Epic Brewing, 3001 Walnut St.; (720) 539-7410; epicbrewing.com

Fiction Beer Company, 701 E. Colfax; (720) 456-7163; fictionbeer.com

Great Divide Brewery Tap Room, 2201 Arapahoe St.; (303) 296-9460; greatdivide .com

Little Machine Beer, 2924 W. 20th Ave.; (303) 284-7893; littlemachinebeer.com

Odell Five Points Brewhouse, 2945 Larimer St.; (720) 795-7862; odellbrewing.com

Ratio Beerworks, 2920 Larimer St.; (303) 997-8288; ratiobeerworks.com

Renegade Brewing Company, 925 W. 9th Ave.; (720) 401-4089; renegadebrewing .com

Spangalang Brewery, 2736 Welton St.; (303) 297-1276; spangalangbrewery.com

Trve Brewing Company, 227 Broadway #101; (303) 351-1021; trvebrewing.com

three days each July 4th weekend, this is the setting for the Cherry Creek Arts Festival, celebrating the visual, culinary, and performing arts.

The *Golden Triangle Museum District* has many of the city's museums, including the spectacular Denver Art Museum, History Colorado Center, the Clyfford Still Museum, and the Kirkland Museum of Fine & Decorative Art, as well as some 50 galleries. The *LoHi* neighborhood borders the South Platte River and includes Elitch Gardens Amusement Park, the Downtown Aquarium, and the Children's Museum of Denver. The Art District on Santa Fe, just south of downtown, has more than 40 galleries, restaurants, and shops. It's the largest concentration of galleries in the city, and is one of several First Friday Art Walk sites. Five Points is one of Denver's oldest neighborhoods, with blocks of Victorian homes and buildings. The main thoroughfare, Welton Street, has 75 businesses and a light-rail system, and is one of the few predominately African American–owned commercial strips in the country.

For a slice of the Vietnamese community, drive along South Federal Boulevard between Alameda and Mississippi Avenues. Dozens of restaurants and shops with signs in Vietnamese line the street. **The Far East Center** at 333 S. Federal Ave. has the highest concentration of Vietnamese stores, with an Asian market, restaurants, a bakery, and a large gift shop filled with unusual items. For more information on these and other neighborhoods, see visitdenver.com/artdistricts.

Few American cities come close to matching Denver's 850 miles of biking, jogging, and walking trails. This extensive network of off-road paved and packed-earth trails covers seven counties, traversing a variety of urban and rural environments. Walking or biking along these routes, you will see why Denver appears on lists of physically fit cities. These pathways are used year-round by people of all ages, shapes, and sizes. Here are some of the more popular ones.

Starting north of Denver, the **South Platte River Greenway Trail** follows the river for almost 30 miles, connecting several riverside parks on its way from Confluence Park to Chatfield Reservoir, and connects downtown to the RiNo district. South of Denver, the **High Line Canal Trail** follows the historic **High Line Canal.** More than 65 miles long, the canal has a wide, mostly dirt trail for much of its length. The **Cherry Creek Trail** begins at Confluence Park in downtown Denver and follows Cherry Creek south for 15 miles to Cherry Creek Reservoir. The **Bear Creek Bike Trail** has few bears these days, but this 20-mile route from the South Platte River to the town of Morrison offers side trails connecting to Chatfield, Red Rocks, and Bear Creek Lake Parks. Stop in Morrison for ice cream and browse the antiques shops. For more information on Denver's extensive bike path system, go to denver.org/things-to-do/sports-recreation/bike-trails.

If you'd prefer to laze away an afternoon on a quiet piece of green earth instead of hiking or biking, you're in the right town. Denver has more than 4,000 acres of traditional parks and parkways ranging in size from tiny to sprawling. Considered one of the largest park systems in America, Denver's green spaces provide locals and out-of-towners a relaxing reprieve from city life. Here are some of the more well-known parks.

Civic Center Park at Colfax and Broadway lies at the heart of downtown, close to the State Capitol building, Denver Art Museum, Denver Public Library, and the 16th Street Mall. Beautifully landscaped with expansive lawns and flower beds, and bustling with life, this is the location for events such as People's Fair, Cinco de Mayo, Taste of Colorado, and the Fourth of July celebration.

Denver for Free

Here are six Denver activities that won't cost a dime!

Colorado Sports Hall of Fame Museum
(Hall is free; tours of Empower Field at Mile High are not.)
coloradosports.org

First Friday Art Walks
denver.org/things-to-do/denver-arts-culture/denver-art-districts

Free Days for Colorado Residents at the Denver Art Museum (first Saturday of every month)
denverartmuseum.org

Hammond's Candy Factory Tours
hammondscandies.com

New Year's Eve Fireworks over the 16th Street Mall
downtowndenver.com/event/new-years-eve-fireworks-2

The 16th Street Mall Free MallRide
rtd-denver.com/FREEMallRide.shtml

Climb the steps of the Capitol to the mile-high marker for a view spanning 120 miles of Rocky Mountains on a clear day. At lunchtime, when office workers flock here, this is a fun people-watching spot.

trivia

The Denver Center for the Performing Arts is the second-largest complex of its kind in the US, with 10 theaters seating more than 10,000 people.

At 314 acres, *City Park* is the largest in Denver. Located a few minutes' drive east of downtown at 17th Avenue and York Street, this mile-long park has flower gardens, fountains, two lakes, a historic boathouse, and lots of grass for picnics, soccer games, Frisbee, and snoozing under a tree. Paddleboats can be rented in summer. Every Sunday at 6 p.m. from June through early August, City Park Jazz presents free jazz concerts in the park. The park is also home to some of the city's top attractions, such as the Museum of Nature and Science and the Denver Zoo.

The *Denver Zoo* has nearly 4,000 animals representing 700 species. Natural habitats, winding paths, and large trees are spread over 80 acres, giving the zoo an open feeling. The newest exhibit, Elephant Passage, is a 10-acre area with five habitats, including the world's largest bull elephant habitat. Animals such as rhinos, tigers, and tapirs rotate through the different habitats each day.

The zoo is open daily. Hours from Mar through Oct are 10 a.m. to 5 p.m. and from Nov through Feb, 10 a.m. to 4 p.m. Admission from Mar through Oct is $17 for guests 12 to 64, $14 for seniors (65 and older), and $12 for children 3 to 11. Admission from Nov through Feb is $20 for ages 12 to 64, $17 for seniors, and $14 for children 3 to 11; children 2 and younger are always free. For more information call (720) 337-1400 or visit denverzoo.org.

One of the city's top museums, the **Denver Museum of Nature & Science (DMNS),** is also located in City Park. DMNS includes both temporary and permanent exhibits, such as "Egyptian Mummies," "Chocolate," and "The Robot Revolution." At the Expedition Health exhibit, take a personal, up-close journey inside your own body as you go through different activity areas while experiencing a virtual expedition up a Colorado peak. In addition, the museum is home to the Phipps IMAX Theater, Discovery Zone with hands-on activities for children, and the Gates Planetarium. The museum is also blessed with an excellent view over City Park toward downtown and the Front Range.

DMNS is open daily from 9 a.m. to 5 p.m. except on Christmas Day. General admission is $19.95 for adults, $14.95 for children 3 to 18 and students with ID, and $16.95 for seniors. IMAX and planetarium tickets are extra. For more information call (303) 370-6000 or visit dmns.org.

One of the city's most relaxing green spaces is the **Denver Botanic Gardens** (720-865-3500; botanicgardens.org). Ranked one of the nation's top botanic gardens, this 24-acre oasis just 10 minutes east of downtown has around 33,000 plants spread over 45 different gardens. The tropical conservatory houses thousands of exotic specimens from the world's equatorial regions. Go to the ecofriendly "green" roof on top of the Offshoots Cafe for sweeping panoramas of Denver and the Rocky Mountains. The summer concert series held here (concerts.botanicgardens.org) is legendary for world-class performers

Black American West Museum & Heritage Center

Did you know that nearly one-third of America's working cowboys in the Old West were Black? The **Black American West Museum** offers a unique and much-needed look at the history of these and other Black people and the roles they played in our nation's past. The museum is housed in the former home of Denver's first Black doctor, Dr. Justina Ford, who delivered more than 7,000 babies during her illustrious career. For more information: 3091 California St., Denver 80205; (720) 242-7428; bawmhc.org.

playing in an intimate setting. Open daily except major holidays; admission fees are adults $15, seniors $11.50, students and children 3 to 15 $11, and children under 3 free.

Cheesman Park, located at Franklin Street and 8th Street, attracts joggers to its crushed granite loop trail around the park. The large grassy expanses are popular with sunbathers and small groups enjoying a quiet afternoon. Families come for the large playground. A large, white-columned memorial fountain on top of the hill is a picturesque landmark and a good place to sit and contemplate those big mountains looming to the west. This is the spot to be in the evenings for one of the best sunset-over-the-Rockies spots in the city.

Just a short drive south of downtown, in a neighborhood filled with early-20th-century brick homes, **Washington Park** is one of Denver's most popular year-round parks. Known as Wash Park by locals, these 165 acres contain 2 lakes, 54 flower beds, a 2-mile loop with separate lanes for foot and wheeled traffic, boathouse, fitness center, soccer and tennis courts, and plenty of big trees. Locals love to work out here, and you can join them by renting a bike or paddleboat. If you're not inclined to take part in the activities, just find a shady spot on the grass and watch it all go past. The Old South Gaylord Street and Old South Pearl Street neighborhoods are both a short, pleasant walk from here. The park can be accessed at South Downing Street and East Louisiana Avenue.

Located 6 blocks east of Wash Park, the **Old South Gaylord Street** shopping district has an eclectic collection of restaurants, bars, and shops blended into a mostly residential neighborhood. A few blocks southwest of Wash Park is **Old South Pearl Street** (southpearlstreet.com), another neighborhood that's been lovingly restored with old buildings converted into restaurants, wine bars, pubs, art galleries, and specialty shops. In summer Old South Pearl is host to various music and food festivals and an excellent Sunday farmers' market. A walk through either neighborhood on a warm summer evening is another of Denver's many pleasures.

Stretching along an 18-block, sometimes gritty run of South Broadway is **Antique Row** (antique-row.com). Beginning just south of Alameda, this eclectic collection of shops is home to one of the nation's largest concentrations of antiques dealers. Just about any kind of collectible can be found here, and sprinkled along the avenue are dozens of ethnic restaurants, used bookstores, art galleries, neighborhood taverns, pizza parlors, avant-garde clothing stores, and much more. The area comes alive at night with a smattering of clubs featuring rock, salsa, swing, and techno. For sustenance during your antiquing, drop into **Maria Empanada** on the corner of Broadway and Louisiana (303-934-2221) for arguably the best empanadas in the city, edible odes to the owner's childhood in Argentina. Just past Evans on South Broadway, Post

A Walk on the Wild Side

Set on some 10,000 acres of rural, rolling grasslands 50 miles east of Boulder at Keenesburg, *The Wild Animal Sanctuary* is home to more than 400 lions, tigers, wolves, leopards, bears, mountain lions, and other large carnivores living freely in large social groupings. The animals have been rescued from abusive or illegal situations and are kept in large, humane habitats and given expert care and exceptional diets. Observation decks and walkways provide numerous opportunities to view and photograph the animals as they roam through 20 large-acreage habitats. Open every day except major holidays and during bad weather. For more information call (303) 536-0118 or visit wildanimalsanctuary.org.

Chicken & Beer (720-466-5699) dishes up down-home fried chicken with all the sides plus craft beer.

Located at Sheridan Boulevard and West 17th Avenue, *Sloan Lake Park* attracts a mixed following: retired folks, young parents pushing strollers, joggers, picnicking Vietnamese families, soccer players, bicyclists, and sunbathers. With 177 acres to spread out in, there is plenty of room for everyone. At the center of it all is enormous Sloan Lake. Quiet during the week, it comes alive on summer weekends. Each July the *Dragon Boat Festival* celebrates Asian-American culture and traditions, and dragon boats race across the lake.

Venturing just beyond the actual city limits, Red Rocks Park, Genesee Mountain Park, Chatfield State Park, and Cherry Creek State Park are all outstanding retreats. For more information about Denver's parks, contact the Denver Parks and Recreation Department's Parks Division through City Services; (720) 913-1311; denvergov.org/content/denvergov/en/denver-parks-and-recreation.

If you want to look down onto Denver from above, take a hike in one of the mountain parks. The Denver Mountain Parks system consists of 31 named parks and 16 unnamed areas totaling around 14,000 acres of mountains and foothills owned by the city. These parks offer a wide variety of geography and activities, and a great escape not far from the city. For more information go to denvergov.org/content/denvergov/en/denver-parks-and-recreation/parks.

The Eastern Plains

Many visitors are surprised to learn that not all of Colorado is filled with mountains, lakes, and alpine scenery. In fact, the flat eastern third of the state looks more like neighboring Kansas and Nebraska than it does the rest of Colorado. Even though it's part of this quintessentially western state, many consider this vast landscape of rolling plains more Midwest than West. Eastern Colorado is one of the most sparsely populated places in the US. The Dust Bowl period of

Comanche National Grassland

After the Dust Bowl catastrophe of the 1930s, the federal government set up programs to protect tracts of land from further ruinous farming and grazing practices. *Comanche National Grassland* was created in 1960 from one of those protected areas, and today more than 460,000 acres of prairie grassland and canyon remain much as they were centuries ago. The area was used by ancient American Indians and remnants of their time here remain, including rock art thousands of years old, as well as the remains of rock shelters and tepee rings. More than 320 species of birds have been recorded here, and several canyons—Picket Wire, Vogel, Carrizo, Picture, and Cottonwood—offer hiking, biking, prehistoric rock art, and, in the case of Picket Wire, dinosaur tracks. For more information go to Pike-San Isabel National Forest & Cimarron and Comanche National Grasslands; 2840 Kachina Dr., Pueblo 81008; (719) 553-1400; fs.usda.gov/detail/psicc/about-forest/districts/?cid=fsm9_032695.

the 1930s was hard on the region, with 2.5 million people moving out of the Plains states. Although eastern Colorado eventually saw a return to agriculture in the 1960s to 1980s, dropping agricultural prices combined with rising farming costs led to a decline in population throughout the region.

Although the eastern third of the state lacks the mountain geography of the western two-thirds, it's blessed with plenty of visually compelling landscapes. Wide open spaces stretch to the horizon, broken by an occasional grain elevator, weighing station, or windmill. The shortgrass prairie greens briefly in the spring and is home to a number of bird species. The air is cleaner here than in the cities. Small towns with feedstores, cafes, and churches are scattered across the countryside. Places like Punkin Center, Last Chance, Cope, and Otis hunker beneath the winter winds and pelting summer hail, fragments of Americana far removed from the big cities. At night main streets close down and fall silent.

Although there are fewer visual thrills here compared with the rest of the state, eastern Colorado has a variety of interesting sights. Probably the most prominent landmark on the eastern plains is the ***Pawnee Buttes.*** Part of the 200,000-acre Pawnee National Grassland, these twin buttes can be seen from many miles away.

A gravel road leads up to the Buttes trailhead. From there, a 1.5-mile path takes you on foot or by mountain bike to the first butte, the western one. The eastern butte lies a quarter-mile east. From a plateau the trail drops to the prairie floor, crossing open pastureland before dropping again into a deep ravine. Cream-colored chalk cliffs form the promontories. This is shortgrass prairie, not much higher than tundra. The steady winds keep plant growth low to the ground. Prickly pear cactus, blue grama grass, sagebrush, and buffalo grass grow no higher than 6 inches. This constant wind, combined with poor farming practices, created the ecological Dust Bowl disaster of the 1930s, when drifts

River Adventures in Northern Colorado

A *Wanderlust Adventure* in Laporte will give you the opportunity to see and feel the *Poudre River* firsthand. Since 1982, this Fort Collins–area outfitter has taken adventurers young and old on Colorado's only National Wild and Scenic River. The 3- and 4-hour trips are guaranteed to give anyone a workout negotiating Class II to Class IV rapids, depending on the section of river. Wanderlust has a trip to fit everyone (minimum age of 7 for easiest trip). Trips run from May through Aug and range in price from $55 to $69 per person. For more information contact A Wanderlust Adventure; (970) 482-1995; awanderlustadventure.com.

of wind-driven topsoil piled up like snow over fences, closing roads and killing crops. The **Pawnee National Grassland** and the **Comanche National Grassland** in southeastern Colorado were created when the federal government withdrew the land from agricultural use and consolidated the parcels into protected terrain.

In his book *Centennial,* author James A. Michener renamed these landmarks the fictitious "Rattlesnake Buttes." The book is based on life in the area during pioneer days. About the buttes Michener wrote, "They were extraordinary, these two sentinels of the plains. Visible for miles in each direction, they guarded a bleak and sad empire."

trivia

Horace Greeley's original concept for his namesake town was a utopian agricultural colony modeled after the Oneida, New York, experimental settlement.

Lack of water and trees do not stop the many prairie species of birds from flourishing in this country. Lark buntings—the Colorado state bird, with its distinctive white wing patches against a black body—thrive here. So do horned larks, meadowlarks, kestrels, larkspurs, mountain plovers, common nighthawks, and long-billed curlews—some of the 200 species recorded here. A 36-mile self-guided birding tour is a great ride over the prairie in a car or on a mountain bike. Cattle share this area with pronghorn; across the prairie there are occasional windmill-powered water tanks for stock. For information contact Arapahoe and Roosevelt National Forests & Pawnee National Grassland, 2150 Centre Ave., Building E, Fort Collins 80526; (970) 295-6600; fs.usda.gov/arp.

The city of **Greeley** (named after Horace Greeley, the newspaper publisher) is 49 miles northeast of Denver, surrounded by agricultural farmlands. The town is infamous for its fragrant feedlots, and the fields beyond the town limits grow sugar beet, barley, and other crops. The twelfth most populous city in the state, it is home to the **University of Northern Colorado** (UNC). The late James Michener was one of UNC's famous alumni and later a teacher there.

He was inspired to write his bestselling novel *Centennial* through his familiarity and on-location research in Greeley and surroundings.

Much of the local sightseeing relates to Greeley's past. At **Centennial Village,** part of the City of Greeley Museums, you can visit dozens of historic exhibits, including a sod house, a homesteader's wagon house, and a one-room rural school. In addition, Centennial Village has graceful Victorian homes. In all, some 35 structures on 8 acres take visitors through the history of the High Plains, spanning the years 1860 to 1930. Open late May to Sept, Fri through Sat, 10 a.m. to 4 p.m.; closed Sun to Wed; Thurs for groups by appointment. Admission is $8 for adults 18 to 59, $6 for 60 and older, and $5 for children 3 to 17; children 2 and under are free, and there's a family rate (max of 5) for $18. For more information call (970) 350-9220 or visit greeleymuseums.com/locations/centennial-village.

Another of the city's museums is the **Meeker Home Museum,** formerly the home of Nathan Meeker, founder of Greeley and the agricultural editor of Horace Greeley's *New York Tribune*. This graceful, two-story adobe home built in 1870 contains many of his furnishings and the plow that turned the first sod in the Union Colony. Learn about his untimely death in the White River Massacre, and how his family struggled to survive without him. Located at 1324 9th Ave., it's listed in the National Register of Historic Places. Open the second Saturday of the month from 10 a.m. to 2 p.m. June–Aug.; $8 for adults, $6 for seniors, $5 for children 3 to 17, and free for children 2 and under. The family rate (5 max) is $25. For more information contact (970) 350-9220; greeley museums.com/locations/meeker-home.

To the west, nestled against the foothills, **Fort Collins** may well be the most sophisticated community in northern Colorado. With 130,000 inhabitants, it is the fifth most populous city in the state. Colorado State University is here, and as with many larger college towns, the city has no shortage of good restaurants and cafes, bars, bookstores, and shops catering to 20-somethings. The city shows up on those annual "Best Small Towns To Live In" lists, and a stroll through the pedestrian Old Town Square and neighborhoods to the south and west will soon show you why. Large shade trees, historic preservation of homes and buildings, outdoor sculptures, fountains, shops, and art galleries give visitors and residents alike plenty of reasons to linger.

In a state famous for its wealth of microbreweries, Fort Collins shines. Two of the best-known, **New Belgium Brewing Company** and **Odell Brewing Company,** offer inside looks at how these finely crafted brews are created. New Belgium is at 500 Linden St.; (970) 221-0524; newbelgium.com. Free tours are offered at 2 p.m. weekdays, 2 and 4 p.m. weekends. Odell is at 800 E. Lincoln Ave.; (970) 498-9070; odellbrewing.com. Since COVID, tours have not returned to Odell, but call to check, as it's likely they'll open eventually.

Try a Yurt Vacation!

Within **State Forest State Park,** 75 miles west of Fort Collins, the **Never Summer Nordic Yurt System** offers highly unique opportunities to cyclists.

Consider staying in a yurt here. Yurts are portable, round dwellings that were first used by nomadic Mongols in central Asia; they sleep six comfortably and are well situated as push-off sites for some great rides.

Among the park's trails are Gould Loop, a 6.5-mile round-trip ride that parallels the middle fork of the Michigan River, and American Lakes Trail, which gains more than 1,500 feet of elevation in its 5.5 miles.

For more information about Never Summer Nordic, Inc., go to neversummernordic .com or call (970) 723-4070. For information about State Forest State Park, visit cpw .state.co.us/placestogo/parks/stateforest.

The Fort Collins region is known for its nearby fly-fishing possibilities. Among others, you might head up the scenic **Poudre Canyon** and the Cache la Poudre River, which is consistently recognized as having some of the finest trout fishing in the state. For more information contact Canyon Lakes Ranger District, Arapaho & Roosevelt National Forests, 2150 Centre Ave., Building E, Fort Collins; (970) 295-6700; fs.usda.gov.

For camping and boating—and even scuba diving—try **Horsetooth Reservoir** west of town. Open year-round, Horsetooth has 1,900 acres of water, which attracts summer crowds with camping, hiking, boating, biking, climbing, or just relaxing with a picnic lunch. To reach Horsetooth Reservoir, drive west on CR 38E (Harmony Road) from its intersection with Taft Hill Road in Fort Collins. Park permits are available from stations throughout the park; cost is $10 per vehicle or $20 per vehicle and boat trailer. For more information contact Larimer County, 200 W. Oaks St., Fort Collins; (970) 498-7000; larimer.gov/ naturalresources/parks/horsetooth-reservoir.

There are many singletrack and paved trail biking options in and around Fort Collins. Pick up a free map of the city's bikeway system, illustrating the 56 miles of local bike trails, lanes, and routes. Maps are available at most Fort Collins bicycle shops, or download it online at fcgov.com/bicycling/ bike-maps.

Close to Fort Collins, **Lory State Park** offers great hiking as well as single-tracks for more advanced bike riders. This former ranch is now a 2,400-acre park with 26 miles of trails that tempt bikers with challenging mountain biking almost year-round; snow is frequent in winter, but abundant sunshine keeps the trails relatively clear.

Just beyond the park entrance at the Timber Recreation Area is the **Timber Trail.** This singletrack, 3.7-mile route is moderately technical, climbing steeply through grass and shrublands to a pine forest. From south Fort Collins, take Harmony Road/CR 38E west. Turn right onto 23N. Proceed north to the T-intersection. Turn left at the stop sign onto 42C. Go north to Lodgepole Drive and turn left. Go 1.6 miles to the park entrance. The park is open daily; hours vary according to the season. Cost is $9 per vehicle.

Horsetooth Mountain Park at the southwest side of Horsetooth Reservoir has a variety of jeep roads and singletrack trails that are popular with local mountain bikers.

South of Fort Collins, **Loveland** is famous for valentines. Each year thousands of cards are sent to the town. Volunteers tuck them in new envelopes, hand stamp them with a Valentine's Day verse, and send them off to the lucky recipient postmarked "Loveland." Cupid has worked here since 1947, ensuring that Valentine's Day cards have that extra touch on each envelope.

Loveland is a pretty city with a small-town atmosphere. With a historic downtown, antiques shops, 27 public parks, and year-round events and entertainment. Among its surprising but don't-miss attractions: **Chapungu Sculpture Park at Centerra**, 26 acres of riverside walking paths lined with evocative stone sculptures by Zimbabwean artists. 5971 Sky Pond Dr.; (970) 962-9990; chapunguatcenterra.com.

West of town, **Sylvan Dale Guest Ranch**, in operation since the 1920s, provides an authentic, Western experience in the Big Thompson River Valley. Included in the price are cabin accommodations, hearty meals, and ranch activities such as riding instruction, trail rides, fishing, trap shooting, and nature walks. Kids and adults can take part in ranch chores, and there's a morning youth program for ages 3–12. Special programs include weeks for adults only or for women only. For details contact Sylvan Dale Guest Ranch, 2939 N. CR 31D, Loveland 80538; (970) 667-3915; sylvandale.com. For more information on Loveland, contact the Loveland Chamber of Commerce at (970) 667-6311; loveland.org.

Western Summertime Celebrations

The *Greeley Stampede* is held from the last week of June to the first week of July, with nine rodeos, parades, and fireworks, as well as events on all downtown plazas. The rodeos are at Island Grove Park, 14th Avenue and "A" Street. For more information call (970) 356-7787 or visit greeleystampede.org. The *Weld County Fair* takes place in late July at the same location, with horse shows and livestock displays, plus various contests. For more information call (970) 400-2066 or go to weldcountyfair.com.

The eastern plains of Colorado saw much travel and bloodshed in the early days of this country. Indians, trappers, traders, settlers, Mexicans, and the Spanish used what was called the Santa Fe Trail, which followed the Arkansas River for many miles. After cutting across the southeast corner of what is now Colorado, the trail reached the area around present-day *La Junta,* then turned south over Raton Pass into New Mexico.

Bent, St. Vrain & Company, a frontier trading and retailing business, built and owned *Bent's Old Fort* near what is now La Junta. Beginning in 1833, for the next 16 years it was the only major permanent white settlement on the Santa Fe Trail between Missouri and the Mexican settlements to the south. The fort was a trading destination for Mexicans, Indians, adventurers, and trappers, and a place to repair wagons; get supplies, livestock, food, and water; and rest awhile after a long and dangerous journey. The famous scout Kit Carson was a hunter for the fort from 1831 to 1842.

The fort provided goods for several groups. Mexico obtained quality manufactured items from the US. Native Americans got cookware, metal, rifles, and other goods. Trappers acquired supplies, a market for their furs, and the company of other people following lonely months of hunting. Bent, St. Vrain & Company traded with all these folks and among themselves. Furs from the trappers and buffalo robes from the Arapaho and Southern Cheyenne made their way back east, where they were sold at a handsome profit.

In the mid-1800s, Bent's Old Fort was caught between resentful Indians and the whites who were moving in on them. The Indian wars began and trade faded away.

trivia

Two of the ornate cast-iron grill panels that rise for eight stories above the Brown's atrium lobby were installed upside down. No one knows whether it was a mistake or sly intention. Can you find them?

First Friday Art Walk

On the first Friday of each month, galleries and studios in Denver's Art District on Santa Fe open their doors for an evening of art viewing and gathering. Art aficionados and those out for a casual night of socializing hobnob with artists, chat, and network. And it's free. The district spans from 13th to Alameda Avenue and from Kalamath to Inca Street. The bulk of galleries are in a very walkable area between 5th and 11th Avenues. The event runs from 5:30 to 9:30 p.m. The area is readily accessible by public transportation, which is highly encouraged. Parking is available in the district, though traffic tends to get heavy on first Fridays. Several businesses and facilities offer parking during First Friday Art Walks only. Call (720) 773-ADSF or vist denversartdistrict.org/first-friday for information on parking and more.

Charles Bent was killed in a revolt in Taos, New Mexico, while serving as governor of the state, and Ceran St. Vrain left to do business farther south. Cholera spread through the Indian tribes.

The fort was destroyed under mysterious circumstances in 1949. Most historians believe that after William Bent tried unsuccessfully to sell the fort to the US Army, he mined it with explosives and gunpowder and blew it up. What was left of the fort was abandoned and fell into ruins.

Original sketches, paintings and diaries, and archaeological excavations were used to rebuild the fort in 1976. Designated by the National Park Service as a National Historic Site, Bent's Old Fort has been constructed as close as possible to its original design, using authentic materials and tools. Today, the adobe structure remains a monument to past and present-day craftspeople whose skill and patience built and rebuilt it again.

Just outside La Junta, Bent's Old Fort stands much as it did more than 160 years ago. To preserve the authentic atmosphere of this trade center, visitor parking is a quarter-mile from the building. The paved walk toward the fort, with its backdrop of cottonwood trees by the Arkansas River, is a stroll into history. In deference to realism, there are no concessions for food, drink, or curios.

Uniformed park employees are often on hand to answer questions. But to get into the spirit of the place, join one of the $3-per-person ($2 for children 6 to 12) guided tours conducted by an individual dressed in period clothes. These "interpreters" stay in character, thanks to the authentic costumes. The tours, which run from June 1 to Sept 1, are fun and informative, giving visitors a feel for life around the fort in the 1880s.

Scheduled special events take place throughout the year, such as Wagons Ho! Trail Transportation through Time, the Fur Trade Encampment, and Hispanic Heritage Day. For more information contact Bent's Old Fort, National Historic Site, 35110 Hwy. 194 East, La Junta 81050; (719) 383-5010; nps.gov/beol/index.htm. Closed most federal holidays. Open June 1 through Aug 31 from 8 a.m. to 5:30 p.m.; Sept 1 through May 31 from 9 a.m. to 4 p.m. From US 50 in La Junta take Highway 109 north 1 mile to Highway 194. Go east for 6 miles to the fort.

For a trip even further back into history—150 million years further back—visit **Picket Wire Canyonlands** in **Comanche National Grassland,** about 25 miles south of La Junta. Picket Wire opened to the public in 1991. The attractions? The clear footprints of dinosaurs on a solidified limestone shelf just a few feet over the Purgatory River, as well as Native American rock art and pioneer ruins. In a quarter-mile stretch there are more than 1,300 dinosaur footprints in four different layers of rock, forming North America's largest dinosaur track site.

Though the area is considered extremely fragile, mountain biking and hiking are allowed in Picket Wire.

You may catch glimpses of the current inhabitants: coyote, badgers, pronghorn, quail, kestrels, orioles. Stay out of the tall grass, which is ideal snake habitat. The dinosaur tracks are marked by small signs pointing the way. Right next to the river, you come to a shelf of limestone that looks like someone mucked around in it while it was wet. On further examination you will discover that these muddlings are dinosaur tracks. Two different types of dinosaur left these track. The immense *Apatosaurus* left big holes like you'd expect from an elephant, only much larger. The meat-eating *Allosaurus* left distinctive three-toed, wicked-looking footprints. Many scientists consider this site to be a national treasure.

Petroglyphs are scattered around the rock canyon walls. These etchings aren't identified by signs; you have to find them on your own. This rock art is anywhere from 375 to 4,500 years old. These are precious ancient artifacts, and they should not be touched.

This region of the state gets very hot in summer. Fill your tank with gas before driving out to the area. Take plenty of water—there is no drinking water in Picket Wire Canyonlands—and a hat while hiking. To prevent rattlesnake encounters, watch where you put your hands and feet. Solo travel is generally not recommended; if you go alone, let someone know where you are going and arrange to check in when you return. The distance to the dinosaur tracks one way is 5.3 miles. Although there are no commercial campgrounds here, primitive camping is permitted anywhere in Comanche National Grassland except in Picketwire Canyon. Contact the Comanche National Grassland, 1420 E. 3rd St., La Junta 81050; (719) 384-2181; visitlajunta.net/play/comanche-national-grassland.

Places to Stay in Denver & the Plains

DENVER

Brown Palace Hotel
321 17th St.
(303) 297-3111 or
(800) 321-2599

brownpalace.com
Expensive
Historic elegance at the edge of downtown.

Capitol Hill Mansion Bed & Breakfast
1207 Pennsylvania St.
(303) 839-5221 or
(800) 839-9329
capitolhillmansion.com

Moderate
Turn-of-the-20th-century opulence in the Capitol Hill neighborhood; family and gay friendly.

Clayton Members Club & Hotel
233 Clayton St.
(303) 551-1500
claytondenver.com

Moderate to Expensive
Hotel guests are treated
like members at this chic,
contemporary gathering
place for locals and visitors
alike.

Crawford Hotel
1701 Wynkoop (inside
Union Station)
(720) 460-3700
thecrawfordhotel.com
Expensive
Lovely boutique hotel
retrofitted into Union
Station during the
renovation. Some rooms
are designed to resemble
the old Pullman cars on
trains.

Curtis Hotel
1405 Curtis St.
(303) 571-0300 or
(800) 525-6651
thecurtis.com
Expensive
Fun, pop-culture boutique
hotel in the heart of
downtown.

Hotel Monaco
1717 Champa St.
(303) 296-1717 or
(800) 990-1303
monaco-denver.com
Expensive
Modern luxury in a
historic building within
walking distance to many
downtown attractions.

Hotel Teatro
1100 14th St.
(303) 228-1100 or
(888) 727-1200
hotelteatro.com
Expensive
Luxurious downtown
boutique hotel with 2
fine-dining restaurants.

Oxford Hotel
1600 17th St.
(303) 628-5400 or
(800) 228-5838
theoxfordhotel.com
Expensive
Richly furnished historic
boutique hotel in the heart
of LoDo.

Ramble Hotel
1280 25th St.
(720) 996-6300
theramblehotel.com
Expensive
Boutique hotel in the
popular RiNo neighborhood
with an uber contemporary
vibe and upscale
furnishings.

**Renaissance Denver
Downtown City Center**
918 17th St.
(303) 867-8100
rendendowntown.com
Expensive
Housed in the historic and
grand former Colorado
Bank Building; combines
history and modern luxury.

Thompson Denver
1616 Market St.
(303) 572-1321
hyatt.com/hotel/colorado/
thompson-denver/denth
Expensive
Urban sleek meets
mountain rustic at this
sophisticated downtown
boutique hotel.

FORT COLLINS

Armstrong Hotel
259 S. College Ave.
(970) 484-3883
thearmstronghotel.com
Moderate
Landmark historic hotel
with complimentary cruiser

bikes in the heart of Old
Town Fort Collins.

**Best Western University
Inn**
914 S. College Ave.
(970) 484-2984 or
(800) 780-7234
bestwestern.com/Moderate
Centrally located in Old
Town across from the
university and close to New
Belgium Brewing.

**Edwards House Bed &
Breakfast**
402 W. Mountain Ave.
(970) 493-9191
edwardshouse.com
Moderate
Elegant, romantic
accommodations a few
blocks from Old Town.

The Elizabeth Hotel
111 Chestnut St.
(970) 490-2600
theelizabethcolorado.com
Expensive
Luxury hotel in the heart of
Old Town.

GREELEY

**Country Inn and Suites
by Carlson**
2501 W. 29th St.
(970) 888-6529
countryinns.com
Moderate
Hot breakfast and wireless
internet included with all
rooms.

Currier Inn Hotel
1221 9th Ave.
(970) 392-1221
greeleybedandbreakfast
.com
Moderate
Ten distinctly decorated
rooms come with delicious

gourmet breakfasts and free wireless internet.

Fairfield Inn & Suites by Marriott Greeley
2401 W. 29th St.
(970) 339-5030
marriott.com
Moderate
Newly renovated, clean hotel with friendly staff.

LA JUNTA

Hampton Inn La Junta
27800 US 50
(719) 384-4444
Moderate
Clean and modern with friendly staff; hot breakfast included.

Midtown Motel
215 E. 3rd St.
(719) 384-8010
midtownlajunta.com
Inexpensive
Clean and affordable, with complimentary wireless internet.

LOVELAND

Best Western Plus Loveland Inn
5542 E. US 34
(970) 667-7810
bestwesterncolorado.com/hotels
Moderate
Conveniently located near I-25, with a dinner restaurant and lounge, complimentary breakfast, free internet access; pet-friendly.

Candlewood Suites
6046 E. Crossroads Blvd.
(970) 667-5444
ihg.com/candlewood/hotels
Inexpensive to Moderate

On-site fitness center, high-speed internet; pets allowed.

Quality Inn & Suites Loveland
1500 Cheyenne Ave.
(970) 427-5249
Moderate
Affordable hotel with easy access to Rocky Mountain National Park.

Places to Eat in Denver & the Plains

DENVER

Avanti Food & Beverage
3200 N. Pecos St.
(720) 269-4778
avantifandb.com
Inexpensive to Moderate
One of Denver's multi-vendor food halls, Avanti offers 7 eateries around communal dining space and 2 bars (downstairs and up) serving 20 draft beers (including microbrews) and more.

Bastien's Restaurant
3503 E. Colfax
(303) 322-0363
bastiensrestaurant.com
Moderate to Expensive
Old school and fabulous, Bastien's, known for its sugar steak, has been a Denver staple for decades. Unlike other steak houses that ding you for every addition, the price of your steak here includes potato, salad, and fresh veggies.

There's more than steak on the menu, too.

Bistro Vendome
1420 Larimer St.
(303) 825-3232
bistrovendome.com
Expensive
Sibling to Rioja across the street, but a somewhat hidden gem on Larimer serving classic French dishes in a charming setting that could almost be in Paris. Menu changes seasonally.

Cart-Driver LoHi
2239 W. 30th St.
(720) 501-2264
cart-driver.com/lohi
Moderate
Cooked in a wood-fired oven, this pizza is arguably the best in Denver. Add creative salads, fresh oysters, and gluten-free options, plus a monthly "cocktail for a cause" that benefits local organizations. Sure, there's local craft beer but a nice wine and spirit list, too.

Chez Maggy
1616 Market St.
(720) 794-9544
chezmaggydenver.com
Moderate to Expensive
Classic French cuisine with a Colorado influence, set inside the Thompson Denver. Butter and cream? Yes, indeed.

ChoLon Modern Asian Bistro
1555 Blake St., Ste. 101
(303) 353-5223
cholon.com
Moderate to Expensive
Asian traditional and fusion

with lunch, dinner, and small bites menu.

Forget Me Not
227 Clayton St.
(720) 259-5369
forgetmenotdenver.com
Moderate to Expensive
Primarily a superb cocktail and wine bar, Forget Me Not has a compact menu of snacks and small plates ranging from comfort food bites to upscale palate pleasers.

Globe Hall Bar-B-Q
4483 Logan St.
(720) 668-8833
globehall.com
Moderate
Globe Hall, down home and focused on serving up excellent barbecue and live music, is proof that Denver's gritty Globeville neighborhood is far more than a drive-by on I-70.

Hop Alley
3500 Larimer St.
(720) 379-8340
hopalleydenver.com
Moderate to Expensive
Regional Chinese and inspired Asian dishes, many wokked or wood grilled—nothing ordinary here.

Lucile's Creole Cafe
275 S. Logan St.
(303) 282-6258
luciles.com
Inexpensive to Moderate
Classic Creole-inspired breakfast and lunch in a fun Cajun setting.

Mizuna
225 E. 7th Ave.
(303) 832-4778
mizunadenver.com
Expensive
Highly rated, seasonal menu from a creative kitchen offering innovative cuisine.

My Brother's Bar
2376 15th St.
(303) 455-9991
Inexpensive
Classic burger place and Denver institution with a long history and a lively back patio local scene—but no sign.

New Saigon Restaurant
630 S. Federal Blvd.
(303) 936-4954
newsaigon.com
Moderate
Consistently voted the best Vietnamese restaurant in town.

Post Chicken & Beer–Rosedale
2200 S. Broadway
(720) 466-5699
postchickenandbeer.com/rosedale
Moderate
If you're craving the kind of fried chicken celebrated on *Diners, Drive-ins and Dives*, this is it. And yes, it has been. Authentic, deeply delicious fried chicken with all the sides, plus craft beer, are served up in a casual setting. There's also a newer Post Chicken outpost in LoHi.

Postino
2715 17th St.
(303) 433-6363
postinowinecafe.com
Moderate
Small bites, an excellent wine and beverage list, and one of the best patios in the Highlands.

Rioja
1433 Larimer St.
(303) 820-2282
riojadenver.com
Moderate to Expensive
Creative Mediterranean-inspired menu with local and seasonal ingredients when possible.

Root Down
1600 W. 33rd Ave.
(303) 993-4200
rootdowndenver.com
Moderate to Expensive
Organic, natural, and local ingredients whenever possible; a top foodie destination with a hip ambience.

Steuben's
523 E. 17th Ave.
(303) 830-1001
steubens.com
Moderate
Classic American regional cuisine and comfort food.

FORT COLLINS

Canino's Italian Restaurant
613 S. College Ave.
(970) 493-7205
caninositalianrestaurant.com
Inexpensive to Moderate

Family-owned Italian restaurant serving from an extensive menu in a homey setting in a historic building.

Coopersmith's Pub and Brewing Company
5 Old Town Sq.
(970) 498-0483
coopersmithspub.com
Inexpensive to Moderate
Innovative pub menu and good beer in a fun setting.

The Still & Whiskey Steaks
151 N. College Ave.
(970) 294-4360
Moderate to Expensive
Mountain-rustic ambience and a menu featuring more than 40 Colorado whiskies, steaks, and more.

GREELEY

Coyote's Southwestern Grill
5250 W. 9th St. Dr.
(970) 336-1725
Moderate
Locally owned, authentic Southwestern and Mexican cuisine with a twist.

Fat Albert's Food & Drink
1717 23rd Ave.
(970) 356-1999
fat-alberts.com
Inexpensive to Moderate
Nice selection of sandwiches, dinners, salads, and desserts.

Rio Grande Mexican Restaurant
825 9th St.
(970) 304-9292
riograndemexican.com
Moderate

This Colorado chain serves fresh and filling Mexican food and legendary margaritas.

LOVELAND

A.K.A. Kitchen
414 E. 6th St.
(970) 617-2325
akakitchennoco.com
Inexpensive to Moderate
Relaxed, family-run restaurant serving locally sourced pub food.

Black Steer
436 N. Lincoln Ave.
(970) 667-6679
blacksteerrestaurant.com
Moderate to Expensive
Consistently voted best place for steak in Loveland; menu includes homemade soups, seafood, salads, and pastas.

FOR MORE INFORMATION

DENVER
Visit Denver, The Convention & Visitors Bureau
1555 California St., Ste. 300, 80202
(303) 892-1505 or (800) 233-6837
denver.org

FORT COLLINS
Visit Fort Collins
1 Old Town Square, Ste. 107, 80524
(970) 232-3840
visitftcollins.com

GREELEY
Greeley Chamber of Commerce
902 7th Ave., 80631
(970) 352-3566
greeleychamber.com

LOVELAND
Loveland Chamber of Commerce
5400 Stone Creek Circle, Ste. 200, 80538
(970) 667-6311
loveland.org

OTHER ATTRACTIONS WORTH SEEING IN DENVER & THE PLAINS

DENVER
Art District on Santa Fe
1001 Santa Fe Dr.
(720) 773-ADSF (2373)
denversartdistrict.org

Elitch Gardens Theme & Water Park
2000 Elitch Circle
(303) 595-4386
elitchgardens.com

History Colorado Center
1200 Broadway
(303) 447-8679
historycolorado.org

Museum of Contemporary Art
1485 Delgany
(303) 298-7554
mcadenver.org
16th Street Mall
16thstreetmalldenver.com

Wings Over the Rockies Air & Space Museum
7711 E. Academy Blvd.
(303) 360-5360
wingsmuseum.org

EADS
Sand Creek Massacre National Historic Site
Approximately 23 miles east of Eads
(719) 438-5916
nps.gov/sand

FORT COLLINS
The Lincoln Center
417 W. Magnolia
(970) 221-6735
lctix.com

GREELEY
Colorado Model Railroad Museum
680 10th St.
(970) 392-2934
cmrm.org

LA JUNTA
Bent's Old Fort National Historic Site
35110 Hwy. 194 E
(719) 383-5010
nps.gov/beol/index.htm

Comanche National Grassland
South of La Junta; ranger office at 1420
E. 3rd St.
(719) 523-6591

ROCKY FORD
Arkansas Valley Fair
(719) 254-7723
arkvalleyfair.com

Index